Women in Daoism

Catherine Despeux

&

Livia Kohn

Three Pines Press

Three Pines Press
303 Cambridge Street, #71
Cambridge, MA 02141
www.threepinespress.com

9   8 7 6 5 4 3 2 1

First Edition, 2003
Printed in the United States of America
⊗ This edition is printed on acid-free paper that meets
the American National Standard Institute Z39.48 Standard.
Distributed in the United States by Three Pines Press.

Cover art: *The Queen Mother of the West and Her Court*. Qing dynasty, 17th century, hanging scroll, ink and colors on silk. From *Daojiao shenxian huaji* (1995).

Library of Congress Cataloging-in-Publication Data

Despeux, Catherine.
  Women in daoism / Catherine Despeux, Livia Kohn.
    p. cm.
Includes bibliographical references and index.
  ISBN 1-931483-01-9
  1. Taoism--History. 2. Taoist women--History. I. Kohn, Livia, 1956-
II. Title.
  BL1923 .D47 2003
  299'.514'082--dc21
                        2003013339

Contents

List of Illustrations

Fig. 1. Xiwang mu with her distinctive headdress, served by an entourage, and sourrounded by the mythical animals of the sun and the moon. Source: Rubbing of pottery tile from Sichuan, first century C.E., Suzanne Cahill, private collection.

Fig. 2. The Queen Mother of the West with two ladies-in-attendance on the balustrade of her heavenly palace on Mount Kunlun. Source: *Zengxian liexian zhuan*.

Fig. 3. The Dipper Mother formally receives the nine stars of the Dipper in celestial audience. Source: *Doumu jing* manuscript.

Fig. 4. The stars of the Dipper.

Fig. 5. Maonü covered in black hairs encountering the immortal in the moutain. Source: *Liexian quanzhuan*.

Fig. 6. The Hemp Lady in immortal splendor with her divine deer. Source: *Liexian quanzhuan*.

Fig. 7. The immortal Zheng Siyuan and his tiger companions. Source: *Liexian quanzhuan*.

Fig. 8. He Xiangu with her ladle containing immortality mushrooms, peaches, and pine branches. Source: *Yuandai Liexian zhuan*.

Fig. 9. A portrait of Sun Buer. Source: *Daoyuan yiqi jing*.

Fig. 10. A map showing the major centers of women's institutions under the Yuan.

Fig. 11. The "Chart of Inner Passageways." Source: *Neijing tu*.

Fig. 12. The flow of yin and yang in the human body, depicted as a mountain. Source: *Duren jing neiyi*.

Fig. 14. Seated meditation, with the characteristic hand positions for men and women. Source: *Neiwai gong tushuo jiyao*.

Fig. 15. The immortal embryo emerges from the head of the practitioner. Source: *Xingming guizhi*.

Fig. 16. Ascension to immortality on a phoenix. Source: *Xingming guizhi*.

Dynastic Chart

B.C.E.	Shang	1766-1122
	Western Zhou	1122-770
	Eestern Zhou	770-221
	Qin	221-206
	Former Han	206-6
C.E	Later Han	23-220
	Three Kingdoms	220-265
	Western Jin	265-317
	Eastern Jin	317-420
	Six Dynasties	420-589
	Sui	589-618
	Tang	618-907
	Five Dynasties	907-960
	Northern Song	960-1126
	Southern Song	1126-1260
	Mongol-Yuan	1260-1368
	Ming	1368-1644
	Manchu-Qing	1644-1911
	Republic (Taiwan)	1911-
	People's Republic	1949-

Acknowledgments

This book grew over the last several years, in close cooperation of the two authors. The idea for the project arose when students and colleagues alike continued to mention the need for a survey volume on the roles and practices of women in the Daoist religion. Since both authors had done previous work on the subject, it was agreed to start with existing writings as a basis and develop the book from there. As a result, much in the present volume reflects prior work undertaken by the two authors, notably Catherine Despeux's *Les immortelles de la Chine ancienne* (1990), and Livia Kohn's "The Mother of the Tao" (1990) and "Doumu: The Mother of the Dipper" (2001). From the root of these works, the book has grown, developing as scholarship expanded and as we became more conscious of issues and historical details.

In the course of writing and editing, the book saw various drafts and underwent many revisions. These were greatly aided by the active comments and suggestions of many friends and colleagues. Stephan Peter Bumbacher read the manuscript with great meticulousness, gave bibliographical additions, added greatly to its overall correctness, and sharpened our vision of various interrelated concepts and issues. Suzanne Cahill carefully went over the entire book in its final version, suggesting improvements and changes to various chapters and paying special attention to the presentation on Xiwang mu. Patricia Ebrey worked through an early draft with great care and had many good ideas for the formulation and problematization of gender issues, especially in the introduction. Beata Grant provided much needed information on successful Buddhist women of the late imperial period and helped with finetuning the introduction. Russell Kirkland made thoughtful comments and gave numerous helpful suggestions to various sections of the book, and in particular the introduction. Liu Xun contributed significantly to our understanding of inner alchemical practices in the Ming dynasty; he helped out with identification of authors and texts, information on twentieth-century masters, and numerous bibliographic resources. James Miller gave insightful comments on terminology and conceptualization, also aiding with questions of editing and translation. Jordan Paper provided various suggestions on the work and added to our understanding of contemporary feminist theology and related issues. Lisa Raphals was supportive of the project. Thomas E. Smith provided translations of passages from the *Liexian zhuan* and also made numerous helpful suggestions on the role of women in this ancient text. Last, but not least, Janet Theiss provided information on the life and fate of a Qing-dynasty Daoist nun, based on official and court notices.

They all took a kind and detailed interest in the project, providing numerous notes and corrections, and helped with formulating problems as much as solutions. Still, they are not responsible for the views or facts described in this book, and all errors and oddities are owned solely by the authors.

Introduction

Daoism is the indigenous higher religion of traditional China. Growing from a philosophical root and developing through practices of longevity and immortality, it has found expression in communal organizations, ritual structures, and age-old lineages. A multifaceted tradition, Daoism in the 2,500 years of its history has related to women in a number of different ways matching the complexity of other religions, where the relationship to the female is often ambiguous and ambivalent. They commonly see motherhood, sexuality, fertility, esoteric knowledge, and secret powers as closely linked with the feminine and evaluate these aspects positively. But many religions also relegate women to inferior status, considering them of a lower nature, impure and irresponsible, and often suppressing them with greater or lesser severity.[1]

The complexity of women's positions is particularly poignant in the Daoist case, since the religion is caught between its ideal cosmological premise of the power of yin and the realities of a strongly patriarchal society following the Confucian model. That is to say, cosmologically Daoism sees women as expressions of the pure cosmic force of yin, necessary for the working of the universe, equal and for some schools even superior to yang. Daoism also links the Dao itself, the force of creation at the foundation of the cosmos, to the female and describes it as the mother of all beings. Within the religion there is a widespread attitude of veneration and respect for the feminine, honoring the cosmic connection as well as the productive and nurturing nature of women.

However, Daoism throughout its history has lived and breathed the social vision of mainstream Confucian society, which was patriarchal, patrilineal, and patrilocal, and saw women as inferior to men. Tradi-

---

[1] On women in various religions, see Plaskow and Romero 1974; Carmody 1979; Falk and Gross 1980; Sharma 1987; 1994; 2000; King 1997; Young 1999.

1

tional Chinese culture relegated women to the inner quarters of the house and prevented them from participating in decision-making and larger social issues (Ebrey 1993, 7-8). In Confucian thinking only sons were valued, since they alone could continue the family line and fulfill the ancestral obligations. Girls, often not even counted among a man's children, were commonly treated with disregard and contempt, considered a burden since they would eventually marry out and continue someone else's bloodline. They were not seen worthy of education, except in household skills, and their natural cycles rendered them impure and unsuitable for major responsibilities.

Women in Confucian China were defined largely through their relationships with men—being either daughters, wives, mothers, or widows. Already the *Liji* (Book of Rites) notes that they had the duty of "threefold obedience." And the classic on Confucian women, the *Lienü zhuan* (Biographies of Eminent Women), ascribed to Liu Xiang (77-6 B.C.E.), says: "A woman needs someone to depend on. While her father is alive, she is dependent on him. While her husband is alive, she is dependent on him. And while her son is alive, she is dependent on him" (3.5a; Bumbacher 1998, 674; O'Hara 1980; Sung 1981; Raphals 1998). According to this model, men had full control over the lives and activities of their womenfolk, determining the training and treatment of their daughters, able to mistreat and divorce their wives at will, and shunning widows as outcasts and socially useless.[2] Wives in particular were easily rejected and divorced, for reasons including sterility, lewdness, disobedience to the parents-in-law, loquacity, stealing, jealousy, and having a repulsive disease (*Lienü zhuan* 2.5a; Gulik 1961, 266; Bumbacher 1998, 678). But many never even made it to the status of wife, reserved for the senior and legally married bride. Others were concubines or "little maids," menial

---

[2] Footbinding was one way in which women were controlled in traditional China. It made them into status symbols and expressions of conspicuous consumption (Ko 2001, 151; see also Levy 1966; Paper 1997, 91-92; Ko 2002, 158; Ebrey 1993, 266). Female infanticide has been common (Gulik 1961, 111; Carmody 1979, 68). Widows were shunned and had low social standing (Waltner 1981, 131). See also Guisso 1981; Holmgren 1995; Watson and Ebrey 1991; Ebrey 1993.

women who had no property rights or status claims (Watson 1991, 233-34).

A moving document of their plight is the poem by the scholar-official Fu Xuan (217-278 C.E.), contained in the *Yutai xinyong* (New Songs for a Jade Terrace), a sixth-century poetry collection:

> Bitter indeed it is to be born a woman,
> It is difficult to imagine anything so low! . . .
> A girl is raised without joy or love,
> No one in her family really cares for her.
> Grown up, she has to hide in the inner rooms,
> Cover her head, be afraid to look others in the face.
> And no one sheds a tear when she is married off,
> All ties with her own kin are abruptly severed. . . .
> Her husband's love is as aloof as the Milky Way,
> Yet she must follow him like a sunflower the sun.
> Their hearts are soon as far apart as fire and water,
> She is blamed for all and everything that goes wrong.
> (Gulik 1961, 111-12)

This rather dismal picture of women's lives reflects the Confucian ideal, held up as a model to strive for but only partially realized in history. In actual fact, women in Chinese society had a great deal of freedom and responsibility. For example, women of the lower classes had to work hard outside the home, not only running households but also working in agriculture and business (Ko 1994). They interacted freely with men and were not restricted to their own homes (Bray 1997). If they ended up in the entertainment world, they were not inevitably chattels of cruel mad-ams, but in some cases found "opportunities to develop their literary, musical, and artistic talents" in this milieu (Ebrey 1993, 5). Women of the upper classes similarly functioned as political and intellectual agents, not only educating their sons but also giving advice to their husbands and thus influencing policy making and social realities (Raphals 1998, 4, 259). These women, moreover, carried responsibility not only for their hus-band's clan but also maintained close relations to their native family, cementing social alliances and forging political bonds (Thatcher 1991, 45). They may not have mixed freely with males beyond their immediate household, but they created women's networks that carried considerable weight in the community (Bray 1997).

Mothers, moreover, were the object of the Confucian virtue of filial piety, which demanded respect for the mother and obedience to her wishes. Not entirely misogynous, Confucians acknowledged the importance of yin, paid veneration to the sacrality of the Earth, and honored their mothers—often matriarchs who ruled the household and educators who shaped the worldview of sons (Bumbacher 1998, 681; Paper 1997, 48).[3] Still, women in traditional Chinese society were usually prevented from reaching more than a limited level of influence.

Also, social rules changed over time, so that, for example, divorce by mutual consent became legal in the Tang dynasty. Women from the Song onward maintained ownership of their dowry and could accumulate wealth in their own right (Ebrey 1991; 1993, 6). In the Ming and Qing women's overall literacy grew to the point that we know of over three thousand anthologies of women's poems from late imperial China (Grant 1996, 53; Chang and Saussey 1999). Widows, far from being only victims and outcasts, were often strong agents who made independent decisions, lauded highly if they remained true to their husband's clan (Ebrey 1993, 5, 204; Holmgren 1981; Mann 1987).

The overwhelming majority of women in traditional China married and did not pursue an independent career (Ebrey 1993, 7). Still, even if a woman remained largely in the inner quarters, this was not necessarily conceived as a limitation and restriction. There was also a dimension of the "marital relationship that emphasizes affection, partnership, and shared responsibility" (Mann 1991, 208; Overmyer 1981, 93), so that being in the house represented a position of safety and refuge. Women forced out of their seclusion due to political upheaval or economic hardship tended to express their yearning for the peace, tranquility, and security of the inner court (see Ko 2001). Staying at home, surrounded by familiar figures and things, performing tasks well under their control served as much to reassure the women's identity and self-worth as it helped to maintain the proper social order. Being a woman in Confucian

---

[3] The importance of women in the education of boys also appears in contemporary Japan, where the trait of *amae* or "loving sweetness" is a key characteristic. See Doi 1973.

China, therefore, although at first glance a lowly and dependent situation, was not without benefits or flexibility. [4]

The roles of Daoist women in this context are complex. Normatively, Daoism reflects the mainstream vision of women, and female lay followers were usually married, subscribed to the program set out by society, and remained subject to Confucian restrictions. In other reflections of the mainstream ideal, there are also some Daoist practices that involve the exploitation of women, either sexually or socially. However, Daoism goes beyond mainstream Chinese values in that many of its strands propose a feminine ideal as cosmic yin and venerate important goddesses and immortals. These serve as models to living women. Daoism, moreover, offers a social alternative for women in that it opens paths to pursue their own goals as independent agents, be it the practice of self-cultivation, service as mediums, nuns, or priests, or attainment of immortality.

The following chapters survey and arrange examples culled from the historical record to illustrate changes in the Daoist perception and social situation of women. The historic record is used in a way similar to how a geologist uses the geological record: by noting changes in morphological structures we can become aware of the "surface conditions" found in different time periods. A recurrent theme that arises throughout is the control over the feminine body. As the definitions and means of control change, so do the roles and opportunities available for women in Daoist culture. Some of the issues raised accordingly include control over sexual bodies, the body of scripture, bodily nourishment, ritual garb, and the body as a gateway between society and transcendence, between microcosm and macrocosm. The volume will show how women in Daoism have appeared in various ideal forms and historical personages, reflecting both general cultural Chinese attitudes and the different organizational constellations within the religion. Without oversimplifying the

---

[4] For more on women in Confucian society, see Gulik 1961; Wolf 1972; Wolf and Witke 1975; Guisso and Johannesen 1981; Overmyer 1981; Kristeva 1986; Chow 1991; Watson and Ebrey 1991; Ko 1994; Bray 1997; Mann 1997; Paper 1997; Raphals 1998; Zurndorfer 1999; Mann and Cheng 2001; Wang 2003. Women who rejected the stereotype tended to get a bad reputation. For example, Empress Wu (Fitzgerald 1955), Zixi (Bland 1910), and Jiang Qing (Witke 1977).

matter, one can distinguish five major visions and roles of women in Daoism, each dominant in a certain period of the religion's history. They are described in chronological order and begin with the vision of motherhood and the goddess, since the earliest extant sources deal with these issues. Women's body cultivation comes last because texts on the subject only appear in the late imperial period. The five roles and images are:

(1) the female as mother, the life-giver and nurturing power of the universe—in ancient Daoism expressed in the philosophy of the *Daode jing* (Book of the Way and Its Virtue, ca. 350 B.C.E.) as well as in Daoist mother goddesses

(2) women as representatives of the cosmic force of yin, complementary to the male or yang, reflecting both the universal presence of yin and its expression in sexuality and fertility—in Han-dynasty longevity practices and among early Daoist communities of the second century C.E.

(3) women as divine teachers and bestowers of esoteric revelations, empowering adepts through instruction and direct interaction—in the Highest Clarity or Purity (Shangqing) movement of the fourth century

(4) women as possessors of supernatural connections, healing powers, and shamanic techniques, leading to the emergence of powerful priests, founders, and matriarchs—in the high middle ages and well into the late imperial period (Tang through Ming)

(5) the female body as the seat of essential ingredients and processes of spiritual transformation, understood in the terms of inner alchemy—in the late imperial and modern periods

The Dao as Mother

The veneration of motherhood in Chinese culture is strongly expressed in the ancient *Daode jing*, a collection of aphorisms associated with the legendary sage Laozi, the Old Master (see Henricks 2000; LaFargue 1992). The text represents the Dao as the great mother, the essential element of water that nurtures all, and possessed of feminine qualities of softness and weakness (Overmyer 1981, 92).

The Dao as mother is where all beings come from and to which they all return, the source and essence of the universe, the all-embracing and nurturing power at the root of all (Reed 1987, 162). Described variously (chs. 1, 20, 25, 32, 34), the Dao is called the womb of the universe that brings forth all and nurtures all; every being is part of a single, integrated organism that ultimately goes back to and is embraced by the Dao (Chen 1974, 57; 1969). People who attain the Dao consequently have total trust in it as their universal mother. They allow all changes and transformations—even death—to happen naturally and place themselves in the mother's position at the mysterious center of the cosmos, where, as Ellen Marie Chen points out, "things at the same time emerge into the activities of life and return to the quietude of death" (1973, 235).

Other scholars also affirm the predominance of motherhood in the *Daode jing*, and some even explicitly associate the Dao with the great mother of mythology.[5] Yet others see the feminine in the *Daode jing* as the true complement of the masculine and find that the realization of the sage in the world, rather than being a reduction to feminine values, lies in the reconciliation of opposites manifest in the embodiment of the Dao and the attainment of life as a consummate person who is neither feminine nor masculine (Ames 1981, 43). This androgynous ideal found in visions of the Dao, moreover, continues in the later tradition, where it appears in the form of various mother goddesses presented below.

Besides the strong emphasis on motherhood, the *Daode jing* also links the Dao with female animals (chs. 6, 10, 28, 61) and uses various symbols that indicate containing and latency—such as the empty vessel (ch. 4), the bellows (ch. 5), the dark unborn (ch. 1), water (chs. 6, 78), and the valley (chs. 6, 28, 32) (Chen 1974, 53). It also emphasizes that the Dao embraces all (chs. 27, 32), evenly spreads its goodness (ch. 32), and cher-

---

[5] See Needham 1956; Erkes in Duyvendak 1954, 56. On the great mother in mythology, see Neumann; 1963; Preston 1982.

ishes all beings with motherly love (ch. 67). It notes that the female over-comes the male by its quality of stillness (ch. 61) and that in order to at-tain union with the Dao one should abide by the female (ch. 28), cultivat-ing the qualities of weakness and softness (Chen 1974, 51).

Here the image of the feminine is not entirely one of giving and nurtur-ing, but contains elements associated with the darker side of yin, things like weakness, stillness, passivity, darkness, emptiness, and withdrawal. It reveals a more shadowy, mysterious, even uncanny side of the fe-male—exalted in the *Daode jing* as the way to overcome and balance the dominant mode of the world, yet also linking women with rather somber and unassuming values. This reflects the mainstream ideal of Chinese culture, where women in general were secreted in the inner chambers and encouraged to develop virtues that made them easy to control, such as chastity, modesty, meekness, and obedience. The *Daode jing*, therefore, in both its strong emphasis on motherhood and its characterization of the female as dark, weak, and withdrawing reflects standard Chinese attitudes toward women. But it also modifies these attitudes by placing a positive value on the female and contrasting it with the male, ruthless and scheming, ways of the world.

Women and Cosmic Yin

Another major vision of the female in Daoism emerges under the influ-ence of yin-yang cosmology in the Han dynasty (206 B.C.E.-220 C.E.). Here women are seen as representatives of yin and complementary to yang, one half of the two forces that govern all life. In some instances yin is even valued more highly—as for example in the system of Chinese medicine where the five organs (liver, heart, spleen, lungs, and kidneys) that store and nurture the vital energy of *qi*, thereby essentially deter-mining people's health and life expectancy, are classified as yin. They are matched by the six yang organs (stomach, bladder, gall bladder, small and large intestine, triple heater), which are active in nature and more involved in digestion and elimination, and classified as secondary in im-portance (see Porkert 1974; Kaptchuk 1983; Liu 1988).

Before the establishment of Daoist community organizations in the second century C.E., yin-yang cosmology was applied on a practical level in the cultivation of *qi* for the attainment of long life and immortality. Practitioners, who did not think of themselves as "Daoists" but some of whom were later canonized by the tradition, used the yin-yang system to modify their diets, breathing, and movements, with the goal of purifying the *qi* within and maximizing its potential, thus reaching the greatest possible vitality. Both men and women participated in these practices, however, men took particular advantage of women in sexual practices, known as "bedchamber arts" (*fangzhong shu*) and first documented in the manuscripts found at Mawangdui and dated to 168 B.C.E. (Harper 1987; 1999).

Geared to enhance men's *qi* by absorbing that of their female partners, these techniques taught men to have intercourse with as many women as possible, preferably young and healthy ones, bring them to orgasm so they would emit their sexual essence—*jing*, a manifest form of *qi*—but never have an ejaculation themselves. Instead, men were to experience arousal and, by applying meditative concentration and physical pressure to the perineum, prevent their sexual essence from flowing out and visualize it rising up along the spine towards the head. Known as "reverting the sexual essence to nourish the brain" (*huanjing bunao*), this method is commonly seen today as a form of sexual vampirism that encourages men to value women only for their *qi* and discard them after use.[6]

The doctrine behind these techniques assumes that women possess an inexhaustible supply of yin and will not suffer from the practice. Not only that, they experience marvelous climaxes through the skilled techniques employed by the men. On the other hand, it is also assumed that women will not voluntarily agree to be thus used, and the literature describes the practices as a form of war which could best be won if the opponent remained ignorant of the game. Thus the *Yufang bijue* (Secret Formula of the Jade Chamber), a medieval text on nourishing life, quotes the Master of Central Harmony (Zhonghezi) as saying:

---

[6] For studies of these sexual practices, which also formed part of Daoism, see Needham 1956; Gulik 1961; Ishihara and Levy 1970; Chang 1977; Chia and Winn 1984; Robinet 1988; Reid 1989; Wile 1992; Chu 1994.

> A man who intends to nourish his yang essence must not per-
> mit women to learn this art. Her knowledge of it will do him
> no good, and can even make him ill. This is the meaning of the
> proverb: "Do not lend another a dangerous weapon."

> In fact, if you encounter a knowledgeable woman, it is best to
> gather up your weapons, because you will not win. Similarly
> the longlived Pengzu affirms that if a man wants to reap great
> profits from the sexual act, he must preferably do so with a
> woman who is ignorant of this art. (In *Ishimpō* 28.5b-6a; see
> Wile 1992; Ishihara and Levy 1970)[7]

With the exception of the Queen Mother of the West (Xiwang mu) and some enterprising early immortals who used similar methods on men, women tend to be victims in this kind of practice, which was known also outside of Daoist circles. If women ever do engage in aggressive sexual behavior or promiscuity, society tends to label them as demonic "fox fairies." Such fairies were believed to be supernatural beings, developed over centuries from foxes or other animals that had accumulated magical powers and learned the art of appearing in human form. To enhance their powers even more and attain full immortality, they had to obtain yang *qi*, ideally from virile young men. Preying on lonely, young schol-ars, they engaged in a sexual relationship with them and eventually brought about their death from exhaustion and *qi*-depletion.[8]

The sexual partner practices of ancient China have long been associated with Daoism in the Western mind. In fact, they evolved as part of lon-gevity practices long before the beginning of Daoism as a religion and were undertaken by all different members of Chinese society. Daoist schools integrated their principles, but had a mixed relationship to them over the millennia—both rejecting and embracing them in different con-texts.

---

[7] The text survives in a Japanese edition of medical and longevity materials, dated to 984. It was not codified in the Daoist canon due to editorial restrictions in later dynasties

[8] On fox fairies and their activities, see Watters 1874; Giles 1916; Krappe 1944; Johnson 1974; Huntington 1993.

For example, among the earliest organized groups of the second century C.E., the Way of Great Peace (Taiping dao) and the Celestial Masters (Tianshi), sexual practices were sublimated in ritual intercourse. Characterized by their strong millenarian belief systems, ritually based hierarchies, moral life-style, and intense community cohesion, these groups formed the backbone of organized Daoist religion as it came to grow over the millennia (see Hendrischke 2000). As in the *Daode jing* and in mainstream culture, mothers and matrons were highly honored and played leading roles as wives of leaders and as senior priests or libationers (*jijiu*) in their own right. Beyond that, younger women were key participants in initiatory rites.

Early Daoists understood sexuality as the most direct way of harmonizing yin and yang, continuing a belief in ancient China that sexual exchange was necessary not only for the individual's wellbeing but also for the proper functioning of the universe. The emperor as intermediary between heaven and earth had a regulated sex life in harmony with the evolution of yin and yang *qi*. "Ladies of the court called *nüshi* were experts in the regulation and supervision of the sexual relationship of the king and his wives. They made sure that the king received them on the good days in the calendar according to the cycle established by the *Book of Rites* for each rank" (Gulik 1961, 42-43). In the countryside, villagers similarly celebrated the renewal of spring with festivals during which sacred unions were commonly practiced (see Granet 1932).

Early Daoists similarly saw the interaction of yin and yang as leading to a state of unitary *qi* and to harmony with the Dao; it could occur as bodily, spiritual, or intellectual intercourse (Reed 1987, 165-66). In either case, each partner had his or her role: the yang creating and engendering, the yin transforming and transmuting. In the sexual act as conceived by Daoists, adepts learned to detach themselves from desire and to dissociate orgasm from pleasure. The act itself was less important than its effect of setting the *qi* in harmonious motion along the inner bodily circuits of the participants, where it provided sustenance and nourishment instead of being wasted either by physically flowing out of the body or through passionate outbursts of emotion. In the sexual act Daoists prioritized the internal over the external, the invisible over the visible, in order to allow full empowerment of the harmony of the two forces, thereby benefiting themselves, their community, and the cosmos at large (Despeux 1990, 36).

Both the Way of Great Peace and the Celestial Masters practiced sexual rites as part of an initiatory rite known as "the harmonization of *qi*" (*heqi*). As far as we can tell from brief notes in later sources, it consisted of a complex ceremony during which male sexual energy (yellow *qi*) and female sexual energy (red *qi*) joined together in accord with cosmic forces (Schipper 1984, 203). The rite was in the quiet chamber (*jingshi*), in the presence of a master and an instructor. Adepts began with slow, formal movements accompanied by meditations to create a sacred space, then established the harmony between their *qi* and the cosmic *qi* through visualizations. For example:

> May each person visualize the *qi* of his cinnabar field [below the navel] as large as a six-inch mirror, leaving the body through open space. Its light progressively increases to illuminate the head and bathe the entire body in radiance, so that the adept can clearly discern the five organs, the six viscera, the nine palaces, the twelve lodgings, the four limbs, as well as all the joints, vessels, pores, and defensive and nutritive *qi* within the body and without. (*Shangqing huangshu guodu yi*, DZ 1294, 2a; Despeux 1990, 29-30)[9]

Next, adepts informed their master and various divinities that they were going to undertake the harmonization of *qi*. This involved ritualistic movements in precise directions and according to astronomically defined positions, as well as the concentration and firm maintenance of bodily essence and vital spirits through the retention of sexual fluids. Reverted away from orgasmic expulsion, these fluids were moved up along the spinal column and into the head, where they supposedly nourished the brain and enhanced the individual's health and the community's harmony. The risen *qi* would also communicate with the gods of the heavens who in turn erased the names of all participating members

---

[9] This text is a fourth-century Highest Clarity document that contains remnants of earlier practices, which date from the second or third centuries (Schipper 1994, 252). Titles in the Daoist canon are abbreviated DZ and numbered according to Schipper 1975; Komjathy 2002.

from the registers of death and instead inscribed them in the ledgers of long life and immortality (see Stein 1963; Yan 2001).

In this practice women functioned as equal partners. They were valued as important members of the community and carried their fair share of responsibility and benefits. Going beyond the ancient evaluation of yin as dark, weak, and withdrawing, the Celestial Masters established a new level of respect and honor for women among their followers. However, neither the Great Peace movement nor the Celestial Masters were able to practice their harmonization of *qi* for long. The Great Peace movement, believing their leader to be the next rightful emperor of China, in 184 rose in rebellion against the Han and was eliminated in a series of military campaigns. The Celestial Masters were caught up in political power struggles and surrendered their domain to the warlord Cao Cao in 215 (see Levy 1956; Kobayashi 1992). Following this, they were forced to migrate to different parts of north China and began to form small enclaves among the larger populace, who tended to view their sexual and energetic practices with suspicion and disdain. In due course several sets of new revelations grew from the mixture of Celestial Masters practices and local beliefs, transforming sexual initiations and shifting the vision of women to another dimension.

Divine Teachers

Both in the "New Code," a set of precepts to reform the Celestial Masters which was revealed to the visionary Kou Qianzhi (365-448) in north China in 415 and 423, and in the Highest Clarity revelations of Yang Xi (330-386) in south China in 364-370,[10] women appear less as equal sexual partners than as teachers and masters of techniques, providers of instruction and secrets for personal and communal cultivation.

For example, a key revelatory deity of the Highest Clarity texts was Wei Huacun (252-334), originally the daughter of a high official and an adept of the Celestial Masters (Reed 1987, 167). Married to a leading religious

---

[10] On Kou's new Daoism, see Mather 1979; Kohn 2000. On Yang Xi and the Highest Clarity revelations, see Robinet 1984; Strickmann 1978c; 1981.

officer and the mother of two sons, she retired to a separate part of the family compound and devoted herself to self-cultivation. In 299, she had visions of several perfected beings who presented her with sacred scriptures and oral instruction and became a libationer with ritual powers and administrative duties. During the war that led to the rise of the Eastern Jin in 317, her family fled to Jiankang (modern Nanjing), after which she spent much of her life in seclusion, receiving further visits from celestial perfected of high rank (Despeux 2000a, 388). Eventually she attained the Dao on the holy mountain of the south (Mount Heng) in Hunan, which at the time was an active center of both Buddhist and Daoist practices (see Faure 1987; Robson 1995). She was accordingly called Nanyue furen (Lady of the Southern Peak) and, after her ascension to heaven, appeared to Yang Xi and revealed numerous texts and instructions (Bumbacher 1998, 690-91; 2000a, 520).[11]

Other important female revealers in the Highest Clarity tradition include the Queen Mother of the West, the Lady of Purple Tenuity (Ziwei furen), and the Lady of Highest Prime (Shangyuan furen). In their role as teachers they continue an ancient tradition first found among texts on longevity practices, and especially on sexual arts, of women appearing as masters and instructors: the Simple Woman (Sunü), the Colorful Woman (Cainü), and the Mysterious Woman (Xuannü), each instructing the Yellow Emperor (Huangdi) and leaving a text on sexual fulfillment behind (Gulik 1961, 121-25).

In Highest Clarity, such learned ladies were known as "perfected women" (nüzhen), parallel to the term "perfected" (zhenren) that is applied to men. But the term zhen, which means "perfect," "whole," "authentic," is sometimes replaced by its homophone zhen*, meaning "virtuous" or "chaste," and occasionally the two words are used interchangeably (Despeux 1990, 32). Thus the Kaihua zhenjing (Perfect Scripture of Unfolding Transformation, DZ 1133) relates the virtues that a

---

[11] For more on Lady Wei, see Homann 1971, 19-21; Strickmann 1981, 142; Robinet 1984, 2:402; Cedzich 1987, 31-34; Despeux 1990, 56-60. On her cult, see Schafer 1977a). A Yuan-dynasty hagiography is found in Lishi zhenxian tidao tongjian houji (Supplement to the Comprehensive Mirror of Perfected Immortals and Those Who Embody the Dao, DZ 298), 3.7a-8a. This text is henceforth referred to as Tongjian houji.

"chaste woman" should cultivate—moral rectitude, filial piety, celibacy after being widowed—reflecting the qualities expected of women in traditional Chinese society, as already described in the *Nüjie* (Women's Precepts).[12]

Following the female role models of traditional Chinese society, Highest Clarity Daoism encouraged sexual abstinence and favored a more detached role for women. Yet it preserved the theme of sexual intercourse as an initiation and rite of communion by transposing it into the realm of the supernatural (Bumbacher 2000a, 521). Yang Xi, the chief interlocutor for the perfected in the *Zhen'gao* (Declarations of the Perfected, DZ 1016), accordingly says:

> When a perfected person is in the presence of a spirit-light companion, he must first prize the union with that light and the love between their two lights. Although they are called husband and wife, they do not practice marital acts. Speaking of them as a couple is merely a way of making understood that which can be revealed. But if the perfected person hangs on to ideas of the yellow and red [actual sex], he shall never see the supernatural spirits manifest themselves, nor have them for companions. (*Zhen'gao* 2.1a; Bumbacher 1998, 691; Despeux 1990, 58-59)

A set of technical instructions for this kind of union has adepts visualize the pure *qi* of the sun or the moon before their eyes, then imagine a goddess in its midst. The goddess grows stronger and more vivid with prolonged practice until she is felt present in the flesh. Pressing her mouth to the adept's, she dispenses celestial vapors to increase his vitality and, after a long courtship and repeated visualizations, might even lie down with him—all in the service of communicating secret celestial knowledge and experiences (see Schafer 1978b). Another variation of this theme of interiorized sexuality was the adept's visualization of the joining of interior yin and yang energies or of male and female divinities within the

---

[12] The *Nüjie* is a Han-dynasty text written by the female scholar Ban Zhao, considered the classic on feminine submission. See Gulik 1961, 98-103; Sung 1981; Kelleher 1987, 144-47; Mann 1991, 213-14; Paper 1997, 63-64; Raphals 1998, 236-46. For other works of instruction to women, see Raphals 1998, 246-57; Handlin 1975; Martin-Liao 1985.

body, such as the father of the Dao in the brain and the mother of the Dao in the kidneys.

Physical sexual practices were relegated to a minor rank and were no longer believed to lead to the highest level of realization. As the *Zhen'gao* says:

> A person cannot attain immortality if he only knows the bedroom arts and the methods of guiding *qi*. One must acquire the methods of the divine elixir, which will suffice to become immortal. Even better, if one gets hold of the *Dadong zhenjing* (Perfect Scripture of Great Profundity), even the way of the golden elixir will become irrelevant. Reciting this text ten thousand times is the best way to become immortal. (5.11b)

In the Highest Clarity, the understanding of immortality shifted away from extended physical longevity and the acquisition of magical powers towards a refined existence in the heavens. For this, scriptural mastery and the proper meditations were much more important than gymnastics and qi-practices. In accordance with this shift, the school had an ambiguous attitude towards sexuality, partly opposing the Celestial Masters. According to the *Zhen'gao*, the Lady of Purple Tenuity exclaims:

> The way of the yellow and the red, the art of commingling *qi*, constitutes one of the minor methods commended for becoming one of the elected as espoused by [the first Celestial Master] Zhang Daoling. The perfected [of Highest Clarity] do not make use of such practices. Although I have observed some people interrupting their decline by practicing these methods, I have never met anyone who has attained eternal life through them. (2.1a)

In Highest Clarity, the physical harmonization of yin and yang was therefore no longer sufficient for the attainment of immortality. Women as a result were seen less as consorts and sexual partners and more as aspects of celestial power who could reveal and teach the secrets of the Dao and who would communicate, closely but not necessarily sexually, with mortal seekers. This role was actively continued throughout the Tang dynasty, when numerous poems attest to the quest of the goddess pursued by Daoists and other seekers (see Cahill 1985; Hawkes 1967).

Founders and Religious Leaders

In the Tang and later dynasties, more and more women took holy orders and joined the religion, populating 550 convents among 1,687 Daoist institutions. Women underwent ordination into the same ranks and through the same ceremonies as men, and acquired the same status. They served both as priests in ritual functions and as nuns to pursue their own personal cultivation, remaining withdrawn and celibate yet also interacting with the society around them. Women from all areas of life joined convents, and Daoism in this period offered a genuine alternative to the mainstream model of women's lives.

Women were also venerated as prophets, healers, mediums, and shamanic travelers to the otherworld. They founded various new movements within the religion and served as matriarchs and leaders of existing ones. In the eighth century, when Daoism began to integrate various local cults—particularly in the maritime and central regions of the east and south—divine women of various sorts, such as goddesses of rivers and mountains, shamans, and cultic founders, grew in stature and often became objects of pilgrimages undertaken equally by men and women (see Schafer 1973).

One example of the development of a local cult under female auspices comes from the school of Pure Subtlety (Qingwei) and its first leader, the Tang priest Zu Shu (fl. 889-904; see Ren 1990, 565-66). After receiving ordination in various Daoist levels, she went to Guiyang where she met the Holy Mother of Numinous Radiance (Lingguang shengmu) who transmitted to her the Way of Pure Subtlety together with techniques of talismans and exorcism. Later followers placed Zu Shu at the head of their ancestral lineage, which was constructed in the thirteenth century (see Despeux 2000a, 390; Boltz 1987, 38-39).

In the Song dynasty, a popular cult grew around the Lady Near the Waters (Linshui furen). Originally named Chen Jinggu, she was born in 767 and, despite being gifted with supernatural powers, died young and pregnant at the age of twenty-four during a rain-making ritual. Her powers began to manifest after her death and she gradually grew into the protector of women, children, and boy mediums. Her cult first developed in her home state of Min (Fujian), then spread widely under the Song. Followers were magicians, controllers of demons, exorcists, and healers who could undertake shamanic travels to the otherworld. As the cult grew, local Daoists and literati adopted it and it still continues in Taiwan (see Berthier 1988; Despeux 2000a, 391).

Another senior women practitioner of the period was Cao Wenyi (fl. 1119-1125), a renowned poet and author of the *Dadao ge* (Song of the Great Dao), whose fame reached the ears of Emperor Huizong (r. 1101-1126) and earned her an invitation to the capital and a formal title. She wrote commentaries to various Daoist texts and was frequently lauded as a "master of tranquility and humane virtue and the perfection of the Dao." Also known as a follower of inner alchemy, she was later venerated by several Qing-dynasty lineages, notably that of Purity and Tranquility (Qingjing pai). This is evident in her appearances at spirit-writing séances and in various inscriptions preserved in the Baiyun guan (White Cloud Temple) in Beijing.

In the late twelfth century, with the Song dynasty under attack by Central Asian forces, the school of Complete Perfection (Quanzhen) arose, its founders openly presenting themselves to the aristocracy as practitioners who would save Chinese culture from the invasion of the barbarians. Women in this school served variously as abbots of major temples, wives or mothers of leading adepts, and key members of local associations. Among its first seven masters there was also a woman, Sun Buer (1119-1182).

Born into a powerful local Shandong family, she received a literary education and was married to Ma Yu (1123-1183), better known as Ma Danyang, and also called "Ma Who Had Half the Prefecture." The couple had three sons and lived in peaceful obscurity until 1167 when the founder Wang Chongyang visited the area. Converted to his creed, they became active disciples and Sun grew to be leader of the local Ninghai association, under the Hall of the Golden Lotus (Jinlian tang). Her merits earned her the Daoist title Serene One of Purity and Tranquility (Qingjing sanren), and she received the third and highest level of Complete Perfection ordination, becoming a senior leader with the right to teach and ordain (Despeux 2000a, 392). Her cult grew over later dynasties.

In these representative cases, women attained high levels of religious standing due to their merit and devotion to Daoist beliefs and practices. They worked closely with men and benefited from possessing mediumistic and healing powers. Honored for their potential motherhood, and spiritual competence, they were seen as valuable assets of the Dao, seats of internal seeds of perfection, and holders of the divine tradition of immortals.

Inner Alchemy

A special women's cultivation is found in the tradition of inner alchemy (*neidan*), the dominant form of Daoist practice since the Song dynasty and a key technique of Complete Perfection.[13] Ever since the early middle ages, Daoists had devoted themselves to the quest for immortality. Along with meditations and the enhancement of *qi*, they pursued laboratory or operative alchemy (*jindan*, "golden cinnabar") on the basis of mineral and vegetable ingredients. In the Tang, they moved dominantly towards internal cultivation, using alchemical vocabulary and processes to express their vision. Inner alchemy, the result of this shift, sought to obtain immortality through psychophysiological methods using the ingredients of the body. Through the union of opposites and a sequence of transmutations, the adept would reunite the two poles of life that combine to form the material and spiritual worlds. Returning from worldly multiplicity to the oneness of the Dao, adepts would achieve mystical fusion and attain the eternal life of the spirit.

Since the Song dynasty, there have been several alchemical traditions. Some combined outer and inner alchemy, others distinguished an outer and an inner phase. Many continued the visualizations of Highest Clarity expressed in alchemical terms. Generally the female body was seen as an ideal receptacle of inner alchemical transformation. Women practitioners essentially followed the same process as men, but they began the

---

[13] On inner alchemy, see Needham et al. 1983; Robinet 1989b; 1995; Lu 1970; Cleary 1987; 1992; Wilhelm 1984; Baldrian-Hussein 1994; Baryosher-Chemouny 1996; Skar and Pregadio 2000.

practices from a different starting point and had an advantage as progress set in. Their specific needs and moves, moreover, gave rise to special practices for women known as women's inner alchemy (*nüdan*).

Inner alchemy in many ways continued to use the basic methods of ancient Daoism: reverting sexual energies to nurture the brain, circulating *qi* inside the body, cultivating the three cinnabar fields (in abdomen, chest, and head) and the five organs, concentrating on key energy points in the body, and meditating on innate nature. It adopted these methods through the Chinese system of symbolic correlation, placing the phases of evolution from the Dao in direct correspondence with the alchemical process of refining gold.

The transmutations of inner alchemy involved three bodily energies— sexual fluid or essence (*jing*), vital energy (*qi*) and spirit (*shen*)—in a process of inversion and return to the Dao (Pregadio and Skar 2000, 488). In the first stage, the adepts join the various opposite (yin and yang) forces in the interior of their body and through them form an divine pearl which grows into an embryo of *qi*. The second stage consists of ten months of symbolic pregnancy, at the end of which the embryo is birthed as a being of light. The birth takes place through the top of the head, because the alchemical process inverts the course of ordinary procedures. In the third stage, this luminous spirit learns to freely leave and enter the body. It is further sublimated and eventually merges completely with cosmic emptiness.

As documented in texts on women's alchemy that arose in late imperial China, differences between the sexes occur only in the first of these three stages. Instead of refining semen by "subduing white tiger" (*fu baihu*) and transforming it into *qi*, women refine their menstrual blood, the "red dragon," by progressively diminishing its flow and eventually stopping it altogether. This is known as "decapitating the red dragon" (*zhan chilong*) and is first mentioned in a text of the year 1310. The cessation of the menstrual flow identifies the adept as both pregnant and prepubescent. Menstrual blood in analogy to the men's semen is sublimated and brings forth a "new blood," which certain texts call the "marrow of the white phoenix" (*baifeng sui*).

Both this term and the expressions "red dragon" and "white tiger" transpose ordinary body fluids to a new and higher level of spiritual power. When the texts wish to indicate the physical substance commonly discharged during intercourse or menstruation, they use ordinary or medical terms, such as *jing*, "semen," *yuexue*, "monthly blood," or *yue-shui*, "monthly flow." As the system does not allow a rupture between matter and spirit, the new symbolic language implies that both a physiological and spiritual transformation takes place, so that in effect the decapitation of the red dragon is physically present as the complete cessation of the menstrual flow (Despeux 2000a, 406). This signals great progress towards the attainment of immortality, the first major step in the return to oneness with the Dao, the initial recovery of primordial energy and inherent cosmic power. In this practice as much as in their roles as goddesses, representatives of yin, divine teachers, and renunciants, women in Daoism are ideally successful practitioners of the Dao who contribute significantly to its purity and activation on earth.

Daoist Women and Chinese Society

Daoism in the course of its history has had a multifaceted and complex relationship with women and the feminine. Following mainstream Confucian society, it accorded great honor to mothers and matrons and placed high value on fecundity, nurturing, caring, and other aspects associated with motherhood. It also followed the Confucian lead in placing married women secondary to their husbands, barring them from joining convents and allowing their initiation into the registers of the Celestial Masters only with the husband's consent.

Daughters similarly were treated in traditional ways and could only join a Daoist association or convent with their family's consent. Since ordination involved not only social changes but financial obligations and pledges, the family was accorded great importance. While daughters of non-Daoist households were known to join the Dao, for the most part young women who developed religious intentions came from a Daoist background and continued the family tradition in their own way. Still, whether of Daoist heritage or not, the religion clearly recognized the possibility that young girls might have spiritual potential and aspirations beyond marriage, and offered them a viable institutional alternative to staying within the confines of male governance. This alternative, moreover, was justified—not unlike in comparable Buddhist arguments (see Cole 1998)—with the notion that the truest and most potent form of filial piety and family service was to care for the otherworldly wellbeing of the ancestors and work for the living through intercession with the gods. Having a daughter join a Daoist institution was thus acceptable and in some cases even desirable

While Daoism had little impact on the lives of wives and mothers and offered limited opportunities for spiritually gifted daughters, it made a substantial difference for widows and divorcees. Often shunned by mainstream society, they found an active role as priests and nuns of the religion, which allowed them to attain ranks equal with those of men and live a life of comparative independence and freedom. Similarly, expelled concubines, former courtesans, and aging entertainers could find refuge and a new lease on life inside the Daoist organization, shifting their focus away from worldly involvement and towards the attainment of inner peace. No longer accountable to either parents or husband, these liminal figures posed a threat to Confucian order but offered great opportunity for the Dao. Mature, competent, and often with means of their own, they established convents, served as priests and healers, and contributed greatly to the shaping of Daoist organizations.

All these Daoist women looked to certain ideals in the shaping of their ideas and practices. Presented in myths, immortals' tales, historical records, and visions of the female body, these ideals show how Daoist women conceived of themselves and how they continued to grow towards greater harmony and oneness with the Dao.

Part One

Goddesses

Chapter One

The Queen of Immortals

The most important and most prominent Daoist goddess is Xiwang mu, the Queen Mother of the West. A potent cosmic deity and representative of the essential force of yin, she resides on the central world mountain of Kunlun and reigns over all the immortals, on occasion descending to the mortal realm and sharing her secrets. The goddess grew from ancient, popular, and shamanic origins. The earliest traces of a figure possibly related to the goddess date from the Shang dynasty (1766 – 1122 B.C.E.) and are found on an oracle bone that mentions an Eastern Mother and a Western Mother. No specifics are given, so these deities could have been mother goddesses, regional protectors, or divinized ancestors (Cahill 1993, 12-13; Frühauf 1999, 8-9).[1]

In the Zhou dynasty (1122-221 B.C.E.), the Queen Mother appears variously. Among the classical philosophers, she is a mythical ruler or inspiring teacher of sage kings. Thus the *Zhuangzi* (Book of Master Zhuang, ca. 250 B.C.E.) lists her among ancient emperors who attained the Dao, such as the creator figure Fu Xi and the Yellow Emperor, founder of culture and civilization. It says: "The Queen Mother of the West obtained the Dao and took up her seat at Shaoguang. No one knows her beginning, no one knows her end" (ch. 6; Cahill 1993, 14). Another philosophical text from the same period, the *Xunzi* (Writings of Master Xun) names her as the teacher of Yu, the mythical ruler who controlled the floods (ch. 27;

---

[1] Other studies of the Queen Mother include Fracasso 1982; Chan 1990; Birrell 1993. A detailed discussion of early sources is found in Frühauf 1999.

Cahill 1993, 14-15; Frühauf 1999, 47). The goddess is venerated among high sages who achieved closeness to the Dao.

A more popular and shamanic image of Xiwang mu emerges from a treatise on mythical geography known as the *Shanhai jing* (Classic of Mountains and Seas). It states that she resides on Jade Mountain (Yu-shan) or Tortoise Mountain (Guishan) in the far west and that she "looks like a human being with a leopard's tail and tiger's teeth. She excels in whistling, her hair is disheveled, and she wears a *sheng* headdress on her head. She has control over starry constellations in the sky, such as the Grindstone and the Five Shards" (2.9a; Mathieu 1983, 1:101; Cahill 1993, 15-16; Frühauf 1999, 22-31). According to another passage, she "leans on a bench, wears a *sheng* headdress, and carries a staff. South of her are three blue-black birds who take food for her as she resides to the north of the void of Mount Kunlun" (12.1a; Mathieu 1983, 1:481; Cahill 1993, 19).[2]

These various attributes and descriptions strongly suggest a tribal, sha-manic deity—half beast, half human, closely interacting with the animal world, served by bird attendants, whistling in total control of breath and sound (and therefore *qi*), and residing on mythical mountains associated with indestructibility (jade) and long life (tortoise). Her headdress, the *sheng* is a square, cornered object that perches steeply atop her head, its shape resembling an axle with two wheels and its symbolism linked with the loom and the art of weaving—the central creative and productive activity of women in traditional China and a sign of wealth and good fortune (Cahill 1993, 16; Frühauf 1999, 33-36) (see Fig. 1).[3]

---

[2] Similar birds are also attributes of another Daoist saint, the Holy Mother of Dongling (Dongling shengmu); they indicate ancient shamanic practices. There is a report, for example, of Deng Yuzhi, a Daoist who lived on the South-ern Peak in the fourth century. One day he saw three black birds dancing and beating a drum like cranes. He said to his disciples, "Since the black birds are there, the assembly of divinities is formed" (*Nanyue zongsheng ji*, T. 2097, 51.1066c; Despeux 1990). The abbreviation "T." stands for *Taishō daizō kyō* and indicates the Buddhist canon. It is followed by the number, volume, and page of the text.

[3] Other Han-dynasty sources that contain descriptions of Xiwang mu in-clude Sima Xiangru's (179-117 B.C.E.) *Daren fu* (Rhapsody of the Great Man), Guo Xian's (d. 33 C.E.) *Dongfang Shuo zhuan* (Biography of Dongfang Shuo), Wang

Fig. 1. Xiwang mu with her distinctive headdress, served by an entourage, and surrounded by the mythical animals of the sun and the moon. Source: Rubbing of pottery tile from Sichuan, first century C.E., Suzanne Cahill, private collection.

In the Han dynasty (206 B.C.E. – 220 C.E.), this fierce and powerful goddess, already imbued with multiple layers of associations and references, became known as a deity with particular potency to protect people from pestilence and famine and grant them long life and immortality. She emerged as the central figure of a peasant cult that arose in Shandong and swept through the country in 3 B.C.E. People flocked together in the thousands, carrying straw effigies and preparing to receive her as their new divine ruler. Amongst a wild scene of torches, beating drums, and shouting, the disheveled, barefoot peasants clambered over obstacles and raced along the high roads, making their way to Chang'an, the empire's capital. Everywhere they sang and danced in worship of the Queen Mother, wearing her talismans in the conviction that she would protect them from disease and death (*Hanshu* 27A.22a; Cahill 1993, 22).

Chong's (27-91 C.E.) *Lunheng* (Balanced Discussions), and Ban Gu's (3-54 C.E.) *Hanshu* (History of the Han Dynasty). The *Dadai liji* (Ritual Record of the Elder Dai) also recounts her exploits. See Frühauf 1999.

From sage ruler and vague shamanic deity, Xiwang mu emerged as a widely worshiped cosmic goddess, with powers not only over stars and beasts but also to bestow healing, protection, and immortality. While shamanic traces still remained in the ritualized trances of her followers, the goddess had grown into a divinely sent messiah and savior.

Goddess of Immortality

The salvific, life-giving aspect of the Queen Mother continued to grow as the Han dynasty progressed. Her image appears frequently in tombs, usually paired with her male, yang counterpart, the Lord King of the East (Dongwang gong). Depicted on murals, paintings, reliefs, tiles, and bronze mirrors, she is ubiquitous and represents creation, cosmic immortality, and easy communication with the otherworld. She is invoked in poems and inscriptions to deliver the souls of the dead to an ancestral paradise or to grant them rebirth among the immortals (Cahill 1993, 24-29; also Loewe 1979; Seidel 1982; Reed 1987, 179; Wu 2000).

At the same time, she is firmly linked with the mythical world mountain of Kunlun, now described as a steep, terraced peak rising from a body of water so weak it will not even float a feather. On its slopes the hanging gardens bring forth the peaches of immortality that ripen only once in three thousand years. On its peak the mighty towers and palaces of the Heavenly Walled City (Yongcheng) overlook the Turquoise Pond (Yaochi), where the immortals hold their banquets (Cahill 1993, 37-38; Sōfukawa 1981). The *Shizhou ji* (Record of the Ten Continents), a fourth-century outline of the Daoist cosmos, describes it:

> Mount Kunlun rises thirty-six thousand miles above the surrounding plain. Its top has three corners and is ten thousand miles wide. It is shaped like a hanging bowl. Its base is narrow and its top wide, thus it is called Kunlun, "high and precarious." . . .

> On one corner of the mountain there are heaps of gold which make up the Heavenly Walled City. It is one thousand square miles in area. In the city there are five golden terraces and twelve jade towers. . . .

> There are also halls of luminescent green jade, mansions of
> carnelian florescence, purple, halcyon, and cinnabar mansions,
> phosphorescent clouds, a candle sun, and vermilion clouds of
> ninefold radiance. This is the place governed by the Queen
> Mother of the West and revered by all perfected officials and
> immortal beings. (10b-11a; Smith 1990, 111-12)

Over the following centuries, the Queen Mother continued to and
emerged as a key deity of the Highest Clarity school. Here she not only
resides in the splendid palaces of Mount Kunlun, but is the ruler of immortals, the controller of fate, the giver of good fortune, and the bestower of celestial blessings. She manages the holy scriptures of the religion, assuring their exactness and providing suitable transmission to
earth; she creates protective talismans; she gives instructions on internal
cultivation; and to the very fortunate she appears in person and bestows
upon them the peaches of immortality which will grant a better and
faster access to the divine realms (see Fig. 2).[4]

Most famous among the people blessed by an appearance of Xiwang mu
is the Han Emperor Wu (r. 140-87 B.C.E.), whom she allegedly visited in
110 B.C.E. with an extensive entourage of celestial attendants and divine
ladies. As recorded in Zhang Hua's (232-300 C.E.) encyclopedic *Bowu zhi*
(Record of Extensive Things; see Stranghair 1973) and later developed in
the fourth-century hagiography *Han Wudi neizhuan* (Esoteric Biography
of the Han Emperor Wu, DZ 292; trl. Schipper 1965; Smith 1992), the
Queen Mother initiated contact by first sending a messenger announcing
her arrival. This gave the emperor time to prepare a room for the meeting, scheduled to occur on the seventh day of the seventh month (Cahill
1993, 54-55).

---

[4] Xiwang mu's role in the transmission of scriptures is outlined in the sixth-
century encyclopedia *Wushang biyao* (Secret Essentials of the Most High, DZ
1138; see Lagerwey 1981, 117-19), 32.1a-12b.

西王母

Fig. 2. The Queen Mother of the West with two ladies-in-attendance on the balus-trade of her heavenly palace on Mount Kunlun. Source: *Zengxian liexian zhuan*.

This date, originally related to the cycle of popular festivals and exorcisms, stands at the midpoint of the year with the cosmic forces in perfect balance. It marks the day when the divine and human worlds touch, and is the optimal date for the exchange of yin and yang (Bodde 1975, 281-88). According to legend, on this day the Weaver Maid and the Oxherd Boy—two stars from different parts of the Milky Way that symbolize yin and yang—meet with the help of a cosmic bridge formed by magpies.

It is also the day when Daoist adepts have closest access to the otherworld, when immortality seekers succeed in their endeavors, and when deities descend to earth. More recently, this date has become a day of celebration for women, the number seven associated with their energy cycles and thus symbolizing the female. In Japan, this date marks a highly popular festival known as Tanabata when people write their wishes on pieces of colored paper and knot them into ornamental branches—certain that this practice will communicate their desires to the gods (Loewe 1979, 120; Schipper 1965, 52-53; Kominami 1991).

On this wondrous date, in 110 B.C.E., the emperor was in full readiness in his holy chamber to receive the Queen Mother, who arrived to the sound of celestial flutes and drums and in the company of numerous divine ladies, dragons, phoenixes, and her three bird messengers.

> The Queen Mother was wearing a long unpadded robe of multi-colored damask with a yellow background; its patterns and colors were fresh and bright. Her radiant propriety was clear and serene. Belted with the great cord of the numinous flying beings, at her waist was a sword for dividing heads.
>
> On top of her head was a great floriate topknot. She wore the cap of the great perfected infants of dawn. She stepped forth on shoes studded with primal rose-gem, resting on phoenix-patterned soles.
>
> She looked to be about thirty years old. Her stature was about average, but her heavenly appearance eclipsed and overshadowed all others. Her face and countenance were incomparable—truly, she was a numinous person (*Han Wudi neizhuan* 2ab; Cahill 1993, 57; Smith 1992, 2:484).

After engaging in a formal banquet and polite exchange with the emperor, the goddess offers him several peaches of immortality, laughing at him when he hopes to plant their pits and grow more of the divine fruit. She also provides the emperor with detailed instructions on internal cultivation and various methods of pursuing the Dao, and supports him with sacred texts and protective talismans. Eventually she takes her leave, wishing him the best in his immortal endeavors. However, in the following years, despite his firm intention to develop his inner truth and attain the Dao, the emperor gets too deeply enmeshed in politics and power struggles. He fails to follow the instructions with discipline and thus forsakes the divine seed that the Queen Mother planted, never attaining ultimate ascension to the immortals (Cahill 1993, 147-68; Frühauf 1999, 75-77).

Several other seekers were similarly blessed by a personal encounter with Xiwang mu. Among them is King Mu of Zhou (r. 1001-946 B.C.E.) who frequently engaged in travel through his realm, on occasion even veering far into the unknown. These journeys are described in the *Mu tianzi zhuan* (Biography of Mu, Son of Heaven, DZ 291; trl. Mathieu 1978), an anonymous historical novel allegedly written around 400 B.C.E. but known in extant sources only since the third century C.E. (Nienhauser 1986, 632-33). The stories are also summarized in the *Liezi* (Book of Master Lie), a collection of Daoist tales and philosophical vignettes from about 300 C.E. On one of these trips, King Mu journeyed all the way to Mount Kunlun, where he visited the Queen Mother. "They toasted each other on the banks of the Turquoise Pond, and the Queen Mother composed a song for the king, which he returned with one of his own" (*Liezi* 3; Graham 1960, 64; Cahill 1993, 48).[5] Following this, the king returned to his realm enriched through the encounter but not quite immortal.

Other famous figures blessed by the goddess are the Yellow Emperor, who receives a powerful talisman that ensures his victory over Chiyou, the Wormy Rebel (Lewis 1990, 165-66);[6] the filial ruler Shun who gains

---

[5] Details of their lyrics are found in the *Mu tianzi zhuan* 3.15-16. See Cahill 1993, 50-51; Mathieu 1978. For a critical discussion, see Porter 1996.

[6] The Yellow Emperor also receives help from a disciple of the Queen Mother, the Mysterious Woman of the Nine Heavens (Jiutian xuannü), who

her admiration because of his outstanding virtue; and the great Yu who only succeeds in taming the floods because he receives active support from the goddess (see Cahill 1993, 109-19). In all these cases, the Queen Mother of the West appears as a helpful and accessible supporter of human endeavors, providing protection and instructions for the attainment of peace and justice in the world and perfection in the supernatural sphere. She is the queen of Kunlun from where she controls all fates, but she is also the giving mother who cares for and protects her subjects. She rules as the mistress of the universe, yet serves as indulgent teacher and supporter of humanity. Part of the creative essence of the cosmos, she is a true mother: first and foremost available to assist people in their spiritual endeavors, never tiring to awaken the divine essence in worthy subjects and by implication all Daoist seekers.

Metal Mother of the Universe

While the image of the Queen Mother in the early middle ages conforms closely to the ideal of the female in Highest Clarity Daoism—the divine giver of instructions and protection—her late medieval representation enhances her stature and makes her even more potent as the highest representative of the pure power of yin. This later manifestation is described by Du Guangting (850-933 C.E.), court Daoist, senior master, and a renowned ritualist.

Born near Chang'an, Du Guangting underwent Daoist training on Mount Tiantai in Zhejiang and lived there in seclusion. In 875, he was called to court by Emperor Xizong and became an editor of imperial memoranda. He also served as a court counsellor and participated in controversies with the Buddhists, eventually rising to the rank of commissioner of Daoist ritual. After the capital was sacked by rebels in 881, he fled with the imperial court to Sichuan, where he edited and compiled Daoist texts and liturgies. Following the court, he returned to Chang'an

---

serves as divinity of war, sex, and everlasting life, and can be seen as a secondary manifestation of Xiwang mu (*Yongcheng jixian lu* 6.2a-4a; *Tongjian houji* 2.1a-3a). See Cahill 1992.

in 885 and again joined fled back to Sichuan a year later. In 901, the Tang exile government was overthrown by a local warlord, who established the kingdom of Shu. Du joined this new regime as royal tutor. He continued to be promoted by the Sichuan king until he retired from official service to Mount Qingcheng, where he compiled, edited, and composed Daoist texts until his death in 933 (see Verellen 1989).

During the later period of his life, Du Guangting wrote a number of important Daoist works, including an anthology of women's hagiographies called the *Yongcheng jixian lu* (Record of the Assembled Immortals of the Heavenly Walled City, DZ 783).[7] Consisting of two *juan* and partly contained in the eleventh-century encyclopedia *Yunji qiqian* (Seven Tablets in a Cloudy Satchel, DZ 1032), this text has the most elaborate presentation of Xiwang mu among Daoist texts, integrating all the different traditions that had accrued around her and emphasizing her cosmic stature and embodiment of yin (see Cahill 1986a).

The text calls her Mother Metal Mother (Jinmu) after the cosmic phase associated with the west, and lists a series of her numinous titles. The hagiography begins:

> The goddess Metal Mother is the Ninefold Numinous and Greatly Wondrous Metal Mother of Tortoise Mountain. Sometimes she is also called the Greatly Numinous and Ninefold Radiant Metal Mother of Tortoise Terrace. Another common name of hers is Queen Mother of the West. (9a)

Stating that "she is, in fact, the incarnate wondrousness of the innermost power of the west, the ultimate venerable of all-pervading yin *qi*," Du Guangting describes her birth as originating from the Dao itself. As the Dao, he says, "was resting in nonaction, it desired to unfold and guide the mysterious accomplishments of creation, to bring forth and raise the myriad beings" (9a). To do so, it took pure cosmic yang *qi* and created the Queen Mother's male counterpart, the Lord King of the East, here known as the Wood Lord (Mugong) and associated with spring and the color blue-green. Then,

---

[7] Suzanne Cahill has made an extensive study of this work see Cahill 1986a; 1992; 2000; 2001. A translation and analysis of the text is forthcoming in *Divine Secrets of the Daoist Sisterhood* (Cambridge: Three Pines Press).

the Dao took the perfected wondrous energy of the innermost power of the west and transformed it into the Metal Mother. The Metal Mother was born on the shore of Yonder River on the Divine Continent. Jue is her surname, and Kou the clan to which she belongs. As soon as she was born, she soared up in flight. Born from the *qi* of highest yin, she rules in the west. Because of this she is also called the Queen Mother of the West.

In the beginning, she derived her substance from great nonbeing. She floated along in spirit and was mysteriously hidden in the midst of the west's confused chaos of primordial energy. Then she divided the pure essence of the great Dao to connect it back together again and form herself a body. (9b)

Consisting of nothing but utterly pure, cosmic energy, the Queen Mother represents the essence of ultimate yin. "She mothers and nourishes all kinds of beings, whether in heaven above or on the earth below, whether in any of the three worlds or in any of the ten directions. Especially all women who ascend to immortality and attain the Dao are her dependents" (9b).

Not left to do all the great work alone, moreover, she is accompanied by a number of assistants and ladies-in-waiting. They also have biographies in Du Guangting's work.[8] Designated as the "women" of the Queen Mother, they are described in terms of their human names—whether given at birth on the human plane or adopted when they descended to deliver divine teachings—and through their celestial exploits, such as attainment of specific methods, ecstatic travels, or connections with cosmic deities. They serve as instructors to humanity and are highly literate, creating poems of great quality, often in large numbers. In this latter trait they resemble the perfected of Highest Clarity who tend to express themselves frequently in verse (see Russell 1985). The ladies, like the Queen Mother herself, represent the powerful and all-knowing nature of

---

[8] Among them are the Lady of Highest Prime (Shangyuan furen; 2.1a-13b), the Lady of Great Perfection (Taizhen furen; 4.1a-10b), the Lady of Numinous Efflorescence (Linghua furen; 3.1a-4b), the Queen of the South Culmen (Nanji wang furen; 2.16a-18a), and the Queen of Purple Tenuity (Ziwei wang furen; 3.6b-15b). See also *Tongjian houji*, ch. 3.

the cosmos, a great reservoir of depth and hidden strength which is transmitted to human beings on special occasions.

The Power of Yin

Xiwang mu is seen as the perfect embodiment of the cosmic power of yin. As such, she comes to fulfill three distinct roles that each symbolize the cosmic dimension of yin and its activation in the world. These roles signify the empowerment of women in different areas of life. First, she is the personification of the Dao and the key administrator of the universe, with powers bestowed directly from the central deity of the world. Du Guangting says:

> The Heavenly King of Primordial Beginning [Yuanshi tian-wang] bestowed upon her the primordial lineage record of the myriad heavens and the Tortoise Mountain registers of nine-fold radiance. He empowered her to control and summon the myriad spirit forces of the universe, to assemble and gather the perfected and the sages of the world, to oversee all covenants and examine the people's quality of faith.
>
> Moreover, she presides over all formal observances in the various heavens as well as at all audiences and banquets held by the celestial worthies and supreme sages. In addition, it is her duty to supervise the correcting and editing of the sacred scriptures in heaven, to reflect divine light on the proceedings. Her responsibility covers all the treasured scriptures of Highest Clarity, the jade writs of the Three Caverns, as well as the sacred texts that are bestowed at ordination. (10b; Kohn 1993, 59; Cahill 1993, 104)

In this role, Xiwang mu has complete authority to run a celestial palace — matching aristocratic women who similarly ran entire palaces and organizations with a strong hand (Paper 1997, 60). She alone is in charge of the important task of gathering the celestials and presiding over formal observances — what any good hostess and mistress of her domain would do in the world — but in addition she also manages the editing, correcting, and processing of the sacred scriptures, the backbone of all Daoist teaching and the holy containers of the religion's essence.

Completely fulfilling this role, the Queen Mother documents in a mythical way the importance of women and their potential to run important aspects of life with competent management and full responsibility. Women are empowered by the goddess because she creates a representation of femininity that clearly involves superior ability and eminent leadership. There is nothing timid or hesitant about this goddess—she provides a model of feminine authority and assertiveness. Just as the image of the goddess encourages women to emulate this part of their inherent potential, so it reminds men of women's competence and inherent power.

In a second aspect, the embodiment of utmost yin through the Queen Mother enhances the appreciation of the female aspect in the human body. She appears in early medieval literature as a body divinity and object of visualization. As the *Laozi zhongjing* (Central Scripture of Laozi, DZ 1168),[9] a meditation text associated with Highest Clarity, says:

> She resides in the center of a person's right eye. Her surname is Great Yin, her name Mysterious Radiance, and her cognomen Supine Jade. One must obtain the King Father and the Queen Mother to guard and preserve one's eyes. Only then can one practice pacing the void above the stars. . . .

> Similarly, the two nipples represent the germinal *qi* of the myriad gods, where yin and yang pour down and bubble up. Below the left nipple is the sun; below the right nipple is the moon. They are also the residences of the King Father and the Queen Mother. Above they rule in the center of the eyes, and play on top of the head. Then they come to rest beneath the nipples and lodge in the purple chambers of the Scarlet Palace [the heart]. (3b-4a; Cahill 1993, 35-36; Schipper 1994, 110)

Xiwang mu, paired with Dongwang gong, is the divine representation of cosmic yin inside the body—seen as a replica of the larger universe,

---

[9] The text is also contained in *Yunji qiqian*, chs. 18-19. For discussions, see Schipper 1979; 1994, 105; Robinet 1993, 135; Ren and Zhong 1991, 924.

complete with stars, gods, rivers, and mountains.[10] The divinities in the body, who simultaneously reside in the stars, represent both the instinctual/demonic and the spiritual/divine sides of the human personality and stand for both yin and yang. Yang is found in the three *hun* or spirit souls, while yin is present in the seven *po* or material souls. The same dichotomy also applies to two sets of three divinities each, the Three Ones (*sanyi*) who represent people's heavenly potential and the Three Corpses or Deathbringers (*sanshi*) who entice them towards evil and make them sick (see Kohn 1997a). By becoming aware of the internal yin and yang tendencies, Daoists learn to reorient their bodies toward purer levels of *qi* and eventually attain direct communication with the heavenly forces. They become one with them and ascend to immortality.

The power of yin in this context is just as important as the power of yang. Both have to be refined and purified equally for the adept to attain wholeness and gain access to spiritual perfection. This holds true equally for men and women. Women, through the goddess residing within, learn to appreciate and enhance their femininity along with the masculine strength that they too possess. Men, on the other hand, understand that they can never be complete without acknowledging and honoring their female self. By visualizing the goddess in the body, moving about and resting near the heart, members of both sexes realize their full potential.

In a third dimension of the Queen Mother of the West, she shows the power of female sexuality. Sexuality, as noted earlier, was understood as the most direct and most obvious way of activating and harmonizing yin and yang. Practiced in a Daoist or longevity setting, sexuality is used to revert *jing* or "essence" into *qi*, which then allows its transformation into *shen* or "spirit." Sexual arousal, and thus intercourse, serves to activate the *jing* deep in the body and bring it to the surface. Only when *jing* is tangible can it be reverted, through concentration and pressure applied at the right moment, into the *qi* that enhances life.

Typically sexual manuals are directed at a male audience, encouraging men to select young partners and change them frequently, forcing women to give up their *jing* without losing their own through ejaculation

---

[10] On the body in Daoism, see Schipper 1978; 1994; Kohn 1991; Andersen 1994; Kroll 1996; Saso 1997; Bumbacher 2001.

(Furth 1994, 135). The Queen Mother, on the other hand, balances this one-sided picture by representing a strong woman who dominates the power exchange, using men—preferably young—to acquire *jing* and revert it to nourish her own health and longevity. Her practice is described in a text entitled "Sexual Instructions of the Master of Pure Harmony," which is cited at length in the *Yufang bijue* (Secret Instructions of the Jade Chamber), probably of Tang origin. The text was lost in China but transmitted to Japan, where it was included in the medical compendium *Ishimpō* (Essential Medical Methods; dat. 984) by the court physician Tamba no Yasuyori. The text says:

> The Master of Pure Harmony says: Beyond cultivating the yang, yin *qi* can be developed as well. The Queen Mother of the West, for example, attained the Dao by cultivating her yin. Whenever she had intercourse with a man, he would immediately get weaker, while her complexion would be ever more radiant without the use of rouge or powder. . . .
>
> When having intercourse with a man, first calm your heart and still your mind. If the man is not yet fully aroused, wait for his *qi* to arrive and restrain your emotions in order to attune yourself to him. Do not move or become agitated, lest your yin-*jing* become exhausted first. If this happens, you will be left deficient and be susceptible to illnesses due to wind and cold. . . .
>
> If a woman is able to master this Dao and has frequent intercourse with men, she can avoid all grain for nine days without getting hungry. Even those who are sick or have sexual relations with ghosts attain this ability to fast. But they become emaciated after a while. So, how much more beneficial must it be to have intercourse with men? (28.7b-8a; Kohn 1993, 156; Ishihara and Levy 1970; Wile 1992, 102-3)

Here the Queen Mother not only embraces her female sexuality, giving encouragement to all women who follow her, but even uses it in an aggressive, exploitative way to enhance her inner essences and thus increase her potential for health, beauty, and vitality (Furth 1994, 134). She dedicates herself selfishly to the attainment of pleasure and power, using enchantment to realize her sexuality and giving free reign to what mainstream society would consider shameful and dangerous. In this version of Xiwang mu's hagiography, sexuality is praised and intercourse with multiple partners is encouraged—preferably with real and living men, not imaginary couplings with ghosts and specters. This creates a scenario highly liberating for women, showing them that their sexuality and their inborn power of yin can be enjoyed for the sake of personal transformation and does not need to be harnessed and contained for reproduction or for the benefit of men.

Cultic Veneration in the Tang

Given her strong enhancement of femininity and the power of yin, it is not surprising that the Queen Mother of the West has been actively associated with women ever since the early middle ages. She is often reported to make appearances in Daoist women's lives, helping and guiding them along their spiritual path. For example, the Queen Mother of Hebei (Hebei wangmu) had regular visions of Xiwang mu, and Xie Ziran, a Tang priestess, received steady guidance from the goddess.[11] The Queen Mother also served as the patron of Daoist lay women and protector of female outsiders—actresses, prostitutes, widows, and nuns— and accordingly received numerous praises in Tang poetry, such as the ode by Li Bo in honor of the Princess Jade Perfection (Yuzhen) who took Daoist vows in 711 (see Benn 1991):

> The immortal lady Jade Perfection
> Often goes to the peaks of great Mount Hua.
> At pure dawn she sounds the celestial drum;
> A whirlwind arising, she soars upward on paired dragons.
> She plays with lightning without resting her hands,
> Traverses the clouds without leaving a trace.
> Whenever she enters the Minor Apartment Peak,
> The Queen Mother is there to meet her.
> (*Quan Tangshi* 948; Cahill 1993, 217)

---

[11] See *Tongjian houji* (3.6a-7a; 5.8b-11b); *Taiping guangji* (Extensive Record of the Taiping Era), a tenth-century encyclopedia (60.40).

In the Tang, the cult to Xiwang mu had spread through the empire, from Mount Heng, the sacred peak of the south where she had a traveling residence, to Mount Hua near Xi'an where the tomb of her earthly remains was believed to be located, and even as far as Mount Wuyi in the southeast. As recorded in the local gazetteer *Nanyue zhi* (Record of the Southern Peak), near the main temple to the mountain there was a Daoist monastery named Qizhen guan (Monastery of Sojourning Perfected), which contained a major hall specially dedicated to her (20.12b).

On a more official level, the Queen Mother was venerated by the state and invoked in connection with a rite known as "tossing the dragons" (*toulong*), which involved the delivery of prayers and petitions to the gods by casting metal images of dragons—the messengers of the divine—into flowing streams (see Chavannes 1919; Kamitsuka 1992). Performed mainly on Mount Tai, the sacred peak of the east and residence of the god of the underworld, the ceremony caused the construction of some major temples and the creation of a pond, still known today as the Queen Mother's Pond—an earthly equivalent of the Turquoise Pond on Mount Kunlun (Cahill 1993, 59).

Another site made holy through this ceremony of "tossing the dragons" and the presence of the Queen Mother is Mount Wangwu in Henan. Residence of Sima Chengzhen (647-735), the twelfth patriarch of Highest Clarity and highest ranking Daoist under Emperor Xuanzong (r. 713-755) (see Engelhardt 1987; Kirkland 1986), this was also the first of thirty-six grotto-heavens (*dongtian*), supernatural passage ways that connected the sacred mountains of the earth with each other and with the realm of the immortals. Xiwang mu was actively worshiped here, and ceremonies in her honor and of communication with the otherworld took place on a regular basis (Cahill 1993, 60).

The Queen Mother also had a sanctuary that received official sponsorship on Mount Hua in Shaanxi. As the sacred peak of the west, this location had the same cosmological associations as the Queen Mother— metal, fall, death, spirits, tiger, and so on. It housed a temple dedicated in her honor (Cahill 1993, 60). There probably existed numerous other undocumented sanctuaries to the goddess, however, written sources and official documents on her cult are rare, perhaps because the more orthodox Daoist government focused on her official worship and tended to ignore her more popular impact, possibly because it feared the cult's revolutionary potential (Cahill 1986b).

Not only venerated by women and officially recognized by the state, Xiwang mu in the Tang dynasty was also the object of male worship. Men pursued her as the queen of immortals and bestower of boons, singing her praises and continuing an ancient shamanic tradition that invoked the goddess to descend and share her powers (see Hawkes 1967).[12] As documented in the *Chuci* (Songs of the South), a collection of shamanic songs and ritual chants from the third century B.C.E., shamans—both male and female—were eager to receive boons from the gods and enter into close personal relations with them, enticing them to descend to earth with prayers, fragrant flowers, dances, and offerings (see Hawkes 1959). The relationship was often couched in erotic and sexual terms, and involved a close union between the human and the divine. The meeting, if it ever took place, was highly formalized, preceded by ample petitions and prayers and accompanied by banquets, music, and the transmission of divine secrets. The departure of the supernatural partner usually left the human desolate and yearning for more—wallowing in misery and resentment for being left alone (Cahill 1985, 199-200).

Later Worship

In the Ming and Qing dynasties, the Queen Mother of the West was linked to the Eternal Mother (Wusheng laomu), a Buddhist-inspired mother goddess of popular religious movements. She created the world in the beginning of time and continues to return to assist her numerous children in leading proper lives and finding perfection, eventually taking them to her western paradise (see Overmyer 1976; Jordan and Overmyer 1986, 20). In this form and following the dominant tendency in late imperial China to "harmonize the three teachings" of Confucianism, Bud-

---

[12] More than five hundred poems invoking her are contained in the *Quan Tangshi* (Complete Tang Poems; see Cahill 1993). For shamanic relations among men and goddesses, see also Schafer 1973; Cahill 1985.

dhism, and Daoism, the goddess represents a mixture of different ideals, joining moral actions and community spirit seamlessly with the pursuit of nirvana and the attainment of health and immortality (Jordan and Overmyer 1986, 24). She is represented under various names in several scriptures, including so-called precious scrolls (*baojuan*). These texts are revealed in spirit-writing séances and addressed to a group of lay followers, made up largely of women and belonging to different religious societies, such as the White Lotus Sect (Bailian pai) or the Unity Religion (Yiguan dao; Jordan and Overmyer 1986, 227).

One major record of the goddess's exploits that was not revealed in a séance but stems from the hand of the senior official Wang Shizhen (1526-1590), a native of Taicang in Suzhou and the author of several Daoist works including a collection of immortals' biographies, the *Liexian quanzhuan* (Complete Immortals' Biographies, ZW 957[13]). His *Jinmu ji* (Record of the Metal Mother), contained in his collected works, the *Yanzhou shanren xugao* (More Works from the Man of Mount Yan-zhou, ch. 68), pulls together information from earlier sources including the *Han Wudi neizhuan*, Du Guangting's *Yongcheng jixian lu*, and the Yuandynasty *Tongjian houji* (DZ 298, 1.9a-21a) (Waltner 1987, 119-20). The occasion of its compilation was Wang Shizhen's involvement with the Daoist experiences of a young woman from his hometown, known as Tanyangzi, who before her bodily ascension to immortality undertook an ecstatic journey to the court of the Queen Mother.

Tanyangzi was born as Wang Taozhen in 1558, the second child of Wang Xijue, a friend and clansman of Wang Shizhen. As he describes in the *Tanyang dashi zhuan* (Biography of the Great Master Tanyang), she is drawn to a spiritual life from early on, and even as a child cuts images of the bodhisattva Guanyin from paper to worship her and regularly chants the name of Amitābha. When her parents betrothed her to a local official's son, she remains detached since she knows that marriage is not her destiny. Indeed, her fiancé dies three months after the betrothal gifts are exchanged. Tanyangzi mourns for her intended and considers herself a widow, which leaves her free to pursue the religious path. As part of this

---

[13] The abbreviation "ZW" stands for *Zangwai daoshu* (Daoist Texts Outside the Canon), a twentieth-century reprint of Daoist texts as found in non-canonical sources. The numbering follows Komjathy 2002.

path, she engages in deep meditations and has various visions. According to one of them,

> One night I dreamed of a Supreme Perfected. Her beauty was extraordinary. On her head she wore a seven-ridged cap; on her feet were embroidered slippers. She was seated beneath a five-colored cloud, with one arm resting on a small arm-rest. Her other hand rested on a white jade zither that had no strings.
>
> At her right there was a Daoist nun, clad in green with her hair hanging loose. On her left there was an old woman, clad in brown. She was more than seventy years old. The younger one pointed to the one in the middle and said: "This is the great goddess whom you have worshiped." (*Yanzhou shanren xugao* 78.2b-3a; Waltner 1987, 111)

The goddess then bestows upon Tanyangzi a character written in smoke which she breathes in and swallows. So blessed, she is able to live completely without taking food and gives up eating, much to the concern of her family, who are also not too pleased by the host of spirits that engage their daughter's attention. However, Tanyangzi continues her chosen path and is subjected to four temptations by the gods, testing her steadfastness in the face of "a lewd book, the erotic attraction to a comely man, attachment to physical life itself, and the sensual potential of her own body" (Waltner 1987, 113).

Eventually she has an enlightenment experience in the form of inner alchemy, feeling the immortal embryo take shape within, then leave her body to journey through the universe. Her spiritual career culminates in her audience with the Queen Mother in 1577. She visits her splendid palace surrounded by clouds and water, where heaven and earth are indistinguishable. She sees the Queen Mother attended by a hundred women-in-waiting and is received as an initiate. She receives the secrets of long life and immortality and learns the date of her impending transformation. When the time comes a few months later, she maintains great calm.

Seated in the shrine to her dead fiancé and accompanied by the prayers of her followers, she leaves her body (Waltner 1987, 115-16).[14]

The Daoist career of Tanyangzi shows the continued power and influence of the Queen Mother in the lives of Daoist women. Merged by the late Ming with Guanyin, the bodhisattva of compassion, and with Wusheng laomu, the goddess who created the universe, she is still distinct in her location, appearance, and function, playing a clear role in the Daoist transformation of the adept. She is majestic and imposing, and serves as the dominant instructor of the female seeker. Not hesitating to exert her powers, she calls the girl to her heavenly abode and presides over her transformation from human to immortal.

More recently, the Queen Mother of the West, again linked with Guanyin and Wusheng laomu, has emerged as a popular deity in Taiwan (see Ho 2003), where she also serves as central goddess of the Compassion Society (Cihui tang), founded after World War II, in 1949 (Jordan and Overmyer 1986, xvii). Called the Metal Mother of the Turquoise Pond (Yaochi jinmu), or simply Queen Mother (Wangmu niangniang), she appears to cult leaders and selected members through the planchette, a form of automatic writing undertaken in trance. Followers obey her instructions, which include ethical rules as well as methods of religious training, and learn to activate her presence through ritual worship, ecstatic dance, trance states, and good deeds. They wear blue-green uniforms as a sign of their membership and find physical healing, social community, and spiritual attainment through the practice (Jordan and Overmyer 1986, xviii).

The Queen Mother of the Compassion Society is too high and transcendent to be depicted as a personal deity and often appears in images as a dragon. She takes an active part in the lives of women and guides them to their greatest personal and spiritual attainment, often bringing about miracles and fortuitous coincidences. For instance, a devotee called Exquisite Fragrance reports how the Mother protects her against various vicissitudes of life:

---

[14] A more detailed study of the life and impact of Tanyangzi is forthcoming: Ann Waltner, *The World of a Late-Ming Visionary: T'an-yang-tzu and Her Followers* (Berkeley: University of California Press).

> Once my husband and I were coming back from the Palace [of
> Mother worship] in the rain. When we reached this little path
> and were about to come in, two kids on a motorcycle came
> along really fast. My husband was riding the bicycle with me
> [sidesaddle] on the back, and the motorcycle hit us in the back
> wheel. I felt as though somebody held my body and gradually
> lowered it to the ground. I was sitting on the ground and
> hadn't been hurt at all. Nor had my husband. . . . The two kids
> tried to run away on the motorcycle, but it wouldn't restart. It
> was as if the Mother wouldn't let them run away. (Jordan and
> Overmyer 1986, 191)

Thus even in the most ordinary situations of daily life women in contact
with the Queen Mother believe themselves protected and cherished in a
supernatural way, gaining the ability to take care of their families, serve
benevolently in society, develop personal wholeness, and attain higher
spiritual levels—fully realizing the power of yin in its different dimensions as represented by the goddess.

The Queen Mother in the Daoist Pantheon

Xiwang mu is undoubtedly the oldest and most import goddess in the
Daoist pantheon. Her impact has pervaded Daoist history and worship,
and even spread to other East Asian countries. Korea has a holy mountain dedicated to her, her image appears in art work of various periods,
and she is venerated as the mother of all women and the protector of
shamans. In Japan, she is worshiped during the Tanabata festival of
double-seven, plays a role in medieval art and theater, and is still paraded around town during popular festivals (see Sun 2003).

A deity of great powers, the Queen Mother matches senior male Daoist
gods in complexity and centrality. She is on par with the Dao itself, personified in the Highest Lord Lao (Taishang laojun). Developed as a divinization of the ancient philosopher Laozi and alleged author of the
Daode jing, this god, like the Queen Mother, rose to prominence in the
Han dynasty and evolved in various forms over the centuries (see Kohn
1998a).

Lord Lao has many of the same characteristics as the Queen Mother. He is of cosmic origins and plays an essential part in the creation of the universe; he is involved in the revelation and presentation of celestial scriptures and secrets to humanity; and he appears as a potent body god that needs to be activated in visualization to attain immortality. He is similarly in charge of human fate and immortality, and he is equally accessible to people, descending variously to respond to prayers and offerings. Like the Queen Mother, he has been credited with the practice and teaching of sexual techniques; and like her, he has undergone different phases of development over the centuries, and is still worshiped as a key deity of Daoism today.

Just as Lord Lao is the Dao, the central power of the universe and all existence, so the Queen Mother is the representative of pure cosmic yin, the essential force of cosmic creation. The structure and patterns of their hagiographies are highly similar, but they differ in two points: unlike Lord Lao, the Queen Mother never took birth in human form and became active as a person on earth; nor did she emigrate and found a religious teaching among other countries and cultures. She accordingly was never honored as the ancestor of a human family and has remained more distant than Lord Lao. Still, in her cosmic dimension and her importance for both the heavenly and human worlds, she is just as central to Daoism as Lord Lao and it is no accident that she shares many characteristics with him.

Chapter Two

The Mother of the Dao[1]

The Mother of the Dao, the divinized mother of the Lord Lao, is a completely different type of goddess than the Queen Mother of the West. Also born from cosmic energies and created through the unfolding of primordial forces, she gives birth to Lord Lao, raises him to do his work as a savior of humanity, and ascends back to heaven where she resides as a distant and benevolent ancestor. Her career—from daughter through wife/mother to teacher and eventually ancestor—matches the ideal life cycle of women on earth and represents the formalized version of a successful Chinese woman's accomplishments. It matches the life pattern of men, who according to the Confucian model should proceed from son through husband/father to official and ancestor, with the main difference that men's careers take them outside the home and into the public sphere while women's demand them to stay in the family compound.

This goddess shows the fulfillment of women as daughters, mothers, and family-centered agents. There is little affirmation of administrative powers or cosmic origins, no emphasis on radical sexuality or the essence of yin, no shamanic undertone or extensive communication between the spheres. Instead, the goddess is a good, steady woman—observing the rules and gaining fame and status through her divine son, whom she carries, teaches, and protects.

The four stages in the goddess's life are clearly distinguished in her hagiography, contained also in Du Guangting's collection of immortal women's biographies, the *Yongcheng jixian lu* (DZ 783). According to this,

---

[1] An earlier version of this chapter appeared in Kohn 1989a.

the Mother of the Dao first arises through the merging of original *qi*, of "all-pervading yin and mysterious harmony" (1.2a) She is formed simultaneously with the essence of the universe, and emerges immediately from the source of all creation. She is called Jade Maiden of Mystery and Wonder (Xuanmiao yunü), a name that emphasizes her purity and virginity as well as her identity with the Dao, which is described as "mystery and wonder" in the *Daode jing*.

After her cosmic emergence, the goddess is transformed into a human female and as such gives birth to Lord Lao in a southern Chinese village, in the country of Chu. She becomes pregnant through the intervention of a supernatural agent, when the essence of the sun descends like a shooting star and enters her mouth while she is taking an afternoon nap. During her long pregnancy, she is always joyful and radiant, then gives birth through her left side while standing upright and holding on to the branch of a tree. All this clearly imitates the hagiography of the Buddha, except that in China the tree is identified as a plum (*li*) and the deity takes his surname Li from it. The goddess is accordingly known as Mother Li (Limu) on earth. She also earns the celestial title Holy Mother Goddess (Shengmu yuanjun), Du Guangting's main name for her.

The third stage occurs when the goddess is asked by the divine child to explain the basic structure, concepts, and methods of the Daoist teaching. In nine sections, the texts reports the goddess's discourse on the situation of humanity and the way to transcendence. Beginning with morality and restraint, the path leads through the cultivation of talismans, drugs, and breathing exercises to the concoction of a cinnabar elixir which will eventually ferry people across to the heavens. As the teacher of the god she is known as the Goddess of the Great One (Taiyi yuanjun).

The goddess enters her fourth and final stage when she concludes her instruction and is received by a heavenly cavalcade of flowery chariots and numerous attendants. Having ascended into the higher ranges of heaven, she takes up her residence there as the Great Queen of Former Heaven (Xiantian taihou) and presides as benevolent ancestor over the wider universe.

The fact that one and the same goddess is named differently according to her station in life and major function in the salvific process of the Dao, is made clear by Du Guangting in the hagiographic section of his collection of commentaries on the *Daode jing*, the *Daode zhenjing guangsheng yi* (Wide Sagely Meaning of the Perfect Scripture of the Dao and Its Virtue, DZ 725). He says:

> The Holy Mother Goddess was the Jade Maiden of Mystery and Wonder as long as she resided in heaven. After she had given birth, she was promoted to Goddess of the Great One. As such she taught Lord Lao the basic principles of reforming the world and spreading the true teaching. (2.21b)[2]

> After the Holy Mother Goddess had given birth to Lord Lao, she climbed into a jade carriage drawn by eight luminants and, followed by a host of transcendent attendants, ascended to heaven in broad daylight. Under the great Tang dynasty, she was venerated properly and given the title Great Queen of Former Heaven. (2.14a)

In the following sections, we will look at each aspect and stage of the goddess's career, presenting the different sources and examining the variants and complexities of her myth.

Jade Maiden of Mystery and Wonder

The expression "mystery and wonder" goes back to the first chapter of the *Daode jing*, where the Dao is described as "mysterious and again mysterious, the gate of all wonders." The phrase *xuanmiao* occurs in the middle ages as a formal name for Lord Lao and as in part of the title of his main hagiography, the *Xuanmiao neipian* (Inner Chapters of Mystery and Wonder), which survives in fragments.[3] The word "wonder" (*miao*),

---

2 A similar statement is also found in the Song hagiography *Youlong zhuan* (Like Unto a Dragon, DZ 774), 3.8a and *Tongjian houji* 1.4ab. See Kohn 1998a.

3 Fragments and citations remain in *Yixia lun* (Discourse on Barbarians and Chinese, *Nanshi* 75, *Nan Qishu* 54, dat. 467); *Xiaodao lun* (Laughing at the Dao, T. 2103, 52.143-52, dat. 570); *Sandong zhunang* (A Pearly Bag of the Three Caverns, DZ 1139, dat. 682), 8.4a; *Miaomen youqi* (Entrance to the Gate of all Wonders, DZ

moreover, also appears in the Chinese name of Queen Māyā, the mother of the Buddha—whose actions are closely imitated in the Daoist story. In the earliest translations, from the second century C.E., she is simply called Miao; in later versions she is usually known as Jingmiao or Qing-miao (Pure Wonder).

The Jade Maiden of Mystery and Wonder appears first in the *Santian nei-jie jing* (Inner Explanation of the Three Heavens; DZ 1205) a justification of Celestial Masters beliefs dated to around 420. It says:

> Intermingling in chaos, the three *qi*—mysterious, original, and primordial—brought forth the Jade Maiden of Mystery and Wonder. After she was born, the mixed *qi* congealed and formed Lord Lao who was born from the left armpit of the Jade Maiden. (1.2b; Bokenkamp 1997, 207)

This divine emergence occurred in heaven, so that the virginity of the Jade Maiden was not compromised, her status as a fresh and vibrant representative of the pure Dao remained intact.

After Lord Lao has emerged from the Jade Maiden, he constructs the universe by forming nine continents that he populates with men and women and for which he decrees suitable religions. The Chinese, since they are formed from strong yang *qi*, receive Daoism; the barbarians in the west and in India, mostly made of yin, are to worship the Buddha; the people of southern Asia, a harmonious mixture of both yin and yang, become believers in yin-yang cosmology. This accomplished, Lord Lao concentrates on the cultural evolution of China. For this purpose he assists every dynasty as a divine imperial advisor or "teacher of dynasties"(Kohn 1998a, 217-34). However, despite this marvelous arrangement the world still suffers from decline, and eventually the god's physical presence in human shape is required on earth.

> In the time of King Wuding of the Shang dynasty, he was born again. He became the son of Mother Li. During the pregnancy of eighty-one years, he continuously recited a sacred scripture. At birth, he ripped open her left armpit. He had white hair

---

1123, dat. 713), 7b; and in Du Guangting's *Guangsheng yi* 2.20b. See Zürcher 1959, 301-3; Fukui 1964; Kobayashi 1990, 382-85; Kohn 1995a, 219-20.

when he was born and thus came to be called Laozi, Old Child.
The *Scripture of the Three Terraces* that we have today is the text
Laozi chanted in the womb.

As regards his return to the embryonic state in the womb of
Mother Li, it must be understood that he himself transformed
his body of pure emptiness into the shape of Mother Li. Then
he took refuge in his own womb. There was never a real
Mother Li. Unaware of this fact, people nowadays say that
Laozi was born by Mother Li. Such is not the case. (*Santian nei-
jie jing* 1.3b; Bokenkamp 1997, 210-11)

Thus the Jade Maiden loses her position as celestial virgin and daughter
of pure cosmic *qi* and becomes a mother, the most important role and
ultimate blessing of a woman. However, since she is ultimately not of
this earth, her physical pregnancy has to remain an illusion. Instead she
is just one conglomeration of *qi* bringing forth another. All physical
forms are merely outer appearances, since the underlying reality of the
true Dao is and remains formless.

Mother Li

Mother Li is the name the goddess receives on earth after giving birth to
Lord Lao. The most common explanation of her name is that she held on
to the branch of a plum tree (*li*) while giving birth, thus creating a family
name for herself and the child (*Yongcheng jixian lu* 1.1b). Another is that
she became pregnant after eating plums, thus making the child the offspring of the fruit (*Guangsheng yi* 2.19a-20).

Historically, the family name Li for Lord Lao—which inspired various
millenarian prophesies and contributed to the rise of the house of Tang,
whose name was Li (see Bokenkamp 1994)—appears first in Laozi's biography in chapter 63 of Sima Qian's *Shiji* (Record of the Historian) of
104 B.C.E. It begins:

Laozi was a native of Quren hamlet in Hu district in the state
of Chu. His surname was Li, his personal name Er, and he was

styled Dan. His was a historian in charge of the archives of the
Zhou. (*Shiji* 63; Lau 1982, x-xi; Fung and Bodde 1953, 1:170)

The biography further describes various figures who may or may not
have been the historical Laozi (see Graham 1990) and concludes with a
list of officials and generals of the Li clan, all claiming to be Laozi's descendants. It is likely that this genealogy of the illustrious sage-
philosopher was created consciously by the Li family who adopted him
as their ancestor, a common undertaking in the Han dynasty (Seidel
1969, 19; Kohn 1998a, 10).

Laozi in due course proceeded to become a divinity, a universal god who
was worshiped as the Dao, taking Mother Li with him on a journey to
exalted supernatural status. Laozi as the cosmic Lord Lao is first described in the *Laozi ming* (Inscription for Laozi, dat. 165 C.E.), a formal
inscription compiled at the occasion of imperial rites to the deity in his
birthplace at Bozhou (Seidel 1969). A similar picture of the god is found
in the *Laozi bianhua jing* (Scripture of the Transformations of Laozi, DH
79),[4] a Dunhuang manuscript dated to the second century C.E. (S. 2295;
Ōfuchi 1979a, 686-88). Rather than an official court statement, this text is
the expression of a popular messianic cult in southwest China. Laozi is
presented as the savior of humanity and the creative and ordering power
of the universe. He has descended again and again as the teacher of dynasties to change life for the better, helping rulers maintain harmony in
the world. Since he has never failed to appear in a timely fashion in the
past, he will certainly do so again, carried to term by Mother Li. The text
has:

> Vague and undifferentiated.
> From this the heavenly and earthly are created.
> His spirit assumes form in the womb of Mother Li.
> Changing his body until the time of happy destiny has come.
> After seventy-two years in his mother's womb, he appears in
> the country of Chu. (Seidel 1969, 63; Kohn 1998a, 12)

In the context of increased veneration for Lord Lao, Mother Li received a
temple of her own and an official statement was engraved on a stele in

---

[4] "DH" refers to Daoist manuscripts found at Dunhuang as reprinted in
Ōfuchi 1979a. The numbering follows Komjathy 2002.

front of it. The stele inscription is known as *Shengmu bei* (Stele for the Holy Mother) and dates from 153 C.E. (Kusuyama 1979, 324). It was recorded by the sixth-century writer Li Daoyuan in his *Shuijing zhu* (Annotated River Classic, ch. 23) with a note saying that it was located near her temple. It says:

> Laozi, the Dao:
> Born prior to the Shapeless,
> Grown before the Beginningless,
> Living in the Prime of Great Immaculate,
> Floating freely through the Six Voids.
> He passes in and out of obscurity and confusion,
> Contemplating chaos as yet undifferentiated,
> And viewing the clear and turbid in union.
> (Kohn 1998a, 39-40; Kusuyama 1979, 307)

The supernatural nature of Mother Li and more mythical explanations for Lord Lao's surname come to the fore in the fourth century, when they appear in the *Shenxian zhuan* (Biographies of Spirit Immortals, JHL 89)[5] by the immortality seeker and would-be alchemist Ge Hong (283-343) (see Güntsch 1988; Bumbacher 2000b; Campany 2002). It says:

> Laozi's name was Chonger or Boyang. He was a native of Quren hamlet in Hu district in Chu. His mother became pregnant when she was touched by a large shooting star. Despite his heavenly origin, Laozi made his appearance in the Li family. . . .
>
> There are also stories that his mother bore him for seventy-two years. At birth he emerged from her left armpit. He had white hair and thus was named Laozi. Other reports claim that Laozi's mother had not been married and therefore he had to take on his mother's family name. Yet others say that his mother stood beneath a plum tree when she gave birth. Being

---

[5] The abbreviation "JHL" refers to the *Daozang jinghua lu* (Record of Essential Blossoms of the Daoist Canon), a collection of texts compiled by Ding Fubao and published in 1922. The numbering follows Komjathy 2002.

able to speak upon birth, the sage pointed to the tree and said: "This will be my surname." (ch. 1; Kohn 1996a, 56-57)[6]

In the following centuries, this elementary story of Laozi's birth is expanded to include several myths surrounding the birth of the Buddha, elevating the goddess from Mother Li to Holy Mother Goddess.

Holy Mother Goddess

The first evidence of Buddhist integration is found in the *Santian neijie jing* cited earlier. It describes Lord Lao's career after his successful appearance in China, outlining his emigration across the western pass, the transmission of the *Daode jing* to the pass guardian Yin Xi, and his conversion of the barbarians. The highlight of the story is his command to Yin Xi to obtain birth in the western land and become the Buddha. The text says:

> The wife of the king of India was called Qingmiao. Once when she was taking an afternoon nap, Laozi ordered Yin Xi to stride on a white elephant and change into a yellow sparrow. In this shape he flew right into the mouth of the queen. To her it looked like a shooting star coming down from heaven. In the following year, on the eighth day of the fourth month, he split open her right hip and was born.
>
> Having hardly touched the ground, he took seven steps. Raising his right hand to heaven he exclaimed: "The chief I am above and under heaven. The three worlds are nothing but pain. What is there enjoyable?" He later realized that all birth is suffering and became a buddha. From that time onward, Buddhism began to flourish in those areas. (1.2b-4b; Bokenkamp 1997, 212)

---

[6] A similar account of is found in the *Daode jing xujue* (Introductory Explanation to the Scripture of the Dao and Its Virtue, DH 66) of the fifth century. See Kohn 1998a, 181.

Unlike the *Santian neijie jing*, which has Yin Xi being born as the Buddha, the *Xuanmiao neipian* describes Laozi in this role. Here the story runs:

> Laozi crossed the pass and went to India. The wife of the king of India was called Jingmiao. When she took an afternoon nap, Laozi strode on the essence of the sun and entered her mouth.
>
> On the eighth day of the fourth month of the following year, he emerged through her left armpit. It was midnight. Having barely touched the ground, he took seven steps. From then on the Buddhist teaching came to flourish. (*Yixia lun; Xiaodao lun*, T. 2103, 52.148b; Kohn 1995a, 105)

Both versions actively integrate the story of the Buddha's birth as found in the *Taizi ruiying benqi jing* (Sutra of the Original Life of the Prince in Accordance with All the Good Omens; T. 185, 3.472-83), translated by Zhi Qian in the third century (see Karetzky 1992). Here the three basic phases of the Buddha's conception, gestation, and birth are embellished with a variety of motifs, all later adopted into the Daoist story. The conception is controlled by the later Buddha himself who changes into a white elephant and appears to his mother in a dream. He is surrounded by the essence of the sun. During the entire gestation period the sun continues to shine and the Buddha himself radiates with a strong light upon birth. Celestial motifs such as the essence of the sun and the shooting star are also plentiful in the hagiography of Lord Lao, influenced certainly by Buddhist sources but also reflecting traditional Chinese mythology which associated mythical heroes with celestial and light phenomena.

More specifically, during the gestation, heaven reveals its delight by producing exceptional bounty on earth. The queen shows her participation in the divine through her continuous joy. In the Daoist version, she is depicted as being of extraordinary beauty and never tiring energy. The actual birth is miraculous and pure, and the just-born bodhisattva is able to walk and to speak. He speaks the classical words: "The chief I am above and under heaven. The three worlds are nothing but pain. What is there enjoyable?" The gods of heaven descend to show their respect and celestial dragons perform purifications for the child, echoing traditional Chinese myths of heroes' births accompanied by divine signs and dragon messengers from the otherworld.

The goddess in this stage of her career is a divine agent on a wondrous mission blessed amply by many supernatural signs and celestial powers. It is the starting point for her elevation to the position of the lord's teacher and instructor.

Goddess of the Great One

Teaching the divine child, the goddess prepares him for his important tasks on earth, ensuring that he can properly fulfill his duties of saving humanity and guiding people to perfection. To do so, she takes on the role of instructor and is called Goddess of the Great One.

The One, first described in ancient philosophical texts, indicates the primordial state of the world right at the time when things and beings are about to be created. As the *Daode jing* has it:

> The Dao produced the One;
> The One produced the two
> The two produced the three;
> The three produced the myriad beings. (ch. 42)

The One represents the principle of unfolding, the primordial state of unified pre-creation, and the underlying force that sustains life. "Oneness," moreover, is the basic characteristic of all there is, the state to which all eventually returns. The *Zhuangzi* says:

> In the Great Beginning there was nonbeing;
> There was no being, no name.
> Out of it arose the One.
> Thus there was One, but it had no form.
> Beings realized and came to life.
> This was called their life-force. (ch. 12; Watson 1968, 131-32)

In the Han dynasty, this underlying potentiality of oneness came to be worshiped as a personified god and identified as an astral deity. Installed as the god of the center of the universe, the Great One was served by the five mythical emperors associated with the five phases and invoked whenever major state affairs were undertaken. For example, Emperor Wu offered a sacrifice to the Great One before embarking on a campaign against the southern states. He fought under a banner showing the sun, the moon, and the Northern Dipper, as well as the Great One in the shape of a flying dragon (*Shiji* 28).

The Goddess of the Great One appears first in the late Tang dynasty in Du Guangting's hagiography of the Holy Mother Goddess. She inherits the characteristics of the ancient cosmic god of the center and also adopts the title *yuanjun* (lit. "Primal Lord"). This title was a common appellation for female deities by the late middle ages, but in earlier texts refers to a male instructor. A classic passage occurs in Ge Hong's *Baopuzi neipian* (Inner Chapters of the Master Who Embraces Simplicity, DZ 1185). Here *yuanjun* is the title of Laozi's teacher. The text says:

> The Primal Lord was Lao Dan's teacher. . . . He is chief of the gods and immortals, and can claim to harmonize yin and yang. He gives orders to ghosts, gods, wind, and rain. He drives nine dragons and twelve white tigers. All the immortals of the world are his subordinates. (4.7b; Ware 1966 ,79-80)

> The scriptures of the gods and immortals are unanimous in that both the Yellow Emperor and Lao Dan studied under the Primal Lord of the Great One in order to receive his secrets. (13.3a; Ware 1966, 216)

This description adds yet another dimension to the Great One—the role of teacher and divine administrator, echoing the central image of the goddess in Highest Clarity. It lays the foundation for Du Guangting's vision of the Goddess of the Great One as Lord Lao's teacher, and is reminiscent of the administrative powers and responsibilities shouldered by the Queen Mother of the West.

The goddess begins with teaching the divine child the cosmic nature and essential composition of the human body, explaining it in terms of the five phases and other components. She emphasizes that "the Six Jia deities make up the human body; only because of them do people have five organs, six viscera, nine palaces, twelve chambers, four limbs, five sections, triple heaters, nine orifices, 180 joints, and 360 bones in their body" (*Yongcheng jixian lu* 1.2b-3a). The time and place of birth, moreover, determine the life expectancy and destiny of people, which can be improved by purification and meditation, moderation and withdrawal from sensory exposure. Elementary practice leads to a social awareness that "begins with the personal body, reaches out to the family, the village, and all under heaven. As a son one should behave with perfect filial piety, as a vassal with perfect loyalty. As a superior one should be all love; as an inferior, all obedience" (1.3b). Good deeds, in accordance with proper virtue, will bring great rewards in terms of personal health, family success, and spiritual attainment. Bad deeds will lead to sickness, disasters, and the underworld prisons (1.4ab).

Next, the goddess explains the psychological makeup of people, dividing them into types according to the five phases: wood people are energetic and impulsive; earth types, benevolent and harmonious; water characters, modest and cautious; fire ones, fierce and violent; and metal people tend towards severity and abruptness (1.5b). Each type has to modify his or her behavior properly to attain the steadiness and calmness necessary for the attainment of the higher stages during which adepts revert their *qi* and concoct an elixir of immortality (1.6b-7a).

> Both the nine cinnabar elixirs and the golden fluid are paths leading to ascension. Those who take the nine cinnabar elixirs will become officials in the heavenly bureaucracy and will be bodily carried up to heaven by cloudy dragons. Those who take the golden fluid will radiate a golden light and rise towards heaven instantaneously. In either case, the spirit elixir will spontaneously come to those firmly established in merit and the accumulation of good deeds. Those who lack in merit and fail to do good can never hope for immortality. (1.8a)

She concludes her extensive teachings by once again emphasizing the importance of having the right destiny and proper guidance. Her teaching is further elaborated in a hagiography found in the *Tongjian houji*. According to this, the goddess does not give birth to Lord Lao but encounters him during his wanderings and shares the basics of inner alchemy with him. Questioned for more information, she declines, emphasizing her central cosmic position—similar to that of the Queen Mother—and the primordial role of the divine secrets. She says:

> I am chief of all the immortals, queen of the wonderful Dao.
> The mysterious and numinous secret arts are all part of the

Great Origin. How could I disgrace myself by revealing them?" (1.8b)

When Lord Lao implores her to part with her wisdom so he can give people divine medicines and help them extend their lives, she stresses that "living with the Dao is very difficult" and requires that one is wise, "pious, obedient, and truly sincere" (1.8b). Lord Lao accordingly goes off to discover the methods for himself, gaining magical powers and great insights into the workings of the universe, which he continues to reveal both while on earth and after his ascension (1.9a).

The goddess in this vision appears as the single authority on the foundations and functioning of the universe. She is the true master of all creation who holds the secrets of the Dao. Lord Lao, on the other hand, despite his heavenly origins is the spirited seeker who must work hard to attain the goal. The message of the text is that there is no way to avoid diligent practice or obedience to the goddess who will teach the basics. However, ultimately anyone must go off on his own to find personal evolution and spiritual attainment. The teaching role of the goddess, even though she has all the secrets and powers of the universe, only goes so far. Even the best mother cannot live life on behalf of her child, she can only give him the best possible start. The goddess in this vision is the carrier of knowledge, tradition, and morality. She insists on being socially responsible, doing good, and perfecting the virtues—echoing the demands of the Confucian social order. She thus supports mainstream morality, yet also guides adepts beyond it towards the goal of perfection.

Great Queen of Former Heaven

The successful seeker of the Dao, originally a member of the heavenly community, returns to his native abode in the end. So do his teachers, though undertaking less strenuous efforts in the process. The Mother of the Dao, her earthly mission accomplished, returns to heaven. Du Guangting describes the scene:

> After the Holy Mother Goddess had finished speaking, immortal officials and spirit attendants arrived with cloudy chariots

> and feathery canopies. Forest-like they assembled around her.
> She climbed into the chariot of the eight luminants and as-
> cended to heaven in broad daylight. (*Yongcheng jixian lu* 1.8b)

This is the highest form of ascension known in Daoism. Receiving a
summons to office among the heavenly bureaucrats, the immortal read-
ies himself or herself and, on the day appointed, is formally met by a
planet- or dragon-drawn cloudy chariot and escorted to heaven by a
large entourage of celestial guards, supernatural horsemen, and divine
attendants. The most famous ascension of this kind is that of the Yellow
Emperor who mounted a celestial dragon together with seventy of his
followers, some of whom tried to cling to the dragon's beard and claws
in a desperate effort at eternal life (*Shiji* 28; see Yü 1964). Lord Lao, too,
ascended similarly.

> Lord Lao strode on a white deer and, rising from the top of a
> cypress, followed the immortal equipage back to the Heaven of
> Great Clarity. Today one can still see the traces of the deer in
> the cypress. (*Yongcheng jixian lu* 1.8b)

By doing so, according to Du Guangting, Lord Lao "demonstrated the
fact that everyone who practices the wondrous Dao will ascend to
heaven" (*Guangsheng yi* 2.13b). In either case, the ascension happens via a
celestial chariot and is connected to a tree—in Lord Lao's case the cypress which, according to local legend, still remained in Bozhou during
the Tang dynasty, showing strange patterns in its top. A well-known
occasion of the same dynasty is the transformation of Qu Boting, commonly called Lad Qu, who ascended to heaven in a public occurrence in
the fifth month of the year 773. He was at that time apprenticed to the
fifteenth patriarch of Highest Clarity, Huang Dongyuan. The event took
place in the courtyard of Taohua guan (Peach Blossom Monastery) in full
view of monastic and lay onlookers. While holding on to the branch of a
chestnut tree, Qu's physical form dissolved and he vanished into thin air
(see Sunayama 1987).

In all these ascensions, the motif of the tree is of central importance—
Lord Lao riding the deer on its top and the young man grasping the
chestnut branch just as the goddess had grasped the branch of the plum
when delivering her child. In many ways the scene suggests that a new

birth is taking place. While the birth of a god in human form is a trans-formation of the divine from the heavenly into the mundane, the ascent of the successful practitioner is his translation into a celestial being. The ultimate break with the world of humanity, this ascent transcends all that is ordinary, common, and normal.

Once established in a new identity, the ascended immortal is given a new title. As a resident and official in heaven, he or she assumes a new role as the guide and protector of living beings—not unlike the ancestor who takes up residence above the clouds and continues, with a posthu-mous title and from an otherworldly perspective, to help descendants for generations. When the Mother of the Dao is promoted to this level, she is accordingly renamed Great Queen of Former Heaven.

Just as some form of worship is organized around the grave and the an-cestral tablet of any deceased householder, so the ascent of Laozi and the goddess give rise to cultic veneration in the area.

> After Lord Lao had ascended to heaven, various emperors throughout history venerated and honored his traces. Thus emperors Xuan of the Han and Wen of the Sui both had tem-ples and halls erected in his honor. Moreover, they ordered their ministers of culture to compose stone inscriptions with the aim of preserving the divine deeds. Thus we have the *Laozi ming* by the Han official Bian Shao and the stele inscribed by Xue Daoheng of the Sui. (*Guangsheng yi* 2.14b; Kohn 1998a, 37)

In addition to these official activities, various miracles began to happen, showing the divine nature of the location and serving to commemorate the presence of the divinities. For example,

> in the old village of Bozhou, several old and inclining trees were suddenly full of sweet dew. Looking up one could see a cloud hovering over them for some time. Then a perfected ap-peared and put an end to all witchery in the area.

> Also, clouds and mist coagulated in the air and engulfed pal-aces and houses. Another time, divine birds appeared carrying arrows in their beaks, magic snow whirled about, spirit drag-ons danced in the middle of the nine wells, and characters were visible on the top of the cypress. (2.14b; see Verellen 1992)

The presence of Lord Lao and his mother transformed the location into a sacred space which is blessed and protected by the goddess in her role as Great Queen of Former Heaven. Having returned to her origins by assuming a high position in heaven, she reaches a new rank and a new dimension of divinity. In this position, her activity consists of protecting the locations of her earthly involvement, encouraging Daoists and prospective immortals to persist in their auspicious undertaking, and supporting all efforts toward goodness in the world. No longer a Jade Maiden preparing for the role of motherhood, no longer a Mother Goddess who gives birth to the deity, no longer even the Great One, ruler of the universe and teacher of secrets, she has progressed far and gone to her ultimate destination.

In contrast to the Queen Mother of the West, the Mother of the Dao is more a mother who realizes herself through giving birth, educating, and launching her child. Where the Queen Mother engages in intercourse for her own cultivation but never gets pregnant, the Mother of the Dao gets pregnant without intercourse and gives birth in a supernatural way described in nonsexual terms. Where the Queen Mother administers the universe, holds sway over the immortals, commands numerous attendants, and supervises the accuracy of the sacred scriptures, the Mother of the Dao has little power in herself but vests her might in her divine son, limiting her activities to his birth, raising, and career preparation.

The Mother of the Dao is the goddess as cultural power, tamed and mellowed in comparison to the cosmic creatrix at the center. She is worshiped in side temples of sanctuaries to Lord Lao and does not appear in ordinary women's lives or serve as the focus of ecstatic cults. She is the ideal female as envisioned in Confucian society, a model and support for women in society, whom she empowers in a specialized and culturally acceptable way—denying sexuality and ecstasy and independent power, yet making an unmistakable contribution to the unfolding of Chinese and Daoist culture. By representing the mainstream ideal of women, she serves as a model to Chinese women in their roles as daughters, mothers, and educators. She demonstrates the path toward being a productive and socially responsible member of society and the universe.

Chapter Three

The Dipper Mother

Both the Queen Mother and the Mother of the Dao were dominant in the middle ages and especially in the Tang dynasty. Following the end of this era, in the so-called Tang-Song transition of the tenth century, a number of important changes occurred, both in Chinese society and Daoism (see Ebrey and Gregory 1993). Social change was mainly due to economic developments, notably the building of better roads and new canals. These increased commerce and opened up the southern part of the country, allowing increased integration with the north. The merchant class prospered and replaced the Tang aristocracy as the dominant force in the economic field, just as a new, scholarly trained and officially examined group of bureaucrats took over the imperial administration.

The growth of commerce and the merchant class had three major effects on the religious scene. First, there was a great increase in lay organizations and lay-sponsored temples and practices—ordinary people joined together for worship, rites, and cultivation practices, sometimes in private homes, sometimes in special community halls. Second, there emerged a much larger market for practical religious aids to daily life, from talismans for building homes and spells for granting a safe passage to exorcisms for healing, funeral rites, and salvific services for the dead. Third, popular practitioners required more direct contact with gods, spirits, and ancestors. As a result trance techniques increased, either through spirit mediums or by automatic writing with the help of the planchette (Kohn 2001a, 136). Daoist goddesses in this climate became a focus of rituals for personal protection and communal benefits, revealing the concrete practices and specific hopes associated with women's deities.

Women in the Song and later dynasties were active movers in all these religious activities, making up a large segment of various popular cults. Although more disenfranchised than under the Tang, bound by tighter moral codes, and hampered by the newly developing custom of footbinding (see Levy 1966; DePee 1999; Ko 2001), they created a forum for female forms of worship that involved concrete interactions with the divine and expressed concerns for the practical wellbeing of the people. As a result, numerous new religious movements, whether popular, Buddhist, or Daoist, emphasized the potency of female leaders and goddesses, and a number of powerful new goddesses appeared.

The Celestial Consort (Tianfei or Mazu), a fisherman's daughter from coastal Fujian, is most prominent among the emerging new goddesses. Refusing to marry, she cultivated her spirit until she was able to project herself and command nature around her, then used her powers to rescue her father and brothers when they were in danger of drowning. After an early death, her spirit powers increased and she became highly efficacious in the safeguarding of fishermen and traveling merchants. Still one of the most popular deities in south China and Taiwan today (Paper 1997, 81-83), she was integrated into the Daoist pantheon in the fifteenth century—receiving a Daoist title and official mission from Lord Lao that empowered her formally to slay demons, dispel disasters, and rescue humans from all kinds of difficulty (see Boltz 1986; Wädow 1992). In many characteristics she resembles Guanyin, the bodhisattva of compassion. Like Amitābha, buddha of the Pure Land and savior of true believers, she makes a solemn vow to rescue all and responds to the devout chanting of her name.[1] According to the *Tianfei jiuku lingyan jing* (Scripture on the Numinous Efficacy of the Celestial Concert in Relieving Distress, DZ 649, dat. 1409), she pledges herself to the service of humankind.

---

[1] For studies of Guanyin and her role in Chinese culture and as a goddess for women, see Chamberlayne 1962; Tay 1976; Blofeld 1978; Stein 1986; Reed 1992; Yü 1990a; 1990b; 1992; 2001a. On Amitābha and his Pure Land, see Matsumoto 1985; Corless 1993; Pas 1995.

> From this day forward, whether a traveling merchant or resi-
> dent shopkeeper seeking assets in doing business, whether
> farmers in their sowing or artisans in their professions,
> whether troops in transit engaged in battle arrays, whether
> there be difficulty in childbirth that is not resolved, whether
> there be disturbances from public wrongs, whether there be
> any abusive language that results in grief and injury, or
> whether there be any malady or affliction to which one is inex-
> tricably bound and from which there is no respite—
>
> Should anyone [so mentioned] but reveal reverence and re-
> spect in his or her heart and call my name, then I will offer
> immediate and trustworthy response and cause them to attain
> whatever it is they wish and to achieve whatever pursuits they
> have in mind. In my travels throughout the celestial realm, I
> will always keep watch over humankind, to the extent that
> whatever is sought on land, in waters, rivers, or at sea—in
> every location—all shall be granted as wished. (Boltz 1986, 224)

Like other divine mothers, the Celestial Consort gives support and reas-
surance to ordinary people, commanding celestial powers on their behalf, rescuing them from difficulties, and granting their wishes. Although part of the creative power of the Dao and residing in the distant
heavens, she is accessible to ordinary folk.

Doumu[2]

Another goddess who rose to prominence in Ming-dynasty Daoism and
has since remained an important mother figure is the Dipper Mother
(Doumu), a stellar deity of high popularity that merges ancient star worship with Buddhist tantric influence.[3] Shrines to her are found today in

---

[2] This part of the chapter is an abbreviated version of Kohn 2001b. The article contains a more detailed analysis and also a full translation of the *Doumu jing*.

[3] Yet another Daoist goddess well known for helping women in their plight
is the Goddess of the Morning Clouds (Bixia yuanjun), the daughter of the Lord
of Mount Tai (Taishan fujun), one of the ancient gods of the dead. She rose to
prominence in the Song dynasty and has especially a local following today (see

many major Daoist sanctuaries, from the Qingyang gong (Gray Sheep Temple) in Chengdu through Louguan (Lookout Tower) near Xi'an to Mount Tai in Shandong. She represents the germinal, creative power behind one of the most central Daoist constellations, the Northern Dipper (Beidou), ruler of fates and central orderer of the universe, which is said to consist of seven or nine stars, called the Seven Primes or the Nine Perfected (Schafer 1977b, 233). She is also the Daoist adoption of the Indian goddess and tantric bodhisattva Marīcī, an offspring of Brahma and personification of light, who serves as the ruler of fates and plays a role in various *dhārani* (sacred spells) sutras in the Buddhist canon (T. 1254-59, 21.255-86; Franke 1972, 63). Depicted with nine arms and possessing various weapons and charms (see Little and Eichman 2000, 282-83), she is the central subject of several rituals, both personal and communal, designed to enhance her efficacious support of the world.

The Mother of the Dipper appears in Daoist literature from Yuan times onward. Her major scripture, the *Doumu jing*, survives in both the Daoist canon of 1445 (DZ 621) and in a Ming-dynasty manuscript dated to 1439 (see Franke 1972). An invocation-based text that grants protection and support to the faithful, it begins with a detailed illustration of the key figures in the text (see Fig. 3).

Shown here, from right to left, is the Dipper Mother, her head surrounded by a glowing halo, seated on the jeweled throne and attended by three ladies-in-waiting, two at her back, one closer to her side. She faces the nine stars of the Dipper, beginning with the two senior stars, clearly marked with name plates as the Highest Emperor Celestial Sovereign (Tianhuang shangdi) and the Great Emperor of Purple Tenuity (Ziwei dadi).

They wear formal, embroidered court robes and elaborate headdresses and hold audience scepters in their hands. Behind them follow the seven lords of the Dipper, so marked in a small name plate at the top of the page. They, too, are dressed in formal garb and hold audience scepters, but their headdresses are merely small crowns. Slightly behind them and

Naquin 1992; Paper 1997, 75-76). Among Buddhist goddesses, the outstanding example is Miaoshan. Her legend and development are studied in Dudbridge 1978; Yü 2001b.

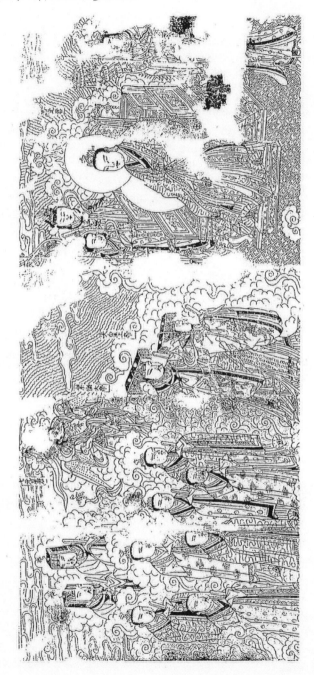

Fig. 3: The Dipper Mother formally receives the nine stars of the Dipper in celestial audience. Source: *Doumu jing* manuscript

above in the picture, are the two additional stars Fu and Bi, secondary emanations of the two great emperors. They are seen only in their upper bodies and wear helmet-like headgear. One final figure, above the first three of the seven lords, is dressed in martial garb and has a more barbarous and violent expression. Not named in a matching plate, he may be a guardian figure in the service of the Dipper lords.

The manuscript then presents the text of the *Doumu jing*. Revealed by Lord Lao, it contains the empowerment of the goddess as an executive of the Dao. After a set of technical instructions on how to recite the scripture and venerate the goddess, it begins by describing her actions in the world, listing the numerous emergencies and problems that she will alleviate and naming her the physician of the universe. It shows her role among the stars, characterizing her as being the essence of water and having the Dipper for her *po* or material soul.[4] She has various different titles, each indicating a different function and power.

The text then focuses on the hagiography of the goddess. Doumu first became the mother of the Dipper when she bathed in the Flowery Pond (Huachi) of heaven. There she was impregnated by nine lotus flowers and gave birth to nine sons. After seven days and nights on earth, she took them up to heaven, where she created divine residences for them and empowered them with mantras and *dhārani* to become rulers of the universe.[5] Worshiping both the Dipper gods and their mother is highly efficacious in many situations and aids the attainment of celestial immortality. The text concludes with a formal prayer, encomium, and *dhārani* to the Dipper Mother, culminating in her holy mantra—*Om, Marīcī swāha*.

---

[4] On the relation of water, the female, and goddesses, see Schafer 1973.

[5] This myth is told in an abbreviated form in the *Doumu jing*. A full version is found in the *Beidou bensheng zhenjing* (Perfect Scripture of the Northern Dipper's Original Birth, DZ 45). See Ren and Zhong 1991, 38-39. For supernatural birth myths in China, see Kaltenmark 1980, 39-45; Birrell 1993. Also Biallas 1986.

The Dipper

The Northern Dipper is a major starry constellation, located close to the Northstar that has served travellers for centuries as an indicator of direction. It is prominent as a heavenly guide and appears in the mythology of many peoples, e.g., as the Great Bear among the ancient Israelites, Arabs, and Romans, and as the Great Chariot among the Greeks (Benhamouda 1972, 52-53). Also known as *fera major* or the "great beast," its main story in Western mythology is associated with the nymphe Callisto, a daughter of Lycaon and princess of the Greek state of Arcadia. Serving in the entourage of Artemis, the goddess of the hunt, she attracted the lustful attentions of Zeus who appeared to her in the shape of Artemis. When Callisto turned up pregnant, Zeus's wife Hera took revenge by having her pulled apart by the hair, then transformed into a big, ugly bear, and banished into the sky. This, then, is the Great Bear of the ancients, a female deity at heart (Benhamouda 1972, 53; see also Marinatos 1998).

The Chinese have seen the same constellation less as an animal and more as a vehicle or device. Sima Qian in his *Shiji* notes that,

> the Dipper is the carriage of the emperor; it is placed in the center, . . . governs the four cardinal points, separates yin and yang, and determines the four seasons. It balances the five phases, arranges the divisions [of time] and the levels [of space], and sets the various measures. (Robinet 1989a, 178; 1993, 212)

Other early sources describe the Dipper as part of the entourage and governing mechanism of the Celestial Sovereign who resides in the center of the sky and rules all from his Palace of Purple Tenuity, often simply called the Purple Palace (Hirohata 1965, 38; Yanagizawa 1967). In human beings, this palace is located in the heart (*Baopuzi neipian* 18; Ware 1966, 302). The color purple represents a heightened dimension of yellow, the symbolic color of the center. Purple represents unlimited power, totality, unity, and the return to the cosmic Dao. It is considered highly sacred, and was worn only by high aristocrats (Porkert 1961, 439-40). A combination of black (great yin) and scarlet (great yang) in the palace of the center (yellow), it is created as an empowering and salvific color that represents the dynamic, yang aspect of the center, while yellow is its passive, yin dimension (Porkert 1961, 441).[6]

The Dipper, part of this mythology of the center, rose to importance in the practices of Highest Clarity Daoism, where it served as the agency that eradicated an adept's name from the registers of death and entered it into the ledgers of life (Robinet 1993, 201). The Dipper was invoked for protection, visualized to descend into the adept's body for inner illumination, and used as a celestial set of stepping stones in ecstatic excursions. Connection to the Dipper was established through chanting the names of its stars and by visualizing these stars as they descend and arrange themselves around the adept—all accompanied by the burning of incense, incantation of scriptures, and application of talismans (Robinet 1989a, 175; 1993, 205).

There are basically seven stars in the Dipper, known in China as the Seven Primes (qiyuan): four form its basic bowl or carriage, and three form its axle (see Fig. 4).

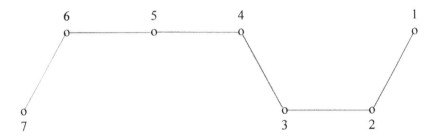

1. Yang Brightness
2. Yin Essence
3. Perfected Person
4. Mystery Darkness
5. Supreme Prime
6. North Culmen
7. Heavenly Pass

Fig. 4: The stars of the Dipper.

---

[6] Seeing the color purple is also an essential aid in visualizing the Dipper in Daoist practice. This is made clear in the *Jiuzhen shengxuan shangji* (Highest Record of Ascension to the Mystery Through the Nine Perfected, DZ 1351), 3a-4a.

Daoists in addition recognize two further stars that are invisible to the non-immortal eye, thereby creating the group of the Nine Perfected (*jiuzhen*). The two stars are known as Sustainer (Fu) and Equalizer (Bi) and can possibly be identified as two of several asterisms in the immediate neighborhood of the Dipper (Benhamouda 1972, 56). Said to be located near its main opening, they serve as guardians and stand watch over the constellation. In later texts these two appear as secondary emanations of the two leading stars of the heavens, the Celestial Sovereign and Purple Tenuity, who are identified as the first two sons of the Dipper Mother and key agents at the head of the Dipper constellation (Noguchi et al. 1994, 547). The various stars, furthermore, have completely different names in the various sources, depending on whether they are astronomic or religious in origin, and from what period they date.[7] They are:

No.	Arabic	Chinese Astronomic	Daoist	Doumu texts
				Celestial Sovereign
				Purple Tenuity
1	Dubhe	Heavenly Pivot	Yang Brightness	Greedy Wolf
2	Merak	Heavenly Cog	Yin Essence	Wide Gate
3	Phecda	Heavenly Armillary	Perfected Person	Prosperous Life
4	Megrez	Heavenly Beam	Mystery Darkness	Literary Song
5	Alioth	Jade Transverse	Supreme Prime	Pure Modesty
6	Mizar	Disclosed Yang	North Culmen	Martial Song
7	Alcaid	Wavering Light	Heavenly Pass	Ruined Army
8		Grotto Brightness	Sustainer	Sustainer
9		Hidden Prime	Equalizer	Equalizer

The Dipper stars are invoked through scriptural recitation and formal rites, preferably undertaken on one's birthday, at new moon, or on generally auspicious days. For example:

---

[7] Arab star names are explained in Benhamouda 1972, 54-56. For Chinese names, both astronomical and Daoist, see Schafer 1977b, 51. Doumu-related names also appear in Qing-dynasty materials on Fengshui and fortune-telling. See Field 1999, 21-22. On the role and importance of Fu and Bi, see Robinet 1989b, 172; 1993, 202; Yūsa 1983, 334.

> To recite the [Dipper] scripture, first develop utmost sincerity
> and purify your mind. Then face east, clap your teeth, and pay
> obeisance in your heart. Kneeling, close your eyes and visual-
> ize the gods [of the Eastern Dipper] as if you physically saw
> the limitless realm of the east. Mysterious numinous forces,
> imperial lords, realized perfected, and great sages—a countless
> host lines up before you. Looking at them will help you over-
> come days of disaster. (*Dongdou huming jing*, DZ 625, 2b; Kohn
> 1998a, 98)

Dipper texts also provide talismans to summon the constellation's gods
to protect life and help in difficulties, assuring the faithful that the perfected will respond immediately and grant a life as long as the Dao itself
(Kohn 1998a, 210). The talismans are used in the presentation of petitions
to the Dipper and contain the power to make its lords respond. To the
present day, talismans and scriptures of the Dipper are activated during
Dipper festivals in Taiwan. They last three to five days and serve to ensure good fortune (Matsumoto 1983, 203; 1997).[8]

Together with the Dipper, its mother Doumu is highly venerated. The
goddess goes back to the Tibetan deity Marīcī, the goddess of dawn and
light. A later version of the goddess Usha of the Aryans in ancient India,
she also appears among the Greeks a Aurora, the goddess of dawn
(Getty 1962, 133; Waddell 1972, 361). Although of Indian origin, she
plays only a minor role in Hinduism, but appears in Tibetan Buddhism
as an acolyte of the Green Tara, the female counterpart or *shakti* power of
the Buddha, and most popularly of the bodhisattva Avalokiteśvara.
Marīcī is placed to his right and called Aśokakāntā (Grünwedel 1900,
142; Getty 1962, 133). She is depicted as sitting on a lotus flower, with a
third eye, three heads, and eight arms. Her Tibetan name is Hod-zer-can-
ma, which means "the resplendent" and refers to her symbolic representation of dawn and the light of universe (Grünwedel 1900, 145; Waddell
1972, 361; Noguchi et al. 1994, 471).

---

[8] Dipper worship also made its way into Japan, where it became popular as
part of Yoshida Shintō. See Sakade and Masuo 1991.

Beyond her association with light and radiance, Marīcī is also linked with seven animals that draw her chariot and are most commonly identified as pigs. Both characteristics carry over into the image of Doumu who also serves as the savior and healer of the world. This characterization is emphasized in the beginning of the *Doumu jing*, which notes that the Highest Celestial Mother of Mystery Prime, the great sage Marīcī, is an Indian goddess who serves as the teacher of dharma kings, controls the light and order of the world, and has an army of celestial generals at her disposal whom she dispatches to bring help and relief to people.

Ritual Activation

The Dipper and its mother are invoked in a formally ritualized setting, either as part of personal cultivation or in the form of communal rites. In both forms, Daoist women participated actively, worshiping the goddess and dedicating themselves to her. Personal cultivation of the Dipper begins by focusing on the nine yin or female powers, potent partners of the nine lords of the Dipper. These goddesses and their accompanying ritual practice are described in the *Jiuzhen dijun jiuyin jing* (Scripture of the Nine Yin [Powers] of the Nine Perfected Imperial Lords [of the Dipper]), a medieval text extant only in a Song-dynasty citation.[9]

According to this, adepts who wish to attain higher powers of immortals, such as invisibility, multilocation, free travel through the cosmos, and control over spirits and demons, must cultivate the inner, female forces of the Dipper. The text lists them one by one, giving their location, rank, name, appellation, and the garb they typically wear. For example:

> In the third star, there is the Palace of Perfect Prime. In this palace resides an imperial lady who controls the six *dun* [gods of time] and the seven *yin* [powers]. She is the Cinnabar Mother of Highest Prime. Her name is Emptiness and Inaudibility of the Great One, her appellation is Sign of Central

---

[9] The text is cited in the early Song encyclopedia *Yunji qiqian* (DZ 1032, ch. 31). For a discussion, see also Robinet 1989a, 172; 1993, 205; Schafer 1977, 138.

Transformation. She wears a cape of green brocade over an embroidered feathery, flying skirt of flowery pattern, and has her top knot in the design "whirlwind clouds."(*Yunji qiqian* 31.10b, 11b)

Each of the nine goddesses has a rank either of mother, lady, consort, or daughter. They have different powers to convey and wear formal garb of a different color, while sporting the same hair style of "whirlwind clouds." Visualizing them forms an essential part of the personal ritual, which begins after proper purification with entering a quiet chamber, burning incense, lying down on one's back, and closing one's eyes. Adepts first see the nine lords of the Dipper in the Purple Chamber of the Great Ultimate (Taiji), located both in the stars and in the center of the head. They envision the Great One and five attendant gods (representing the five phases) in the six spheres surrounding the Great Ultimate. After placing the stars of the Dipper in the heart for proper illumination, they focus on the nine goddesses appearing in the Hall of Light (*mingtang*), a head cavity about one inch inside the forehead from the point between the eyebrows.

One by one, beginning with the goddesses and moving on to the Great One, the deities are taken from their various locations and moved up into the Purple Chamber, where they stand at attention before the nine lords. Then the entire assembly is transformed into one single figure, which in turn changes into the shape of a newly born infant called the Lad of Impermanence (Wuchang tongzi). In his hand, he grasps the nine stars of the Dipper, on his head he wears the sun, in his mouth he holds the moon. Using the combined radiance of these celestial bodies, the Lad irradiates the adept's entire body. Feeling that everything in and around them becomes bright red and submerged in fire, adepts no longer have any awareness of where their body begins and ends or what and who they are. This is the state when they attain complete oneness with the lords and goddesses of the universe. They stay in this state for a prolonged period, then emerge to clap the teeth twenty-four times, swallow the saliva nine times, and chant a laudatory incantation (31.12a-13a).

The ritual of activating the nine yin powers of the Dipper lords is undertaken both by male and female practitioners. It can be seen as a reversal of the myth of the birth of the Dipper through Doumu. An individual figure in the beginning, she emerges from the purple center and cosmic potentiality of the Dao, then diversifies by giving birth to nine sons who manifest themselves as celestial rulers in the stars. The ritual, in a reverse process, begins with the multiplicity deities and states of the body, then joins them in the central, purple chamber in the head, to eventually merge them into one single figure. This figure like the goddess stands at the root of creation, representing the most elementary principle of the universe, i.e., continuous change or impermanence. At the end of the ritual, it permeates and irradiates the entire being of the adept, creating an inner state that matches the flowing nothingness of the cosmic primordiality from which the goddess first arose. The oneness with cosmic principle attained in the ritual can therefore be seen as a way of recovering the creative potential at the beginning of time and, by extension, as an activation of the goddess and her powers within the individual.

Communal Practice

Communal and public rituals involving the Dipper Mother are described in the *Xiantian doumu zougao xuanke* (Mysterious Rites of Petitioning the Dipper Mother of Former Heaven, DZ 1452), a Yuan-dynasty work (Ren and Zhong 1991, 1149). It presents short ritual instructions interspersed among lengthy recitation texts and describes an elaborate ritual sequence consisting of eight parts.

First, there is the *Introit*, when the incense burner is brought in, the altar is purified, the celebrants and officiating priest enter the sanctuary, and a dedicatory prayer is chanted (1ab). Next, during the *Announcement*, the priest bows several times and offers a formal invitation to the goddess and her extensive entourage, including numerous heavenly emperors, immortals and sages as well as dragons and phoenixes, to descend and participate in the ritual. Incense and a talisman are burned as flower petals are scattered (2a-4a). Third, the *Invocation* praises the gods on high and calls upon the stars of the Dipper to accept the invitation and take part in the rite. Several talismans are burned (4b-7b).

The fourth step in the ritual is the *Lighting of the Lamps* of the Dipper, both on the altar and in the heart/mind of the priest. This signifies the gods' descent into the sacred area. They are invoked to take away sickness and misfortune, bring the dead back to life, destroy specters and evil spirits, and give peace to all. As the lamps shine forth, so the bodies of the celebrants are illuminated. An offering is made, incense is burned, the priest bows repeatedly (8ab). Fifth, a *Memorial* is dispatched to the Dipper Mother, addressed with numerous elaborate titles (including her Indian name Marīcī), in which she is praised as controlling the Seven Primes, governing thunder and lightning, radiating a light brighter than the sun and the moon, and asked to descend to the altar to liberate all from sickness and afflictions, dissolve evil and bad fortune, and bring happiness throughout. A cloud-script talisman of purple radiance is burned to establish communication with her, the entire congregation chants an invocation in her honor, then the priest in silent communion visualizes her descent (9a-11a). This descent is fully activated in the sixth section of the ritual sequence during *Spells*, when the priest chants a series of holy *dhārani*, moving to the left and right and raising alternate hands (11a-12a).

The seventh part is the central focus of the ritual, the *Petition* to the goddess, now present in the holy community. She is praised extensively and the story of her life is told. She is then asked to eradicate all the celebrants' sins, take their names from the registers of death and transfer them into the ledgers of life, rectify yin and yang, steady the cosmic order, and generally give health, longevity, prosperity, and happiness to all. At regular intervals during the recitation of the petition, flower petals are scattered and the priest bows to the goddess (12a-16b). The ritual concludes with the priest engaging in an ecstatic heavenly journey to the Dipper and issuing a formal *Mandate*, a celestial order which activates a messenger who delivers the petition to its proper place in the celestial realm. It is thereby fully legalized and carries the weight of divine power. A five-colored talisman is offered for protection, and the goddess, the seven stars, and the assembled celestial entourage are sent back to their heavenly homes. Universal order is in renewed harmony, and good fortune has been attained (17a-18b).

In both forms of rituals involving the goddesses of the Dipper, the goal is the attainment of harmony, in the self and the universe. The central powers of the Dipper lords are focused in the constellations goddesses and activated through them. They become vibrantly present to practitioners in visualization and ritual communication, and empower them with their divine light, irradiating their entire body and self and dissolving sins and ego-focused problems. As adepts are filled with the power of the Dipper consorts or the Dipper Mother, their fate is made whole and raised to the level of the immortals, while the world benefits from great blessings and universal good fortune.

The Nature of the Goddess

The Dipper Mother in her various forms, roles, and ritual appearances is quite different from the Queen Mother of the West and the Mother of the Dao. Although a mother figure like the other two, her power does not emanate from being the ruler of immortals, a body god, or a sexual power, nor is she solely a mother whose main purpose and success in life is the birth and raising of a son. She has power in her own right as a representative of cosmic light and ruler over human fate; but she is also the mother of nine sons, rulers of the central constellation of the Dipper, whom she conceives supernaturally, raises both on earth and in heaven, and installs in their proper celestial function.

In many ways the Dipper Mother symbolizes the movements of fate and the universe, combining in her figure both earthly and celestial existence, multiplicity and unity, descent and ascent, detached rulership and active involvement. She has power over life and death and is in complete charge of the transformations. She is nonsexual yet sexual in her enjoyment of the Flowery Pond. She is different from earlier goddesses in that she represents the *po* or material soul of the Dipper, thereby also including the instinctual, animalistic nature of human beings. Doing so, the Dipper Mother stands for the totality of human life, encouraging the inclusion and integration of emotions and instincts, the active acknowledgment of the darker aspects of reality, both within and without.

This totality, moreover, is activated in ritual, both individual and communal, and described in detail in extant literature, which is also highly informative regarding the rites associated with other gods and goddesses of the Ming dynasty.[10] This wealth of information is due in part to increased literacy and widespread use of printing, which made both the creation and dissemination of information easier and encouraged people to document rites in detail (see Ko 1994). It has also to do with the wider spread of ritual activity among the populace, leading to a greater degree of standardization and a wider use of services. Even in the middle ages Daoist rites were elaborate affairs that often lasted for several days, but they tended to be only held on special occasions and were usually sponsored by the state or by major religious centers. In late imperial China, they were celebrated more frequently and more widely, villages joining together to defray the cost and ordinary people participating more actively. As a result, texts became necessary to record the details of the rites, and scholars have benefited from this abundance of information.

The Dipper Mother, in accordance with these trends, is a much more popular goddess than the Daoist goddesses of the middle ages. She is visualized and praised in ritual, seen to be personally present at the ceremony and working to actively intervene in people's lives. She enables both male and female adepts to unify their inner natures and join the Dao through personal cultivation and communal rites. Her role is both that of a distant ruler of destiny and representative of cosmic light but also that of the direct helper of ordinary people. She can be quickly called upon with an easily repeated mantra and activated immediately through potent talismans. Rushing to provide assistance to suffering humanity, she is—more than the other goddesses—believed to be a trusty partner in the human enterprise and close supporter of all endeavors.

---

[10] For example, the rituals associated with Mazu are outlined in several texts in the Daoist canon (see Boltz 1986), as are those linked with the City God (Kohn 1997b), the God of Literature (Kleeman 1994), the martial god Xuanwu (Seaman 1987; Lagerwey 1992), and the Wutong spirits (Cedzich 1995).

Part Two

Immortals
and
Ordinands

Chapter Four

Ancient Immortals

In this second part of the study, the focus shifts away from celestial divinities and cosmic goddesses to real women who lived in the world and followed the path of the Dao. Aside from the many lay followers, on whom information is scarce and often consists of only a general mention or a list of precepts, women active in the Daoist tradition appear variously, as priests, renunciants, and immortals.

The oldest records recount stories of female adepts who followed the path of self-cultivation and attained high levels of perfection, which in some cases led to conflict with family and society. These are the women immortals of ancient China, notably of the Han (206 B.C.E.-220 C.E.) and Jin (265-420) dynasties. They appeared at a time when Daoism only began to organize as a religion and therefore they had no forum or social context. There was, as yet, no sacred hierarchy or monastic institution in which they could become priests or nuns. As a result, these early woman immortals are lauded mainly for their magical achievements and efforts at cultivation. They are described in records that deal largely with men but often also note the superior powers of women. Female practitioners, like their male counterparts, emerge as active representatives of the early ideal of immortality.

Immortality

The notion of immortality (*xian*) indicates a state of having gone beyond the limitations of this world and ascended to a higher level; it is a form of transcendence to a divine realm that is closely connected with the origins of the universe. To attain this state, practitioners live in separation from society, engage in techniques of physical and spiritual control, have their mind set on interaction with the spirit world, and acquire magical powers as they advance in their training.

This training usually involves a variety of longevity techniques (*yangsheng shu*), breathing exercises, diet control, gymnastics, sexual hygiene, absorption of solar energies, and meditations (Kaltenmark 1953, 9; Engelhardt 2000, 101-03). Like hermits in other parts of the world, immortals undertake these practices with great seriousness. They live in the wilderness, dress in garments of leaves or deer skins, fast by living on pure *qi* or eat raw food they find in the woods (Eskildsen 1998, 20-21). They are symbolically associated with birds in the lightness of their bodies and their ability to fly (Kaltenmark 1953, 10). Being close to nature immortals attain extended longevity and continuous vigor and eventually reach the paradises, luscious mountains surrounded by extensive bodies of water, the most prominent of which are known as Penglai and Kunlun (see Sōfukawa 1981).

The insights or powers immortals gain in their training allow them to understand the workings of the Dao and exert control over natural phenomena and divine agents. However, immortals do not use their magic often; if they do, it is on a whim and not for the benefit of the community or the empire. In this point they differ from the *fangshi* or magical practitioners who use similar techniques but employ them gainfully and for social promotion (see Ngo 1976; DeWoskin 1983). Also, while *fangshi* often serve as formal teachers and state servants, immortals are never limited to socially fixed roles. They can be implored to share their secrets but will act entirely on their own terms.

Immortals are at home both in the world and in the heavens. Accepting life and death as a single flow, they take neither too seriously and make the best of all they meet, exhibiting a happy attitude and playful way of being. They are perfected companions of the Dao, realized ones who have fulfilled their potential, true persons that have become fully human and thus superhuman. They are calm and uninvolved, yet when they take action they do so in just the right way. Immortals seem to do the most outstanding feats with ease and no particular effort, fully in control of themselves, yet charming in their compliance with others (see *Zhuangzi*, ch. 6; Watson 1968, 78-79). Their powers, moreover, are similar to the abilities of shamans. They can heal the sick, exorcise demons and sprites, make rain and stop it, foretell the future, prevent disasters, call upon wild animals as helpers, and remain unharmed by water and fire, heat and cold. Control over the body, a subtle harmony with the forces of nature, as well as an easy relationship with gods and spirits, ghosts and demons, are equally characteristic of successful shamans as of the immortals of the Dao.

In addition, immortals may also engage in magical activities, feats that characterize them as wizards. They are shape-changers who can appear in any form they please. They can multiply themselves be present in more than one place. They can become visible and invisible at will and travel thousands of miles in an instant. Controlling not only themselves, they also have power over nature. They can make rivers flow backward and mountains collapse. Plants, animals, and people die at their command and come back to life if they tell them to do so. They transport buildings to far-off places, open up mountains and reveal grottoes (Kohn 1993, 280). In all these arts, immortals use their powers less for the benefit of humankind than for their own pleasure, as a demonstration of their might. They are unique and playful beings, transcendents in a realm beyond the world who yet appear in the human sphere and interact in society.

Immortals were not part of Chinese culture from the beginning but emerged in the Warring States period (479-221 B.C.E.) and came to flourish under the Han. As Michael Puett contends, they are the visible manifestation of personalized practices of self-divinization, which arose independently, neither due to cross-cultural contacts nor the remnants of an earlier form of shamanism, but rather as a response to the cultural environment of ancient China. In this development, the vision of Chinese immortals is similar to the immortality of the soul in ancient Greece (see

Bremmer 1993). In both cases, the idea of the gods as otherworldly and identical with the dead was replaced by programs of self-divinization in this life, first within a monistic, energy-centered cosmos, later in more dualistic terms, to allow the complete transcendence of bodily existence and freedom from all earthly connection. Ritual practices of old were accordingly transformed and adapted to suit the new vision, permitting the integration of self-divinization into the ritual system (see Puett 2002).

Not many sources remain that describe immortals and their practices. The first appear in the Han dynasty, written by aristocrats and court writers—such as Sima Qian's *Shiji* and the *Liexian zhuan* (Immortals' Biographies, DZ 294), attributed to Liu Xiang (77-6 B.C.E.). Additional information on immortals is found in later dynastic histories (see Ngo 1976; DeWoskin 1983), hagiographies, such as Ge Hong's *Shenxian zhuan*, and technical manuals, e.g., his *Baopuzi neipian*. As in most classical histories and mainstream biographical collections, anecdotes in these texts tend to focus on male protagonists, and only about ten percent mention or describe women. [1] Still, even in these meager sources, certain patterns emerge: classical forms of women's bodily transformation, their magical powers, and their interaction with family and society.

Bodily Transformation

The key characteristic of immortals is the transformation that happens in and to the body of the practitioner. Refining their inner *qi* to higher levels of subtlety, immortals become etheric beings, feathery, sometimes hairy, with no need to eat or drink and completely invulnerable to heat and cold, fire and water. Light as ether, they can appear and vanish in an instant, and despite their advanced years look young, fresh, and radiant.

---

[1] A selection of immortal women's biographies was also published in a separate collection known as *Xiannü zhuan* (Biographies of Immortal Women). The text survives in citations, notably in the tenth-century encyclopedia *Taiping guangji* and summarizes earlier sources. Similar recounts appear in Du Guangting's *Yongcheng jixian lu, juan* 6 (8a-19b) and *juan* 4 (10b-13a), as well as in the Yuan-dynasty collection *Tongjian houji* (2.11a-13b, 4.6a-15a, 5.2b-3b, 5.4ab).

The main techniques leading to this wondrous state involve the refinement of *qi*, which is taken into the body as breath, food, and sexual energy. Immortals practice control in these areas. First, they harness the breath through methods of "expelling the old and inhaling the new" (*tugu naxin*). An early example of this path is Zhu Yi, also known as Woman of Great Yang (Taiyang nü). Practicing controlled breathing, she reached high longevity, and even at the age of 280 still looked as if she was only seventeen. She had a complexion like peach blossoms, a mouth of cinnabar redness, vibrant and smooth skin, glossy black hair and eyebrows. Working together with an advanced master, she completed the elixir of immortality and ascended to heaven with him (*Shenxian zhuan*; Campany 2002, 357). Another lady immortal who gained longevity through breath control was Lu Quan, the Woman of Great Yin (Taiyin nü). Learning from the Master of Great Yang, she inhaled cosmic *qi* in the form of liquid light and attained a body that radiated with the glory of the five phases. Eventually she ascended to heaven (*Shenxian zhuan*; Campany 2002, 324-25).

Similarly successful yet involuntarily forced into the practice of breath control was the daughter of Zhang Guangding. When she was four years old, a major disaster struck her home town and her parents had to abandon her in an old tomb. Three years later the family returned to collect her bones for proper burial. But they were in for a surprise.

> When they went and looked into the tomb, they found the girl still sitting there. On seeing her parents, she recognized them and was very happy, but they first thought she was a ghost. Only when they entered the tomb did they discover that she was indeed not dead. When asked how she had survived, she replied that when her initial food supplies were exhausted she first became very hungry. On noticing a creature in the corner that stretched its neck and swallowed its breath, she tried doing the same thing and became less and less hungry. (*Baopuzi neipian* 3; Ware 1966, 57; Reed 1987, 174)

The creature turned out to be a large tortoise, an animal known for its exceptional longevity. By imitating its breathing and swallowing techniques, the little girl survived—in a manner also followed by many immortals.

Food intake is another major way of achieving bodily transformation. Sometimes this just means the ingestion of a magical potion, as in the case of the Maiden of the West River (Xihe shaonü). The niece of the respected immortal Bo Shanfu, a recluse on Mount Hua, she received a wondrous elixir from him when he noticed that she was sick a lot. Although already seventy years old at the time, she returned to youth and regained a radiant complexion. When she was 130, she was observed hitting an old man with a stick. He turned out to be her son who could not keep up with her. She eventually ascended to heaven from Mount Hua (*Shenxian zhuan* 7; Güntsch 1988, 203; Campany 2002, 486).

In other cases, achieving immortality through food means the ingestion of only natural substances, such as roots, nuts, berries, or pine needles. An early example for this is Chang Rong, who lived in the mountains and ate only ash raspberry roots, thereby maintaining the complexion of a twenty-year old for several centuries (*Liexian zhuan* 2.5b; Kaltenmark 1953, 152-53). Even more famous is Yu Jiang, better known as Maonü, the Hairy Woman. A palace woman under the First Emperor of Qin, she saw the collapse of the dynasty approach and took refuge on Mount Hua. There she met the immortal Gu Chun, who taught her how to eat pine needles and survive in the wilderness—thus gaining the ability to live without solid food and become immune to cold and heat (*Liexian zhuan* 2.7b-8a; Kaltenmark 1953, 159-60). Several hundred years later, she was discovered by a group of hunters.

> They saw a naked person covered with black hair. They wanted to capture the creature but it passed over pits and valleys like a thoroughbred and could not be overtaken. Then they did some spying in the region, surrounded the place, and captured it. When they had established that it was a woman, they questioned her . . .

> Calculations showed that this woman, having been the concubine of Prince Ying of Qin, was more than two hundred years old. When she was brought back to court to be fed grains, their odor nauseated her for several days, but then she got used to them. After about two years of this diet, her body lost its hair, and she turned old and died. (*Baopuzi neipian* 11; Ware 1966, 194; Reed 1987, 174; see Fig. 5)

Fig. 5: Maonü covered in black hairs encountering the immortal in the mountain.
Source: *Liexian quanzhuan.*

Maonü in due course became a highly venerated and respected immortal. She is typically shown in a leafy gown and with hairy legs. To the present day, there is still a temple dedicated to her on the northern slope of Mount Hua, the Maonü Grotto (Porter 1993, 69).

A third major way of controlling *qi* as it enters and leaves the body is through sexual hygiene. In many cases this means the practice of celibacy for the preservation of sexual energy and its circulation and refinement within the body (Eskildsen 1998, 38-40). The *Liexian zhuan* records two cases of immortals rejecting marriage in preference of remaining single and celibate. Both Jiuke and Xuansu were offered the comely daughters of merchants and noblemen, but rather than marry they would disappear in the night (*Liexian zhuan* 1.16ab, 2.16b; Kaltenmark 1953, 122, 191-92).

Sexual hygiene, as noted earlier, could also involve work with partners. Men would have relations with numerous women in order to obtain their *qi* so they could augment their own stock by guiding the precious substance through the body for greater energetic refinement. In the early records, Master Rongcheng is famous for this method. He would absorb seminal essence from the Mysterious Female, following the *Daode jing* dictum that the "valley spirit that does not die" (ch. 6) and thereby preserving his life and nourishing his *qi* (*Liexian zhuan* 1.3b; Kaltenmark 1953, 55-56).

Another immortal who engaged in active sexual practices was Wen Bin. He married frequently, discarding his wives as they grew old. One of his former spouses, however, continued to visit him persistently, until he realized that she really loved the Dao. He accordingly acknowledged her efforts, and said: "Had I realized earlier, I would not have sent you away." He then taught her his diet, and a hundred years later the couple reappeared, still youthful and vigorous (2.9ab; Kaltenmark 1953, 165-66).

Among women practitioners, the *Liexian zhuan* emphasizes the story of the wineseller Nü Ji:

> She once met an immortal who had stopped by her house to drink wine and left a book on five scrolls of silk as a pledge [in lieu of cash]. Ji unrolled and examined the book, which pre-

sented techniques for nourishing inner nature through sexual intercourse.

Ji privately copied the text's essentials, then had another room built where she invited various young men to drink her delicious wine and spend the night with her practicing the techniques described in the book. After thirty years of doing this her facial complexion was once again as it had been when she was twenty.

Several years later the immortal returned. Laughing, he told Ji, "Appropriating the Dao without a teacher [is like] having wings but not flying!" She proceeded to abandon her home and follow the immortal. No one knows where they went. (2.14a; Kaltenmark 1953, 181-82)

As these cases show, women were equally able to attain immortality and used the same methods—refining *qi* through breath, food, and sexual hygiene. They were also used by female adepts according to later hagiographies, notably Du Guangting's *Yongcheng jixian lu* and the thirteenth-century collection *Tongjian houji*. Here the most elementary technique is the rejection of ordinary food (*bigu*), a practice also common among spiritual women in medieval Europe (see Bynum 1987). Practitioners typically begin by reducing their intake of grains and vegetables, then gradually replace them with sesame, mica, pine needles, and other plants and minerals. Eventually the refined body needs very little nourishment and can subsist on pure *qi*, which is taken in and controlled mainly through breath. Sexual practices are applied mainly in the form of internal circulation and transmutation of *qi*, leading to the complete transfiguration of the person from human to immortal.

Magical Powers

As part of the process of transfiguration many immortals gained magical powers. The *Liexian zhuan* records three incidents involving the acquisition of such powers in women. One concerns the imperial consort Gouyi furen, a lady of rather mysterious background.

> When she was young she loved clarity and tranquility. She lay down ill for six years, and her right hand curled into a fist. She drank and ate little. Men who were skilled at observing [the patterns of] *qi* announced the appearance of a noble person's energy in the northeast. After a search they found her and brought her to the palace. She was majestic in appearance. (2.2a; Kaltenmark 1953, 139; also *Shiji* 49).

When courtiers finally managed to pry open her right fist, it contained a hook made from jade which was considered an omen of superior virtue and heavenly blessing, documenting the magical relationship she had to heaven.

Another story in the *Liexian zhuan* is the tale of the consorts of the Jiang river (Jiangfei), who once encountered the official Zheng Jiaofu and let him have the pendants on their belts, only to reclaim them through supernatural means later, after vanishing suddenly into thin air (1.11b-12a; Kaltenmark 1953, 96-97). Yet a different magical feat is mentioned in connection with Duzi, "the daughter of a wine-merchant in the marketplace. Her eyebrows were naturally connected, and her ears were thin and long. Everyone considered her different and said that she was a celestial person." Duzi patronizes her father's wineshop, she follows him out at night to pick fruit, and they are pursued by townspeople wherever they go, but no one can catch up with them (2.2b; Kaltenmark 1953, 142; see also Smith 1998; Bumbacher 2000a, 65-69).

While these magical feats in the *Liexian zhuan* tend to be small occurrences, the *Shenxian zhuan* contains extensive discussions of women's powers in two stories. First, there is the tale of Zhuan He, the Woman of Great Mystery (Taixuan nü). Finding the world a sad place to live in, she left society to find enlightened teachers and pursue the Dao. She obtained the arts of an immortal known as the Jade Master and practiced them diligently for several years. As a result she attained extended longevity while yet maintaining the looks of a young girl. She also became well versed in various magical abilities. As the text says:

> The Lady of Great Mystery was able to enter the water and not get wet. Even in the severest cold of winter she would walk over frozen rivers wearing only a single garment. All the time

her expression would not change, and her body would remain comfortably warm for a succession of days.

She could also move government offices, temples, cities, and lodges. They would appear in other places quite without moving from their original location. Whatever she pointed at would vanish into thin air. Doors, windows, boxes, or caskets that were securely locked needed only a short flexing of her finger to break wide open. Mountains tumbled, trees fell at the pointing of her finger. Another short gesture would resurrect them to their former state. . . .

The Lady of Great Mystery could travel ten thousand miles, yet at the same time continue to stay nearby. She could transform small things to be suddenly big, and big things to be small. She could spit fire so big it would rise up wildly into heaven, and yet in one breath she could extinguish it again.

She was also able to sit in the middle of a blazing fire, while her clothes would never be touched by the flames. She could change her appearance at will: one moment she was an old man, then again a small child. She could also conjure up a cart and horse to ride in, if she did not want to walk. . . . Eventually she ascended to heaven in broad daylight. (Kohn 1993, 291-92; Güntsch 1988, 201-2)[2]

This account presents the immortal abilities mastered by the Lady after following an immortal master and undergoing extensive training over several years. Not only young looking and full of vital energy, she was able to control her inner *qi* to the point of influencing her own shape and location and that of other things. No longer affected by cold and heat, water and fire, she could vanish and appear at will, travel far in an instant, and be in multiple locations at the same time. She could also extend this power to other people and objects, moving houses and temples, making things appear and vanish, causing objects to grow and shrink, open and close, rise and fall—all determined by the pointing of her fin-

---

[2] This biography is found only in *Shenxian zhuan* editions of the Ming dynasty, following the version of the *Nüxian zhuan* as recorded in *Taiping guangji* 59.363. Earlier fragments are very short (Campany 20002, 541-42).

ger, the extension of her *qi*. Like modern masters of Qigong who can manipulate objects and people to move in certain ways by the mere movement of their *qi*, she was able to exert total control over herself and her environment, being fully in charge and highly empowered, a strong representative of women's competence in the immortal arts.

Another woman with magical powers, and probably the most important female immortal of the *Shenxian zhuan* is Magu, the Hemp Lady.[3] Allegedly born under Emperor Ming of the Han (r. 57-75 C.E.), she attained immortality and traveled widely through the cosmos, taking time to sojourn in the paradises of Penglai and Kunlun, and living long enough to "see the Eastern Sea turn to mulberry fields several times over."

Her main legend describes her presence in the family of the Daoist Cai Jing in the company of the immortal Wang Fangping, a high ranking officer on Mount Kunlun in charge of the celestial registers of life and death. Wang had recognized in Cai the "bones of immortality" (*xiangu*) and other physiognomic signs of celestial quality (see Kohn 1996b). He bestowed upon him transcendent teachings, enabling him to shed his mortal form and ascend. A century later Cai returned for a visit and prepared the household for Wang's supernatural arrival on the seventh day of the seventh month. The immortal duly appeared, to the accompaniment of wondrous music and surrounded by a divine entourage of thousands of soldiers and mythical beasts. "He was wearing the headdress of the far-off journey and a crimson robe, complete with a tiger-head belt bag, a five-colored sash, and a sword" (Campany 2002, 261).

After his arrival Wang sent a divine messenger to invite Magu who joined them as a youthful beauty (see Fig. 6).

> Magu appeared to be handsome woman of eighteen or nineteen; her hair was done up, and several loose strands hung down to her waist. Her gown had a pattern of colors, but it was not woven; it shimmered, dazzling the eyes, and was indescribable—it was not of this world. (Campany 2002, 262)

---

[3] The biography was originally part of Wang Fangping's, and only later formed a separate tale. For translations and discussions, see Güntsch 1988, 206-10; Despeux 1990, 61-63; Bumbacher 2000b, 799; Campany 2002, 259-64.

麻
姑

Fig. 6: The Hemp Lady in immortal splendor with her divine deer.
Source: *Liexian quanzhuan*.

After bowing to Wang, the Hemp Lady ordered a "traveling feast" (*xing-chu*), a supernatural banquet made up of the finest delicacies of the empire and the heavens, including such wondrous treats as unicorn meat. "The servings were piled up on gold platters and in jade cups without limit" (Campany 2002, 263). Following this, Magu performed various magical feats, throwing a handful of rice, each grain of which turned into a pearl in support of the young daughter-in-law who had just given birth; and reading Cai Jing's mind who hopes to use her claw-like fingernails to have his back scratched. Before their departure, moreover, the two immortals provided the family's neighbor with a divine talisman, designed to extend life, dispel misfortunes, exorcise demons, and heal diseases (Campany 2002, 263-64).

This extensive story of the magical power of the immortal Magu and her male partner contains shamanic, mediumistic, and exorcistic elements. The two immortals arrive to the sound of celestial music made by fifes and drums, instruments often used in exorcisms on earth. They descend in the company of numerous celestial troops and animals, invoking the presence of the high powers of heaven into the world, just as a shaman would call down the gods to be present for a ceremony or exorcism. Wang in particular wears the formal garb of exorcistic power, including a headdress symbolizing the freedom of heaven, a tiger-head pouch, and a sword, while Magu has partly disheveled hair, showing her shamanic and semi-demonic nature,[4] and is characterized as having bird-like fangs, an indication of her animal nature and ultimate wildness. Rice is thrown to dispel demonic influences, associated in the story as much as in the human world with the dangers surrounding liminal situations, such as weddings and childbirth. Demons of all sorts are controlled with talismans, which also grant long life and heal diseases.

The shamanic and interactive nature of Magu is also expressed in her cult, centered in the regions of Anhui and Jiangsu, where she still had an active following until at least the thirteenth century (*Tongjian houji* 3.5ab;

---

[4] Disheveled hair was a major characteristic of demons and baleful spirits, as well as of maniacs and mad people in this world (see Ōgata 1995). This symbolism, as well as the accompanying control over human hair, is a common theme in various cultures (see Hiltebeitel and Miller 1998).

Despeux 1990, 62). Cultic records appear first in the Tang dynasty, when a sacred mountain was named after her: Mount Magu in Wu prefecture in modern Jiangxi. A stele erected there was noted by the local prefect and Highest Clarity adept Yan Zhenqing (709-786) in 768. He recorded its inscription in his *Wuzhou Nancheng xian Magu shan xiantan ji* (Record of the Immortal Altar on Mount Magu, located in Nancheng District in Wu Province), now found in his collected writings, the *Yan Lugong wenji* (Collected Writings of Yan Lugong, 13-7a-9a). It essentially recounts the main story of the Hemp Lady, matching the *Shenxian zhuan* narrative and later accounts, such as in Du Guangting's *Yongcheng jixian lu* (4.10b-13b).

Beyond her local fame, Magu was also closely associated with Lady Wei Huacun. As documented in the *Nanyue zongsheng ji* (Record of Scenic Places on the Southern Peak, DZ 606), the two divine ladies served jointly in the entourage of the Perfect Lord of the Southern Peak (Nanyue zhenjun) and were housed in a hall near his main sanctuary on Mount Heng. The Lord was one of a series of mountain gods that had been officially appointed under the Tang to protect and bless the empire. Sima Chengzhen in his *Wuling jing* (Scripture of the Five Numinous Lords) describes them as different from all other deities and insists that they be offered regular offerings that yet must never contain any animal parts (1a).[5]

Beyond her two major sanctuaries, Magu also appeared to Daoist adepts. An example is Deng Ziyang, Daoist of the Datong dian (Hall of Great

---

[5] The sponsoring of sacred mountains as state-supporting institutions began in the Sui dynasty (589-618), which first set up Buddhist temples on them, as well as also in the capitals and at important holy sites of the state. The Tang continued this practice, and in 666, Gaozong established one Buddhist and one Daoist monastery in every prefecture and on every holy mountain of the empire (Forte 1992, 219). Emperor Xuanzong (r. 713-755) expanded the practice further. In 738, he had state temples and monasteries, named Kaiyuan (Opening Prime) after his reign title, erected in all major districts and holy locations of the empire. The role of these institutions was less to spread religion than to create a sanctified imperial network throughout the country (Benn 1987, 135; Forte 1992, 235-37). The Perfect Lord of the Southern Peak is part of this system. For more on this mountain in Chinese religion and Buddhism, see Faure 1987; Robson 1995.

Unity). In 739, he had a vision of a celestial chariot drawn by dragons and tigers, in which two divinities were riding. As it was coming close, he recognized the immortal and realized that he was going to die soon. He promptly formalized his wish to be buried on Mount Magu, near her shrine, which resulted in the construction of a monastery there. In 746, a yellow dragon was spotted in the vicinity, another indication of the immortal lady's blessing. More appearances followed, continuing into the Song dynasty, when Magu was given numerous honors and formal titles—in many cases linked with both Wei Huacun and Xiwang mu (*Quan Tangwen* 338.3442; Despeux 1990, 65).

In Complete Perfection Daoism, Magu served as the model and prime example of what women could attain. Ma Danyang, one of the Seven Perfected and husband of the woman leader Sun Buer, wrote:

> Lady Daoists, listen to me now, and listen well:
> Learn all from the Hemp Lady,
> So you too can reach the pure and clear,
> Using her wondrous and excellent practices.
> Never mind about being sharp and bright, never mind at all:
> Act the fool and simpleton without,
> As you grow more spiritual within.
> The great work done, you'll soon be off to Jade Capital!
> (*Jianwu ji* [Collection of Gradual Awakening], DZ 1141, 1.20b)

Later linked with various lineages of women's inner alchemy, Magu has remained an important example of a successful woman immortal who gained great control and achieved eternal life, enjoying heavenly ease for herself and bringing delights and blessings to all.

Social Interaction

Successful immortals—as much as other women—did not operate in a vacuum. However accomplished, they continued to interact with society, influencing the people and events around them. More so than men who could become hermits and leave their social bonds behind fairly easily, women were connected deeply to family and society and often under-

took their immortal self-cultivation in cooperation with a male partner—
be he mentor, father, or husband. In some cases, however, women with
power were resented by the people around them and found themselves
in conflict with their clan.

Several passages in the *Liexian zhuan* portray women as partners of immortals, who help them obtain realization. Most popular and prominent
among them is the Flute Master (Xiaoshi), who taught the daughter of
Duke Mu of Qin to play the flute and imitate the songs of phoenixes. Secluded in a tower on Mount Hua, they attracted phoenixes and other
supernatural creatures with their delightful tunes. One day they joined
the birds and flew off to heaven (1.17a; Kaltenmark 1953, 125). To the
present day, the central peak of Mount Hua is named Yunü feng (Jade
Maiden Peak) after this divine lady, and a shrine is active there in her
honor (Porter 1993, 73).

A divine couple is also described in the biography of Master Redpine
(Chisongzi), who was pursued by Red Emperor's young daughter. Joining up with her, he transmitted his secrets, and she also obtained immortality. They departed to heaven together (1.1a; Kaltenmark 1953, 35).
Then there is Yuanke, who was originally indifferent to the daughters
offered to him by various merchants but converted to marital bliss when
he was engaged in the production of silk. The *Liexian zhuan* says:

> As the silkworm season approached a beautiful woman came
> during the night, called herself Yuanke's wife, and described
> the silkworms' appearance. Together she and Yuanke gathered
> the silkworms, finding one hundred twenty. The cocoons were
> as big as jars; reeling silk off a single one took sixty days to
> complete. When they were finished, they left together for
> places unknown. (2.4ab; Kaltenmark 1953, 148-49)

Another, similar tale is told about the elderly Hu Zixian, who, just before
he "left," called out to an old wineshop woman to get dressed for an audience with the underworld ruler. They flew off into the empyrean, riding on two straw dogs that turned into dragons (*Liexian zhuan* 2.11b-12a;
Kaltenmark 1953, 172-74).

These tales show the close cooperation between male and female partners in the attainment of transcendence. Another story emphasizes their

posthumous connection. The immortal Hanzi follows his dog into a cave and emerges into an otherworldly realm. There he meets his deceased wife, who is now in charge of cleaning fish for the immortals' kitchen. She hands him a box containing talismans, fish eggs, and medicines, and instructs him to give it to a certain magistrate. Hanzi makes repeated visits and eventually stays, thus attaining immortality through cooperation with his wife (2.15ab; Kaltenmark 1953, 187-88).

A slightly different slant on male-female cooperation is found in the *Shenxian zhuan* with the story of Fan Furen, the wife of the immortal Liu Gang. They both practice Daoist arts, and each claim superiority over the other. In one instance, they engage in pronouncing spells over two peach trees in their courtyard until the tree which Liu Gang incanted over flees across the fence. Then they exhale over a basin of water, using their *qi* to make it come to life. Liu manages to create a carp but his wife bests him by bringing forth an otter which eats the carp. Later they encounter a tiger during their travels and find that Liu is vulnerable to its attack. Lady Fan, on the other hand, easily seizes and binds the beast. Despite their continued competition, they ascend to heaven together, although not with equal grace. Liu Gang only manages to jump off into the clouds after climbing into a tree, while Lady Fan simply sits on her mat and is elevated. The story, although humorous, is a testimonial to the competition women experienced in their practice of immortal arts, especially when they were gifted with great potential and inherent superiority (ch. 7, Güntsch 1988, 211-12; Campany 2002, 147-48).

A more severe record of the same theme appears in several other biographies, such as that of Cheng Wei's wife. Obedient and subservient to her husband and family, she goes out of her way to do a lot of good, helping them out with her magical abilities. For example, when her husband finds that he does not own a set of proper clothes for his official duties, she magically conjures up a bolt of fine silk and creates a new gown for him. When he tries his hand at alchemy without success, she mixes a bunch of herbs with mercury and produces silver. Instead of being grateful for his wife's skills, however, Cheng Wei starts pestering her for her secrets, wanting to acquire the power for himself. She consistently denies him access, not seeing any "immortal's bones" in him, and in the end has to flee from the relationship by shedding her mortal coil and ascending to heaven (ch. 7, Güntsch 1988, 205; Campany 2002, 139-40; Cleary 1989, 9).

Another story that points in the same direction is the biography of the Holy Mother of Dongling (Dongling shengmu), also found in the *Shenxian zhuan*. She was a disciple of Liu Gang, Lady Fan's husband, and with his help attained many magical powers. She was able to "appear and disappear at will, change shape, transform, and conceal herself from view" (Campany 2002, 146). She was also an accomplished healer, much sought after in the community. Her husband, Mr. Du, however, had none of these abilities. Searingly jealous of his wife's powers and social position, he denounced her to the magistrate as lecherous and wicked. The Holy Mother was arrested and put into jail but escaped into immortality by flying out the window, leaving only a pair of slippers behind (*Shenxian zhuan* 7; Güntsch 1988, 216-17; Campany 2002, 146; Cleary 1989, 11-12).

In the wake of her unusual life and as a result of her continued great powers, the Holy Mother of Dongling became the object of a cult. The founding of her first shrine occurred after she appeared to a traveling merchant, as recorded by the Song official Yue Shi in his *Taiping huanyu ji* (A Taiping-Era Record of the World; see Hervouet 1978, 128). He says:

> During the Liang dynasty, a merchant passing through by boat one night dreamed that a woman said to him: "I am the Holy Mother of Dongling. I have followed my sacred image down the current to this spot; it is now in the water beneath your boat. If you take my image ashore here and establish a shrine for it, I will richly reward you."
>
> When the merchant woke, he looked around and found that it was as he had dreamed. He took the image ashore and raised a shrine for it. (Campany 2002, 147; also *Tongjian houji* 4.4b)

More shrines to the Holy Mother arose over the centuries and became the locations of miracles and healings. They were commonly populated by wondrous, blue birds, seen as her spirit messengers and indicators of her presence.

The dynamics at work in these transformations of wronged women into efficacious supernatural agents has to do with the power of cosmic *qi* inherent in them. Gifted by the Dao with an unusual strength of *qi* and acquiring control over it through self-cultivation and religious discipline, these women could and should be of great service to the world. If they are not permitted to fulfill this role due to social constraints and the narrow-mindedness of men, they transcend the human realm and exert their powers from the other side. The wrongful behavior these women are subjected to during their lives are attempts to suppress their *qi* but only succeed in making it stronger. This shows that neither the Dao nor the powers of yin can be subjected to human rules and social limitations. The women, part of the Dao and in harmony with the greater forces of the cosmos, appear inherently superior and come out victorious.

Not limited to Daoism, the posthumous, supernatural empowerment of women who were maligned and mistreated during life is a common theme in Chinese folk religion. An early case is found in the story of the Plum Maid (Meigu) who lived in the third century B.C.E. She had the power to walk on water and perform other feats, but was killed by her husband after she committed a minor offense against ritual propriety. Since then, she has appeared hovering over lakes and rivers, especially on the first and last days of the lunar month. Having been killed herself, she ensures that no animals suffer the same fate and anyone found fishing or hunting in waters protected by her is condemned to losing his way and drowning (*Tongjian houji* 2.13ab; Miyakawa 1979, 85-86; Reed 1987, 175). Other cases of a similar nature were recorded by DeGroot in the late nineteenth century. For example, in one story the daughter of a noble family flees to a deserted island to avoid marriage and preserve her spiritual integrity. She works many miracles, including bringing victory to the Chinese naval fleet. She also causes a dry staff to grow green and fragrant, showing her powers by overcoming the laws of nature and humanity (DeGroot 1910, 159-60; Main 1975, 203-4).

In all these cases, female immortals emerge as competent and equal in potential and powers to their male counterparts, although they are sometimes forced into, or hindered in, the practice by social constraints or the jealousy and concerns of their male relatives. As immortals and practitioners of self-cultivation, they actively choose the path of the Dao and pursue it with determination, developing great skills and rising far above the ordinary. In this regard they are not entirely unusual in ancient Chinese culture, where records such as the *Lienü zhuan* show that women could be considered powerful and competent, not only as managers of households but also as educators, advisors, and agents of intellectual, political, and ethical values whose counsel influenced the development of families and states (Raphals 1998, 4).

In both mainstream biographies of eminent women and in Daoist tales of female immortals, the ideal often overshadows the reality, and it is hard to know where legends end and realities begin. In general, ancient sources only report outstanding and unusual cases, documenting things that would not normally be seen and are thus worthy of special mention. Also, the selection of tales depends on the location and social standing of the subjects in question, not every woman practitioner being sufficiently well known in her area to come to the attention of a person with official connections or a literary education.

The stories about Daoist women must be taken with a grain of salt. They are written in a language that does suggest historical facts but these facts are difficult to discern among the obscuring mists of legends and religious ideals. Given the fantastic nature of these stories, it is questionable how many real, living women were in fact powerful practitioners, equal or even superior to men, shining beacons of Daoist attainment. On the other hand, the fact that many were worshiped in shrines and as masters of cultivation in later centuries shows that the empowerment of women was an ideal beyond simple fantasy that lived in Daoist lives and minds. Magu in particular is held up as the model for later practitioners, her beauty, moral rectitude, magical powers, and immortal standing all giving hope and guidance to active followers. The ancient immortals, whether real women or idealized figures, therefore, exerted a strong influence on the vision of women's attainment and stood as classical models for the control of *qi*—their practices and powers continuing in different forms over the centuries to come.

Chapter Five

Medieval Renunciants

The middle ages, from the late Han through the Tang dynasties (2nd to 9th c. C.E.), saw the emergence of various Daoist schools and communal organizations—from the Great Peace movement and the Celestial Masters in the late Han through the schools of Highest Clarity and Numinous Treasure in the Jin and Six Dynasties to the integrated ordination system of the Tang. Women were active in all these schools and organizations from the beginning, both as individual practitioners of self-cultivation and as functionaries with ritual and administrative powers. In accordance with the changing patterns of Daoist organization, they were married, matriarchal priests at first, then—with the emergence of Daoist monasticism in the sixth century (see Kohn 2003)—increasingly took on the role of ordained nuns, a function that came with priestly rank and ritual empowerment. These women made up about one third of the total population of registered Daoists, lived in their own convents, and offered an independent and alternative way of life to the women of mainstream Chinese society.

Priests of the Celestial Masters

According to the founding legend of the Celestial Masters, in the second century C.E., the immortality seeker Zhang Daoling learned a secret alchemical recipe in a trance and tried to obtain the necessary but costly ingredients. He failed and moved to Sichuan. There, on Mount Heming, he entered a deep trance and, in 142, had a major vision of a deity who introduced himself as Lord Lao, the personified Dao. The god informed Zhang that the end of the world was at hand, and ordered him to teach the people how to repent and prepare themselves for momentous changes by becoming morally pure so they could serve as the "Dao people" (*daomin*) or "seed people" (*zhongmin*) of the new age. The god closed the "Covenant of Orthodox Unity" (*Zhengyi mengwei*) by appointing Zhang as his representative on earth with the title "celestial master" (*tianshi*) and giving him exorcistic and healing powers as a sign of his divine status (*Shenxian zhuan* 4; Giles 1948, 60-64; Güntsch 1988, 136-42; Campany 2002, 349-54).

Zhang followed the god's orders and proceeded to preach to the people and heal the sick. As a token for his efforts, he took five pecks of rice from his followers, who included large numbers of local people and ethnic non-Chinese. The tax earned the sect the nickname "Five Pecks of Rice Sect" (Wudou mi dao). Over the years he assembled a sizable following which he arranged into twenty-four districts, each governed by a ritually determined administrator known as libationer (*jijiu*) and run by lesser functionaries, the so-called demon soldiers (*guizu*). All leadership positions could be filled by Han Chinese or ethnic minorities of either sex; the wives of leaders, moreover, were known as "female masters" (*nüshi*) and placed in charge of teaching the women.[1] At the bottom were the common followers, organized and counted according to households and responsible for paying the organizational tax in rice, silk, paper, brushes, ceramics, or handicrafts.

---

[1] The term *nüshi* first appears in the fourth century but seems to have been used earlier. It is found in the *Shangqing huangshu guodu yi* (DZ 1294), 3a; *Shenzhou zhibing kouzhang* (Oral Petitions for the Healing of Diseases Through Divine Incantations, DZ 1290), 34a; *Dengzhen yinjue* (Secret Instructions on the Ascent to Perfection, DZ 421), 3.8a. The latter points out that when the formulas of the Celestial Master Zhang Wei were transmitted to Wei Huacun, adepts entered the quiet chamber and informed the three masters: the celestial master, the female master, and the personal master. The author adds that this was practiced also before the Han, the main difference being that the female master did not have to be the master's wife. For more details on the early Celestial Masters and their organization, see Levy 1956; Stein 1963; Kleeman 1998; Hendrischke 2000.

In addition, each member, independent of sex, from early childhood on underwent formal initiations at regular intervals and was equipped with a "register" (*lu*) of spirit generals for protection against demons—75 for an unmarried person and 150 for a married couple (Maspero 1981, 443; Overmyer 1981, 97; Schipper 1994, 87; Bumbacher 1998, 689). Some of these initiations, as noted earlier, were called "harmonization of *qi*" and involved formally choreographed intercourse between selected non-married partners in an elaborate ritual. Practitioners thereby, as well as by being married and having offspring (Bumbacher 2000a, 516), enacted the cosmic matching of yin and yang in their bodies and thus contributed to greater universal harmony. As a later polemical record describes it, referring to the *Huangshu* (Yellow Book), an old manual on *qi*-related practices:[2]

> During the rituals held at new and full moon, Daoists attend on their preceptor in their private chambers. Feeling and intention are made akin, and men and women engage in joining together. They match their four eyes and two noses, above and below. They join their two mouths and two tongues, one with the other. Once then yin and yang have met intimately, essence and energy are exchanged freely. Thus, the rites of men and women are performed and the Dao of male and female is harmonized. (*Guang hongming ji* 12, T. 2103, 52.172b; Kohn 1995a, 148)

A similar description is also cited in another polemic:

> As the four eyes, four nostrils, two mouths, two tongues, and four hands are clasped together, one concentrates the mind to make yin and yang join—twenty-four times, in accordance with the twenty-four energies of the year. Through this practice one realizes the perfect formula in the cinnabar field.

---

[2] The *Huangshu* is an ancient sexual manual revealed to the first Celestial Master Zhang Daoling, later revised and expurged under Highest Clarity Daoism. The later version still exists as the *Dongzhen huangshu* (Yellow Book of Perfection Cavern, DZ 1343) and contains a description of the original revelation (1b-2a, 12b). The ancient work survives only in citations, especially among Buddhist polemics. For more, see Kobayashi 1990, 199; 1992; Bumbacher 2000a, 514-17; Yan 2001.

> But make sure to keep it to yourself and never let it leak out.
> Nor must you harbor jealousy. The practice will protect you
> from all dangers and disasters. You will be called a perfected,
> go beyond the world, and live forever. (*Bianzheng lun*, T. 2110,
> 52.546a)

Here the emphasis is not only on the harmonization of yin and yang
which will lead to stabilization of the cosmos and greater communal integration but also on the personal attainment of long life and immortality,
linking the communal practices back with the self-cultivation activities of
the immortals of old. As was the case with self-cultivation, women in
these rituals were necessary partners and benefitted in the same way
from the techniques.

For these techniques to be efficacious, it was essential that all ritual intercourse remained free from ordinary sexual feelings and desires. The
Zhenren neili (Esoteric Rites of the Perfected) says:

> Do not fail to observe the proper order of attendance in the in-
> ner chamber. Do not harbor desire for the ordinary way [of in-
> tercourse] nor fail to observe the teachings of [sexual] control.
> Do not lust for relations with outsiders nor fail to observe the
> rituals of the proper nourishing of the inner chamber. Do not
> lust to be first nor fail to observe the rules of cultivation of the
> inner chamber. (*Bianzheng lun*, T. 2110, 52.545c)

The emphasis on qi-control in these sexual rites is further enhanced by
the strong instructions on meditative detachment, breath control, and the
regulated swallowing of saliva contained in the same text (Kohn
1995a,148). In all these activities women were central and continued to
play an essential role.

Despite their importance only few women have earned hagiographies in
the Celestial Masters tradition. Surviving documents tend to focus on the
relatives of the first leaders and were probably created later.[3] Other

---

[3] A case in point is the notice on Zhang Daoling's wife, Lady Sun (Sun
Furen) as female master in the *Wushang biyao* of the sixth century (DZ 1138,
84.10b). Her story is retold in Du Guangting's *Yongcheng jixian lu* (6.4a-5b). It
notes that she successfully cultivated the Dao on Mount Longhu and received a
tiger-dragon elixir method from the Yellow Emperor. So prepared, she joined the

works, however, make it clear that men and women had the same rights in performing and guiding rites, such as the presentation of petitions (*zhang*) and the writing of talismans (*fu*) (Bumbacher 1998, 686; 2000a, 515). In addition, the rituals prescribed the same actions for all participants independent of gender, with some minor differences that took account of the yang nature of men and the yin nature of women.

For example, yang corresponds to the left side of the body while yin matches the right, so men began all ritual moves with the left and women with the right. "When a man and a women receive the registers of the three generals displayed on the altar, the man takes them from the left and the woman from the right," the *Shangqing huangshu guodu yi* prescribes (15a, 12b). Similarly, the *Shoulu cidi faxin yi* (Observances for the Proper Order and Tokens in Receiving Registers, DZ 1244, 17b) says: "After the ceremony, the master takes the man's left hand and the woman's right."

The division of roles and specificity of directions continues ancient Chinese models that provided for a special coming-of-age ceremony for girls, the hairpinning ceremony, parallel to the capping for males (Paper 1997, 57; Overmyer 1981, 97). The *Liji*, moreover, emphasizes the power of women while outlining the geographical and directional division of the sexes:

> The celestial movements provide teachings . . . [At the sacrifices] the ruler is at the [top] of the steps [of the eastern hall]; the principal wife is in the [most western] chamber. The sun comes up in the east; the moon comes up in the west. This is the differentiation of yin and yang and the principle of husband and wife. The ruler [facing west] offers wine in a vessel decorated with an elephant; the wife [facing] east offers wine in a vessel [with clouds and mountains]. The rituals proceed with mutuality above and the musicians respond to each other below. Thus harmony is achieved. (Paper 1997, 58)

Celestial Master and ruled by his side, until their joint ascension in 155. She received the title Lady of the Eastern Peak (Dongyue furen) and was honored by her son and grandson who took over the governing of the cult after her husband. She also has a brief biography in *Tongjian houji* 2.13b-14a as do her daughters and granddaughters (2.14a-15b).

Women were thus essential in the performance of ancient rites as much as in the organization of the early Daoist movement of the Celestial Masters. Serving as wives of masters, as libationers, or fulfilling ritual and administrative roles, they had equal access to religious advancement and political influence and as matriarchs often came to govern the organization. They also tended to work closely with their husbands as equal partners. An example is the wife of Liu Ningzhi, described in the later collection *Daoxue zhuan* (Biographies of Students of the Dao).[4] Born into the family of a high official, she married a follower of the Celestial Masters, and the couple proceeded to pursue the Daoist path, first by giving away their riches and supporting the poor, later by withdrawing into the mountains and practicing self-cultivation. The biography mentions that they had the same ideals, worked closely together, and did not lose their marital harmony even in difficult times (Bumbacher 1998, 687).

Women among the Celestial Masters were seen as essential to the balance of yin and yang in the cosmos, honored as partners in marriage and in the ritual harmonization of *qi*. They held their own as members and leaders of the community, and were not treated with obvious discrimination. To the present day, Celestial Masters Daoism propagates cultivation techniques that are not gender specific and includes many female deities in its pantheon, even among its generals and other supernatural military. Although priests that officiate at rituals are exclusively male, both sexes follow the same rules and rise through the same ritual ranks (Reed 1987, 176; Saso 1978, 156-60).

---

[4] This collection of Daoist biographies from the fourth and fifth centuries does not survive independently but is extant in citations, collected and translated in Bumbacher 2000a. It continues the tradition of both the *Liexian zhuan* and *Shenxian zhuan* in terms of the Daoist tradition, but also follows the Confucian *Lienü zhuan* (Raphals 1998, 87-112; Paper 1997, 65) and the Buddhist *Biqiuni zhuan* (see Tsai 1994) in its realistic and historically accurate reporting. With the *Daoxue zhuan*, women in Daoism emerge from the legendary and individual into the realistic and communal.

Early Medieval Renunciants

With the arising of the Highest Clarity (Shangqing) school in the fourth century in the southern part of China around Mount Mao near Nanjing, personal self-cultivation came to the forefront of organized Daoist practice, and adepts—in some cases with their entire families—retired to the mountains to attain communion with the Dao and celestial immortality.

The Highest Clarity cosmos expanded the supernatural world of the Celestial Masters—populated by deities, ancestors, and demons—to include a new layer of existence between the original, creative force of the Dao and the created world. This celestial layer consisted of several different regions, located both in the far reaches of the world and in the stars, and imagined along the lines of the immortal paradises Penglai and Kunlun. It was populated by divine figures: pure gods of Dao who were emanations of original cosmic *qi*; immortals who had attained celestial status through effort and the proper elixir; demon kings, converted spirits who had risen to rank and power; and ancestors who had entered the realm through death. These divine figures were arranged hierarchically, transforming the Daoist otherworld into a vast celestial bureaucracy—the dead were administered in the Six Palaces of Fengdu, immortals under the rule of the Southern Palace (Nangong) beyond the Northern Dipper, and pure gods of Dao in the heaven of Highest Clarity itself. Practitioners strove to become part of this bureaucracy, rising gradually through the ranks: from demon officer, through underworld ruler, to sage, immortal, and perfected (Robinet 1984, 1:131-34).

As community was discerned in celestial terms, practices privileged individual salvation yet took place in a communal setting. Women practitioners in this organization were seen either as celestial teachers, along the lines of the matriarch Wei Huacun and the court ladies of the Queen Mother of the West, or as religious practitioners in their own right. That is to say, women appear both as deities and divine agents and also as living, human agents of the religion.

As celestial teachers or revealing deities, women met human adepts as they journeyed from the real world to the imaginary. Idealized, they belonged to the otherworld, the world of gods, and supported adepts as intermediaries, preceptors, and counsellors. Thanks to the assistance of these women, adepts could undergo the metamorphoses that led them to the rank of perfected. This assistance came in the form of mediation and transformation, and was indispensable for immortal success. An early example of a celestial teacher is mentioned in the *Shenxian zhuan*. According to this, the immortality seeker Jie Xiang had entered the mountains during his quest for immortality when he encountered a beautiful woman, about fifteen years old and clad in a multicolored gown. The woman demanded that Jie return some colored stones he had picked up on the mountain and purify himself for three years. When these tasks were complete, the divine woman taught him alchemical methods by revealing a pertinent scripture, and Jie attained magical powers and immortality (Campany 2002, 192).

Celestial teachers were usually divinized human women who had undertaken the journey to heaven on their own and had achieved high rank in the otherworldly hierarchy. Elevated to superior status, they sometimes became the objects of cults. Hagiographies abound with examples of these women who obtained perfection through a variety of practices, from reciting canonical texts to breathing techniques and visualizations. Prominent among them are the various ladies associated with the Queen Mother, such as the Lady of Highest Prime and the Lady of Numinous Efflorescence, but gifted earthly women who practiced arduously and attained perfection are also included (see Cahill 1990).

Women practitioners, i.e., living, human adepts of the Dao, formed the other main dimension of female presence in this form of Daoism. They could pursue Daoist realization either by joining the lay organization of the Celestial Masters in cooperation with their families or by leaving ordinary society and becoming students of advanced masters. According to the rules of the reformed Celestial Masters of the fifth century, as recorded in the *Zhengyi fawen taishang wailu yi* (Highest Observances for Outer Registers According to the Code of Orthodox Unity, DZ 1243), there were five categories of women who qualified for the reception of registers:

1. Unmarried daughters living at home who might decide, in agreement with their parents, to receive ritual teachings from a master. This would not prevent them from marry-

ing later, but they would carry their ritual status with
them into the union.

2. Daughters who leave home because they do not wish to
    marry can join a group of likeminded adepts and study
    with a master, preferably with an unmarried woman mas-
    ter but definitely not with a male master living alone.

3. Married women who join their husbands in undergoing
    the ceremonies and receiving registers or who follow their
    own master if he is of exceptionally high virtue.

4. Single women, including widows who have vowed not to
    remarry, virtuous or wealthy spinsters, older women
    without sons, or those too poor or sick to be married. They
    can enroll with a master and pursue their personal salva-
    tion.

5. Daughters who return to live at home, either because their
    husbands died, who have been divorced, or whose horo-
    scopes turn out incompatible. Following the proper pro-
    cedures, they can devote themselves to study with a mas-
    ter. (1a-4a; Overmyer 1981, 99-101; Despeux 1986, 63-66;
    1990, 19; Strickmann 1978a, 470; Bumbacher 1998, 688-90;
    2000a, 515)

In each case, the text provides the full wording of a formal vow that the
new student of the Dao is to make when she joins her master. For example, the vow for unmarried daughters states:

> Grateful for the weighty kindness of the Dao from which I ob-
> tained life, I, an unmarried daughter, in such and such a year,
> with a devoted mind take pleasure in the Dao. Although I am
> ignorant I embolden myself to advance, and now take refuge at
> the master's gate.
>
> I beg you to bestow success upon [my quest]; relying on the
> ritual teaching, I maintain faith and sincerity, and offer these
> phrases to be heard. I request to receive such and such a regis-
> ter so that I can devote myself to religious practice according to
> the ritual teaching. Bowing down, I desire that [you], enlight-

> ened master, will deign to give me permission. Respectfully ut-
> tered. (1a; Overmyer 1981, 99)

The other vows are similar, and also include pledges specific to the situation. For example, in the case of women who do not intend to marry or
remarry the vow includes a permanent dedication and pledge: "For my
whole life I will continue the light, offering incense morning and evening." In the case of married women, it swears the adept to sincere devotion, while "I attend to holding the basket and broom" (Overmyer 1981,
100). The Daoist organization, therefore, provided women of all different
categories, whether established fully in the social framework or not fit-
ting easily into the mainstream mold, with the option of religious training as a supplementary or alternative life style. Women's motivation for
entering into the religious state accordingly had to do with a basic orien-
tation away from the world, either manifesting as a deep urge to attain
the higher states of transcendence and salvation or to escape a difficult
social or personal situation (Bumbacher 2000a, 504-65; see also Grant
1996, 30-31).

The proper procedure for entering a convent involved announcing the
intention to one's relatives, who in Daoism as much as in Chinese Buddhism had to agree to the move (Tsai 1994, 70). Next, the renunciant-to-
be would set up her own hermitage or go to live with a teacher, who was
either another woman or a lay, married priest. In either situation, she
should avoid contact with ordinary people, gather herbs to sustain herself, and generally remove foulness and confusion to find peace of mind.
After this period of purification, another training period followed at a
larger institution—often organized as double-houses— leading to several
levels of ordination, which granted personal independence through the
ability to perform rituals, set up her own convent, and attain senior rank
in an existing institution (Kohn 2003, 82).

While occupying the status of a hermit and in separation from society,
women like men had to observe certain basic behavioral rules, spelled
out in the *Daoxue keyi* (Rules and Observances for Students of the Dao,
DZ 1126):

1. Do not order others about or try to teach people.
2. Do not engage with nobility in the pursuit of fame and gain.

3. Do not practice heterodox prohibitions or exorcistic acts. ˙
4. Do not heal or divine for money, parading your skills about.
5. Do not share your seat with members of the other sex and stay away from outsiders.
6. Worship the Heavenly Worthies of the ten directions at the six daily periods.
7. Do not eat grain or *qi*-based food after noon—water, minerals, fungi, and herbs are permitted.
8. When walking through the woods to gather herbs, snap your fingers every three steps and sound your chime every ten steps to remember the local gods and immortals.
9. If you attain some steps in the Dao, do not praise and exhibit yourself.
10. Remember your parents' kindness in raising your body. (11b-12a)

Here the practices undertaken by the immortals of old have been formalized and institutionalized into rules and forms of proper behavior. Distance from ordinary folk is required to guarantee freedom from temptation. There is a sense of humility and detachment, a devotion to nature and the gods as well as gratitude toward the parents whose support is considered essential. Ordinary food, moreover, is increasingly replaced by herbs and the ingestion of *qi*, and daily life is governed by a devotional schedule that creates a strong relationship to heaven.

Very little information has come down on the lives and activities of Daoist renunciants in the early middle ages but a few cases have been recorded. One example is the story of Qian Miaozhen, a woman from Jinling near modern Nanjing. According to the *Maoshan zhi* (Annals of Mount Mao, DZ 204), she was born around the year 500 and left her family to lead the life of a hermit. She devoted herself to the recitation of the *Huangting jing* (Yellow Court Scripture, DZ 263), a major meditation manual and invocation of body divinities. She spent thirty years in Yankou Grotto near Mount Mao where she died, leaving one prose text and seven poems behind. A temple was built, and women established a cult to her (15.3b).

Another story, recorded in the *Daoxue zhuan*, tells of Song Yuxian who felt a religious calling from an early age and decided to pursue the Dao even in the face of an already arranged marriage.

When she became marriageable, her parents made arrangements to give her to the Xu clan. But she secretly prepared holy vestments. When the time of her wedding came, she mounted the carriage, went to her husband's gate, and was apparently getting ready to enter the six [wedding] ceremonies. But in fact she changed into her Daoist clothes—a yellow linen skirt and coarse woolen cloak—took her magpie-tail incense burner, and refused to play the wife's part in the ceremonies.

Guests and hosts were equally startled, but none, not even the family of her intended, were able to bend her will. Eventually they let her go back to her native house, from where she became a recluse. (Bumbacher 1998, 683; 2000a, 295-96)

Other records surviving in the *Daoxue zhuan*, which had a separate chapter on women and outlined the lives of nine female recluses of the early Highest Clarity tradition, show that women typically followed a calling toward the religious life that they felt early in life—tending toward austerities and cultivation practices even as children and refusing integration into ordinary society. This emphasis on the childhood tendencies of later renunciants reflects a common pattern in the biographies and hagiographies of men, who are commonly praised for their precociousness. It stands in contrast to classical women's biographies, such as the *Lienü zhuan*, which do not present childhood phenomena about their subjects. The fact that religious women are stylized in ways similar to men shows that they were seen more like men in traditional Chinese society, a phenomenon also apparent in their high degree of personal development and social independence.

Daoist women usually left the family with parental consent but if necessary went against the will of their elders. This was also the situation for Buddhist nuns as documented in the case of Tao Tanbei. According to her biography in the *Biqiuni zhuan* (Biographies of Buddhist Nuns, T. 2063, 50.934-48), dated to 516 C.E., she practiced filial piety by taking good care of her mother and did not wish to be married. When her mother arranged for a marriage anyway, she refused all nourishment in protest. After a week of starvation, she was weakened to the point that family and bridegroom took pity on her and allowed her to join a convent (Bumbacher 1998, 685).

Once separated from society, Daoist renunciants tended to retreat to the mountains to study with learned hermits—unlike Buddhist nuns who joined convents located in the suburbs of major communities. In seclusion they engaged in practices similar to those of the ancient immortals, i.e., control of *qi* through the regulation of sexual energy, breath, and diet. In addition, they also undertook the recitation of religious texts, such as the *Huangting jing* mentioned earlier, reflecting the more organized structure and literary unfolding of the religion (Bumbacher 2000a, 498-503).

Again like their ancient sisters, Daoist renunciants of the middle ages attained long life, youthfulness, and magical powers, and were often accompanied by animal companions. Xiao Lianzhen, for example, was noted not only for her advanced dietary techniques and extreme youthful vigor but also for her tiger companion—a feature for which other immortals are also famous (see Fig. 7). As the *Daoxue zhuan* says:

> Xiao Lianzhen entered Mount Yi and studied the Dao. At the age of forty, she had reduced her diet to cypress leaves and various flowers, from which she made pills. She also took mulberry leaves, mixed them with various other herbs, such as atractylis, simmered them, and ate them.
>
> As she reached the age of eighty, her hair turned black again and her teeth grew back. She regularly recited the *Huangting jing* and always had a tiger companion. It crouched and stayed in front of her bed. When she wanted to move about, she urged the tiger forward with a stick and it went obediently, like a dog. (Bumbacher 2000a, 504)

Another known religious woman of the early Highest Clarity tradition was the aunt of Zhou Ziliang. Although her personal name has not been recorded, she was a strong devotee and played an important role in the ascension of her nephew, described in Tao Hongjing's (456-536) *Mingtong ji* (Record of Exploring the Otherworld, DZ 302). Born in 470 as a daughter of the Zhang family of Hangzhou, she was adopted into the Xu family of Wenzhou when her mother remarried after her father's death. The Xus were followers of the Celestial Masters, and the girl was introduced to their practices early on, taking her first initiation at age ten.

Fig. 7: The immortal Zheng Siyuan and his tiger companions.
Source: *Liexian quanzhuan*.

A few years later, following the proper procedures, she announced her wish to leave the householder's life and set up her own hermitage, studying with various local teachers.

Her nephew Zhou Ziliang, born in 497, came to stay with her and was inspired to take up the Dao. In 504, when she was 35, government restrictions on Daoist practice forced her to take a husband, if only in name, and she "fell into the ways of the world" and gave birth to a son. This caused her much shame and distress, and in 505 she left her husband and returned to her family in Wenzhou, where she and Zhou encountered Tao Hongjing a few years later. Eventually they followed him to Mount Mao for continued intensive practice, and Zhou succeeded in ascending to the immortals (Strickmann 1978a, 468-69; 1979, 159-62; Doub 1971).

Women such as these were common in Highest Clarity, as the *Maoshan zhi* attests. In providing a list of monastic residences on the mountain, it notes that among fifty-seven abbots there were eighteen women who ran communities of various sizes (8a; see Schafer 1980). The renunciants of early medieval Daoism, therefore, continued the activities and aspirations of the ancient immortals in a more organized, communal setting. Following the Daoist path, these renunciants reached toward a lofty status in both this world and the next.

Daoist Women of the Tang

The Tang dynasty has often been called the "Golden Age" of Chinese history and was certainly the heyday of religious and especially Daoist activities. Tracing their ancestry to Lord Lao, the imperial Li family greatly favored the religion (Barrett 1996; Kohn and Kirkland 2000). Especially under Emperor Xuanzong (r. 713-755), Daoism with Highest Clarity as the dominant form was recognized as the leading religion in the state, and in 724 the emperor elevated the works of Laozi, Zhuangzi, Liezi, and Wenzi to the rank of canonical writings on par with the Confucian classics.

In 741, the emperor ordered the foundation of an academy for Daoist studies in the two capitals and in each prefecture, creating a Daoist counterpart to the Confucian state examination system. In 736, he also founded an office of Daoist ritual within the Bureau of the Imperial Family that officially made all ordained Daoists members of the imperial clan. It recorded the names of Daoist temples in the capital, the various rituals practiced, and the number of Daoists throughout the empire. Anyone becoming an ordained Daoist had to hold a formal ordination certificate which allowed him or her to travel through the country and register with various religious institutions. The list of renunciants, moreover, was copied to the Ministry of Rites, the Department of Foreign Affairs, and the various prefectures of the empire. It records that in the eighth century there were 1,687 Daoist monasteries, 1137 for men and 550 for women (*Tang liudian* 4.15b-16a; DeRotours 1968).

Within the religion, the formalization of its status and the great support of the state led to an integration of the various schools, known now as the Three Caverns (*sandong*). The integration further led to a formal ordination hierarchy, first described in the *Fengdao kejie* (Rules and Precepts for Worshiping the Dao, DZ 1125), the key manual on Daoist priesthood and monastic organizations of the early Tang (see Reiter 1998; Kohn 2004a). While the various ranks are complex and involve many different scriptures and ritual utensils, the system can be summarized as consisting of the following seven major divisions (see Benn 1991, 72-95):

School	Rank
Zhengyi (Celestial Masters)	Register Disciple
Taixuan (Great Mystery)	Disciple of Good Faith
Dongyuan (Cavern Abyss)	Disciple of Cavern Abyss
Laoxi (Daode jing)	Disciple of Eminent Mystery
Sanhuang (Three Sovereigns)	Disciple of Cavern Spirit
Lingbao (Numinous Treasure)	Preceptor of Highest Mystery
Shangqing (Highest Clarity)	Preceptor of Highest Perfection

The first three ranks were those of lay masters, the last three were monastic, and the middle rank (Disciple of Eminent Mystery) signified a transitional stage that could be held either by a householder or a recluse.

Ordinations into these ranks began early, with children being initiated into the Celestial Masters level and receiving registers of protective generals. After that, each level required extended periods of training, the guidance of an ordination master, and several sponsors from the community. Once an ordination date was set, the candidate went into seclusion to purify for some time, then appeared at a specially constructed three-tiered altar platform and received the three major signs of his or her new rank, i.e., the scriptures, precepts, and ritual methods pertaining to the respective level, as well as a new religious name and a set of formal vestments. In return, ordinands gave pledges as gifts to the institution and swore to obey the rules and serve the Dao (see Kohn 2004b).

Women underwent these ceremonies in much the same way as men and acquired the same ritual status and power—serving both as priests in ritual functions and as nuns in personal cultivation. In this respect medieval Daoism is significantly different from other monastic traditions, where women were considered secondary to monks and typically had to obey many more rules. In medieval England, for example, the dominant order of the Cistercians refused to acknowledge any female recluses, and convents—affiliated with other orders or part of double-houses—inevitably were smaller and less wealthy than male houses. Nuns had to allow male priests into their compounds to receive the sacraments and could never attain the same status or the same freedom of movement as monks. The monastic calling, accepted as worthy and noble in men, was seen as a betrayal of their natural function in women, and many had to enter the religious life against their parents' will (Burton 1994, 86; Kohn 2003, 80).

In Buddhism, too, nuns were made to observe additional rules and restrictions, such as having to show deference to any monk, no matter how young or inexperienced. They also had to spend the rain retreat under male protection, invite a monk to perform the biweekly ceremonies, confess their transgressions to both the orders of nuns and monks, and undergo ordination through both. They could be admonished and criticized by monks, but had no right to reprimand them (Wijayaratna 1990, 159-60; Paul 1985, 85-86). Their *Vinaya* rules are almost twice the length of those of monks, and the only canonical document authored by them is the *Therīgāthā* (Verses of Elder Nuns), a collection of seventy-three poems

(Wijayaratna 1990, 161; Murcott 1991). Chinese Buddhist nuns were similarly subject to restrictions and additional rules (Tsai 1981; 1994), although the overall flourishing of religious institutions in the Tang allowed them to attain high status and a greater respect in the religious life (see Li 1989; Levering 1992; Grant 1996).[5]

Daoist female renunciants in general were more fortunate than their Buddhist or Christian counterparts. Medieval Daoist sources make no difference between male and female ranks, accomplishments, status, or clothing. Du Guangting in his collection of women's hagiographies emphasizes that men's and women's paths are equal (Cahill 1990, 36), and the *Fengdao kejie* continuously uses the phrase *daoshi nüguan* — "all Daoists, whether male or female" — to refer to ordained practitioners (Kohn 2004a). The two consistent differences between male and female Daoists lie in their garb and in the ritual sequencing. They show their different positions in the universe in terms of yin and yang.

For example, while all Daoists wore the same vestments, women were crowned by a more elaborate headdress, the "capeline, an uncommon word for a type of woman's headgear" (Schafer 1978a, 11). This is one reason why women practitioners are called *nüguan* or "female hats." The term does not appear until the Sui-Tang, when it was probably coined to replace *nüguan* or "female officer," the standard expression used in the Six Dynasties, in order to avoid confusion with the common appellation of female palace attendants (Schafer 1978a, 10-11). The more elaborate hat for women can be traced back to early representations of the Queen Mother of the West with her characteristic *sheng* headdress. Fanciful headgear was also common among immortal ladies, documented in Highest Clarity and Tang visualization instructions. Daoist renunciants adopted it in emulation of their illustrious models.

Other differences between male and female practitioners include somewhat more extensive purifications for women before the performance of rituals and the ceremonial emphasis on the use of the right rather than

---

[5] While Buddhist nuns attained more respect in the Tang, female Chan masters appear only in the Song. When the court prohibited the traditional *Vinaya* practice of dual-ordination, women began to control their own institutions. See Hsieh 1999; 2000.

left side of the body, matching the cosmic positions of yin and yang. Also, since yang numbers are odd and yin numbers are even, in the performance of rites lead by women, two officiants perform the celebration rather than just one. As the *Xuanmen shishi weiyi* (Ten Items of Dignified Observances for the Gate to the Mystery, DZ 792), an early Tang guideline of monastic behavior says:

> At all assemblies of the divine law, one male officiant should stand up front, bow three times, then kneel formally and, folding his palms over his chest, announce: "To commence the such-and-such rites, this humble master so-and-so asks all to be seated." Should the assembly be female, the same procedure applies with two women Daoists asking all to be seated. (6a)

In regard to their daily lives, Daoist nuns tended to observe sexual abstinence and remained in seclusion pursuing a life of cultivation, meditation, and charity (Cahill 1990, 28-29). They continued earlier *qi*-practices by controlling their food, sexual energies, and breathing, and expressed their devotion by reciting sacred scriptures and engaging in visualizations and ecstatic journeys (Cahill 1990, 31). Through acts of charity they helped the poor, rescued animals, and fed the hungry, creating a sense of moral integrity and social responsibility. In their overall status, they were a great deal more independent than contemporaneous married women and could, if they so wished, lead rather unconventional lives, shaping their schedules to their needs and freely interacting with people of their choosing. They could also run businesses and build or remodel convents (Bumbacher 1998, 692). Their exceptional freedom evoked both admiration and criticism—poets were singing the praises of pure ladies they envisioned as living goddesses, while stern moralists condemned the splendid costumes and free manners of "female hats" (Schafer 1978a, 6).

A rather controversial figure is Yu Xuanji (844-868), a girl from a common family who was married as second wife to a young scholar studying in Chang'an, then expelled by his first wife after he went back home. Returning to the capital, she made a living as a courtesan for a while, then took holy orders as a Daoist nun and joined the Xianyi guan (Monastery of Universal Propriety).[6] Her talents and literary skills garnered her much admiration, but criticism rose far and wide when she was executed for murdering her maid. Her poems make it clear that she was by no means at ease with life in any of its forms and that she chose the Daoist convent for the security and stability it offered (Cahill 2002).

As Daoist convents could serve as convenient locations to hold women otherwise unfit for society, nuns were associated with courtesans, singing girls, divorcees, widows, impoverished aristocrats, and other female misfits. The convenience of the convent was also used by the imperial court, which regularly co-opted religious institutions for its own purposes. For example, the princess Taiping, daughter of Empress Wu Zetian, had no intention of joining a Daoist convent but, in 670, at the tender age of six, was given to one nonetheless "as a means of ensuring her grandmother's bliss in the afterlife." She did not stay very long, either, but was married in 681 and continued to engage in various conspiracies for political power until her execution in 713 (Benn 1991, 10; Schafer 1978a, 5).

Another prominent case where a Daoist convent served as temporary expedience is that of Yang Guifei, Xuanzong's great love and consort. As Edward Schafer describes the events, the emperor,

> disconsolate since the death of his wife . . . on 1 January 738, ultimately came to realize that the only woman who could replace her was already married to his son Li Chang, Prince of Shou. He thought it quite appropriate that the young couple should be separated, and that the divorcee, Yang Yuhuan, should undergo a period of purification and religious instruction in a Daoist convent under the new name of Taizhen, "Grand Realized One." Later, on 17 September 745, she was released from these disciplines and designated Noble Consort (Guifei). (1978a, 6; see also Benn 1991, 11-12)

---

[6] This convent was founded by Princess Xianyi, the 28th daughter of Emperor Xuanzong. Married several times to influential court figures, the princess became a Daoist nun in 762. Her convent was a magnificent palace that inspired renowned Tang painters and served as a Daoist refuge for the wives of local dignitaries (Despeux 1990, 37).

Then again, some imperial women took serious vows and used the convent as a way to honor their late husband's memory and attain perfection for themselves. Thus, Chen, an imperial concubine of the tenth century, exclaimed at the deathbed of the emperor in 923: "As my body cannot be buried with you, I will have my head shaven and become a nun" (De Groot 1892, 2:756; Main 1975, 268). These women echo the attitudes of dedicated practitioners, such as the Flower Maid (Huagu), Huang Lingwei (ca. 640-721). As recorded in several stele inscriptions, compiled by Yan Zhenqing, the Daoist-cum-magistrate who also recorded the information on Magu (Kirkland 1991, 48), she came originally from a commoner's family in Fujian and had her mind set on the Dao from an early age. Instead of being credited with the common Confucian virtues, she was described as attractive and graceful, and received her first level of ordination at age twelve at the Tianbao guan (Monastery of Heavenly Treasure)—a career that seems to have raised no eyebrows in her immediate environment.

Undergoing further training, including *qi*-control through diet and breathing, she became quite accomplished and experienced altered states and visions of immortals. She was also responsible for the restoration of the Linchuan shrine to Wei Huacun, the divine revealer of the Highest Clarity scriptures (Schafer 1977a), and is generally evaluated as a woman of superior piety and exceptional courage, who possessed great humility and confidence. She was, moreover, of indomitable energy and very self-reliant, full of the wisdom of experience and dedicated to her own self-realization. Her career documents to what degree the Daoist religious life presented an opportunity for personal growth outside of the traditional family context and shows how free a woman could be in medieval China, traveling through the country and organizing shrine worship without apparent ecclesiastical or other social constraints (Kirkland 1991, 63-64).

Huang Lingwei also attained magical powers and succeeded in ascending bodily to the immortals. As her biography in the *Yongcheng jixian lu* has it, after her passing in 721,

> her flesh and muscles were fragrant and clear, her body and *qi*
> were still warm and genial. A strange fragrance filled the
> courtyard and halls. Her disciples followed her orders and did

not nail the coffin shut. Instead, they simply covered it with crimson netted gauze.

Suddenly they all heard a massive stoke of thunder. When they looked at the coffin, there was a hole about as big as a hen's egg in the gauze, and in the coffin itself only her shroud and some wooden slips were left. In the ceiling of the room, there was a hole big enough for a person to pass through.

They presented an offering of a gourd at the place of her ascension. After several days it sprouted creepers and grew two fruits that looked like peaches. Each time the anniversary of her death came around, wind and clouds swelled up and suddenly entered the room. (*Yunji qiqian* 115.11ab, 116.7b-8a; Cahill 1990, 33-34; also *Tongjian houji* 4.16a)

A similar story is recorded about Wang Fengxian (ca. 835-885), a daughter of poor farmers. Graced by visions of gods from an early age, she exhibited magical powers. Refusing to marry, she hid from her pursuers in a Buddhist temple and dedicated herself to the Dao. She no longer took any nourishment, performed potent rituals, traveled widely to holy mountains, and went on ecstatic excursions to the stars. At the age of 48, she transformed into an immortal, an event accompanied by celestial cranes and the manifestation of wondrous fragrances. "At the time she had not eaten for thirty years. She had a youth's complexion and snowy flesh like a virgin" (*Tongjian houji* 3.13a; Cahill 2001, 25).

Daoist nuns and priestesses under the Tang dynasty came from all walks of life and found themselves in rather beneficent circumstances, able to pursue their particular calling and talents, be they organizational, literary, communal, or spiritual. These women underwent a basic training, followed a fundamental code of rules, and worked towards the enhancement and cultivation of *qi*. In doing so, they continued the practices of ancient immortals and earlier renunciants, but were blessed by a more extensive social network and greater personal freedom and responsibility. Female practitioners were more numerous than in earlier times; they were fully accepted as priests in the official Daoist hierarchy. Although less active on the political scene than their male counterparts, Daoist women were not nearly as restricted as the women of mainstream Chinese society, and also enjoyed more personal freedom and respect in the Tang than under other Chinese dynasties.

The Princesses' Ordination

This sense of personal freedom and acceptance into the Daoist hierarchy can also be observed in the most prominent event involving Daoist women of the Tang: the ordination of the two princesses Gold Immortal (Jinxian) and Jade Perfected (Yuzhen), Emperor Ruizong's (r. 710-712) youngest daughters by his third consort, Lady Dou, and sisters of Emperor Xuanzong. All other women of this generation had been married politically and remained embroiled in the constant scheming and intrigues of the time. The two youngest hoped to escape this fate and, after the downfall of Empress Wu, were permitted to follow the religious path. As Charles Benn says, "the cloister offered the Princesses a haven which the family could not. As nuns they were less likely to be implicated in the strife, stress, and reprisals that prevailed at court during their youth" (1991, 9).

They began their training in 705 and soon received the first levels of ordination, then entered the second highest rank of Numinous Treasure in a majestic set of rites celebrated in 711, documented in detail in the supplement to Zhang Wanfu's *Chuanshou jingjie lueshuo* (Brief Outline of the Transmission of Scriptures and Precepts, DZ 1241, 2.18a-21a). In preparation of the ceremonies, a three-tiered altar, 3.5 meters high, was specially erected. The altar was supported by golden pillars, entered through ornate gates marked by purple and golden tablets, and surrounded by blue-green silk cordons (Benn 1991, 22; Schafer 1985). Its floors, although consisting of plain tamped earth, were covered with brocade cushions and intricate mats; its ramparts were lighted by seventeen types of lamps and four different sorts of candles, often giving forth special effects, such as "purple-flaming orchids" or "thousandfold moonbeams" (1991, 27-28).

Each level had at least three tables. One was for incense burners, made from jade or gold and burning various aromatics, like aloeswood, frankincense, sandalwood, cloves, and camphor (Benn 1991, 29). The second served as a lectern for the officiant's recitation of the memorial and the precepts. And the third was a place for the pledge offerings to be made. Each table, moreover, had a scarlet kerchief and a blue-green cover, substitutes for smearing the lips with blood and cutting off a lock of hair in the sealing of oaths, practices that had been part of blood covenants in antiquity (1991, 31).

More ornamentation was also present in the wrappers, cases, and bags used for the scriptures. They were made from precious substances and covered with designs of celestial kings, immortals, mountains, rivers, clouds, dragons, phoenixes, and other sacred images (Benn 1991, 31). The pledges—understood to appease the gods of the five directions and ward off malign influences during the delicate transition—were extensive and rich, including 72 lengths of variegated silk net, 240 lengths of purple silk net, 480 lengths of coarse silk, 240 strings of cash, 200 ounces of gold, 25 lengths of five-colored brocade, 120 catties of incense, 500 ounces of blue-green silk thread, 24,000 sheets of memorial paper, 12 scraping knives, 38 knives and kerchiefs, 6 gold dragon plaques, and 54 golden buttons (Benn 1991, 32-35). Such enormous wealth given to the Daoist institution is, of course, exceptional and found especially in ordinations held for members of the imperial family and other high-ranking aristocrats. Still, even ordinary members had to contribute, not only to help with the upkeep of temples and rituals, but also to document their deep devotion and allegiance to the Dao.

The princesses' ordination ceremony began with the recitation of sacred texts for fourteen days and nights. When the prayers commenced, petals of good fortune and wondrous snow began to fall. When the true writings were unrolled, auspicious clouds came to hover over the holy space. On the fourteenth night at the fourth watch, Lord Lao himself descended upon the altar and visited with the princesses. On the day of transmission, five-colored clouds appeared and eight perfumes scented the air. The princesses joined the Dao in the full splendor of their high status, empowered as priests and encouraged as adepts of immortality (see Despeux 1986; Benn 1991).

Daoist women renunciants of medieval China appeared in a variety of roles and contexts, setting an example for a life that allowed women to fulfill their spiritual urge for transcendence or escape from difficult social situations, developing responsibility and autonomy far beyond their mainstream sisters. For the most part, women took their vows seriously and, once ordained, did not return to lay status or engage in worldly affairs. But in some cases, convent ladies and courtesans were not only neighbors but partners, engaging in social and intimate exchanges with men and living a life of comparative freedom and unconventionality.

The latter does not diminish the religious seriousness of women's lives but shows that, in medieval Daoism as much as in other traditions, religious institutions, once established and accepted, came to serve society in ways not always on par with their original intention. Rather than being detrimental, the fact that Daoism could allow these variances from the ideal without battles, purges, or reform movements is a sign of the religion's depth and maturity as an institutional paradigm. The variety of life styles Daoism makes available to women—from courtesan to saint—places the ideals of the religion within a human context, and allows us to witness the actions of the more serious practitioners with a clearer focus. The larger social picture that develops in medieval Daoism, it appears, honors women as equal participants in the creation of cosmic harmony.

Chapter Six

Founders and Matriarchs

With the end of the Tang dynasty, the integrated ordination structure and state-supported institutions of Daoism collapsed. Temples declined, lineages ceased to exist, and techniques and doctrines were suspended. Individual practitioners no longer had specific key places to congregate or officially recognized masters to follow. They were on their own, wandering from one sacred mountain to the next, connecting with isolated hermits, perhaps finding a stash of old texts, or discovering certain efficacious techniques by trial and error. Occasionally a few were fortunate enough to secure the support of a local ruler—who was usually more interested in alchemical ways of making gold than in spiritual pursuits— and proceeded to reconstruct a temple center of old.

These practitioners had no financial cushion to fall back on, and thus had to find ways of serving communities for a fee so they could continue their quest. As a result—and coinciding fortuitously with the needs of the growing merchant class, bolstered by a population growth, improvements in infrastructure, the beginnings of paper currency, and increased literacy (Ebrey 1993, 2; Ebrey and Gregory 1993)—Daoists, in competition with wandering Buddhists, tantric ritualists, and local shamans, began to offer rites of healing, exorcism, and protection. They issued spells and talismans for concrete goals, and undertook funerals and communication with ancestors to set people's minds at rest. Daoists of this type became common in the Song dynasty and were known as *fashi* or ritual masters (Davis 2001). They grew famous locally at first, continuing local cults of the Tang and creating a following in a specific region (Schipper 1985). Once established, their groups gradually grew to national importance, deities and founders were honored with formal titles, and scriptures were accepted into the imperial repository (Hymes 2002).

Such recognition of local cults was especially prominent under Emperor Huizong (r. 1101–1125), the last ruler of the Northern Song dynasty and a great supporter of Daoism. He sponsored and collected Daoist art and actively engaged in Daoist painting (Ebrey 2000). He also wrote commentaries to several Daoist scriptures, notably the *Daode jing*, which was highly venerated by Song rulers in general. Huizong also organized Daoist rites for state protection and good fortune, and inspired many Daoists to come forward and present their views and texts. In 1114, he initiated the compilation of a Daoist canon to replace a lost collection originally compiled in 1023, of which today only the encyclopedia *Yunji qiqian* remains.

Following the teachings of Lin Lingsu (1076–1120), Huizong became a stout believer in the Daoist dispensation of Divine Empyrean (Shenxiao) and believed himself to be the elder son of the Jade Emperor, known in the heavens as the Great Emperor of Long Life (Changsheng dadi). This god was believed to bring about a new age of peace with the help of Daoist talismans, diagrams, sacred lamps, seals, pennants, and rituals. Unfortunately Huizong did not find much success in his endeavors. His reign ended with the invasion of the capital by the Jurchen in 1125, and his Daoist collections and aspirations were lost (see Strickmann 1978b).

Still, the cults and practices survived and continued to flourish in various ways, growing both locally and nationally and integrating the ancient teachings with contemporary shamanic and exorcistic practices. Many of these cults, moreover, were either founded or led by women.[1]

---

[1] A Buddhist-based cult of a similar nature is the veneration of Guanyin in the form of Miaoshan, a young woman of the eleventh century who refused to take a husband and had numerous visions of the goddess. Responsible for numerous miracles, she was venerated first locally and then more widely. Numerous sources and literary accounts record her exploits. See Dudbridge 1978; Yü 2001.

Early Founders

One such school that was exceptional in its reliance on women, both in terms of ritual performance and religious membership, was the Way of Loyalty and Filial Piety (Zhongxiao dao) or Way of Pure Brightness (Jingming dao). The school arose in Jiangxi and traced itself back to the two medieval sages Xu Xun (ca. 239-292) and Wu Meng (d. 374).

As outlined in the later hagiographies *Xiaodao Wu Xu er zhenjun zhuan* (Biography of the Two Perfected Lords Wu and Xu of the Way of Filial Piety, DZ 449) and *Yulong ji* (Record of Jade Beneficence, in DZ 263), Xu Xun began his career as a local prefect in Sichuan but later resettled in Jiangxi, where he became known as a healer and exorcist. In times of epidemic, he saved thousands from pestilence with the help of talisman water and also was effective in ridding the area of harmful serpents and dragons (Boltz 1987, 70-71; Baryosher-Chemouny 1996, 29-30). Wu Meng similarly was famous for his dragon-slaying capabilities, but he was also well known as a filial son. Both were venerated locally in the Xishan region of Jiangxi, their cult centering around a shrine known as the Youwei guan (Monastery of the Floating Curtain).

By the early Tang the temple had fallen into disrepair but was restored in 682, then grew in popularity. Under the Song emperor Zhenzong (r. 998-1022), it was flourishing and received the more formal name Yulong gong (Palace-Temple of Jade Beneficence). Huizong acknowledged the cult on a national level and provided the founders with extensive titles and imperial honors, having a seven-day *jiao* offering celebrated at the shrine. The scriptures and hagiographies of the cult were later codified by Liu Yu (1257-1308; see Boltz 1987, 72, 75).[2]

Although the tradition does not recognize a first matriarch, it acknowledges a woman as the key preceptor of Xu Xun: Mother Chen (Chenmu), a resident of the Huangtang guan (Yellow Hall Monastery) near modern Nanjing, which she founded through an oracle. Throwing a piece of straw into the air, she announced: "Wherever it lands, there I shall build

---

[2] For further discussions of the cult, see Akizuki 1978; Barrett 1996, 96-97; Skar 2000, 417-18.

a sanctuary" (*Tongjian houji* 2.10b). Connecting spiritually with Xu Xun, she became his main preceptor and her temple grew into a major center of the school (Despeux 1990, 22).

A full-fledged woman founder is found in another Song-dynasty school, the Way of Pure Subtlety (Qingwei dao), a creative combination of Daoist teachings with exorcism and popular ritual. It was codified in the twelfth century through the work of Nan Bidao (b. 1196), who appears as its ninth patriarch. He received the key methods passed down from the founder Zu Shu (fl. 889-904), then developed them into the Pure Subtlety system. As described in the hagiographic *Qingwei xianpu* (Account of the Immortals of Pure Subtlety, DZ 171) by Chen Cai of the Yuan dynasty, Zu Shu originally came from Lingling in Guangxi. Of unusual dark complexion and very tall, she was drawn to spiritual practice from an early age and left the family in her teens (Boltz 1987, 69). Twice she was blessed with divine revelations. The first time she encountered the Holy Mother of Numinous Radiance (Lingguang shengmu) who taught her methods of talismans and exorcism, not unlike those used in the Divine Empyrean school. The second revelation came from Goddess Wen and involved the spiritual ordination into the major ranks of the medieval hierarchy (Ren 1990, 565-66).

Zu Shu combined medieval Daoist methods with talismanic and exorcistic methods of the Song dynasty and thereby developed the Way of Pure Subtlety. In essence it can be described as a form of thunder rites (*leifa*), a popular method of exorcism and protection that invoked the deities of the celestial Department of Thunder (Leibu). The latter was an agency administered by officials that governed sickness and good fortune and had a direct impact on human events. Thunder stands for the entire complex of thunderstorms, including lightning and other potent cosmic forces. Thunder officials were known by name and highly venerated, and petitions and memorials to them were essential in ritual practice at the time.

The techniques of Pure Subtlety allegedly originated in the same celestial sphere as the methods of Divine Empyrean and other new schools of the time. The central revealing deity here was Highest Emperor of Primordial Beginning (Yuanshi shangdi), residing in the Heaven of Pure Subtlety. He was supported by an extensive pantheon, hierarchically organized, with large numbers of goddesses in his immediate environment, a sign of the matriarchal heritage of the school. Below this level were the various saints of the traditional schools and patriarchs of Pure Subtlety, important for the school but clearly secondary to the central power of feminine divinity (Boltz 1987, 70).

Unlike Wei Huacun, whose family background and role as libationer is known, we know nothing about either Mother Chen's or Zu Shu's home background and family life. The little we do know about their activities makes them seem like southern shamans and religious visionaries. They were dedicated to the Dao and served as transmitters and organizers of divine methods, creating a new synthesis from the teachings of old in conjunction with local shamanistic and exorcistic techniques.

Matriarch of Women's Alchemy

Another prominent Daoist woman of the Song dynasty is Cao Wenyi (fl. 1119-1125), most famous for her classical erudition and poetry. Originally called Cao Daochong, she is described briefly in a fragment of the *Luofu shan zhi* (Gazetteer of Mount Luofu) cited in the Qing-dynasty encyclopedia *Gujin tushu jicheng* (Complete Illustrated Collection of Things Old and New, 292.2b), and has a biography in the *Tongjian houji* (6.1b-3a). According to these sources, the renowned poet was so famous that even Emperor Huizong had heard of her. He duly called her to the capital and gave her the formal title "Perfected of Literary Withdrawal" (Wenyi zhenren).

Brief notes in Song bibliographies attest to her quality as an author and mention that she wrote commentaries to various Daoist texts, including one on the *Xisheng jing* (Scripture of Western Ascension, DZ 726) and one, in two scrolls, on the *Daode jing* (Loon 1984, 104, 106). The latter remains in fragments and is cited in a collection of twenty *Daode jing* commentaries by Peng Helin of the Southern Song, the *Daode jing jizhu* (Collected Commentaries to the *Daode jing*, DZ 707; pref. 2.1b). The collection begins with an exegesis by Emperor Huizong and contains works by various illustrious Song scholars. Among these, Lady Cao is the sole

134 / Women in Daoism

woman, described in the introduction as "Cao Daochong, master of tranquility and humane virtue and the perfection of the Dao." A note adds that "her secular name was Xiyun and she was a woman Daoist of good standing whom people called Immortal Lady Cao. The emperor gave her the title 'Great Master of Literary Withdrawal into Clear Emptiness' and called her 'Master of Tranquility'."

Lady Cao was later venerated by several Qing-dynasty lineages of women's inner alchemy. This is evident in her appearances in spirit-writing séances and in various inscriptions preserved in the Baiyun guan in Beijing. One school in particular honors her as patroness, the school of Clarity and Tranquility (Qingjing pai). Its main inner-alchemical program is described in a lengthy poem attributed to Cao, the *Dadao ge* (Song of the Great Dao). This poem has survived in two different versions, a short stanza cited in the *Changsheng quanjing* (Complete Scripture of Long Life, DZ 1466) of the Southern Song, and a more extensive opus, found in the *Qunxian yaoyu zuanji* (Collection of Essential Sayings by the Host of Immortals, DZ 1257) by Dong Jingchun of the early Ming.

The first version of the *Dadao ge* consists only of one stanza that describes the fundamental vision of inner alchemical transformation. It says:

> Spirit is inner nature; *qi* is destiny.
> So that the spirit does not gallop far away, let the *qi* be firm.
> Originally the two are mutual and close,
> How could they ever be dispersed—the primordial handle of
> all life. (*Changsheng quanjing* 13a)

The text focuses on the cultivation of "inner nature" and "destiny" (*xingming*), identified with spirit and *qi* (*shenqi*). Closely interrelated, the two signify the psychological and physiological aspects of human beings, inner nature referring to the mental, meditational dimensions of personality, while destiny indicates its more bodily aspects. Closely connected, both have to be developed equally until a level is reached that is often described in terms of "clarity and tranquility" (*qingjing*). This level of equilibrium is reflected in the notion of the "handle of life," the fundamental way of being in the world, i.e. a state where the mind has been freed from desires and is completely absorbed in the Dao.

While this version of the poem is commonly attributed to Cao Wenyi, an earlier citation of the verse under the title *Lingyuan pian* (The Numinous Source) appears in the *Daoshu* (Pivot of the Dao, DZ 1017; 16.1a), a collection of inner alchemical treatises, dated to about 1150. Here the poem is not associated with Cao Wenyi but with He Xiangu, a famous immortal who originally lived in the early Tang dynasty. As her hagiography describes, He Xiangu was in her early teens when she encountered an immortal in a dream who instructed her to live on powdered mica. She followed his directions, vowed to remain a virgin, and entered the Dao, attaining magical powers and healing faculties. Empress Wu tried to meet her, but the monarch's envoy was unsuccessful in finding the immortal who preferred to remain in seclusion and only occasionally appeared in wondrous visions above a shrine to Magu (*Tongjian houji* 5.8ab; Giles 1948, 127-28; Yetts 1916, 781-83).

In the Yuan dynasty, He Xiangu became the only female member of the famous Eight Immortals (Baxian), a group of eccentric and happy Daoists who respond to pleas in emergencies, grant favors and protection, and appear variously in séances and personal visions. They remain highly popular today, as symbols of long life and happiness. As such they still appear on cards for auspicious occasions and in shops and restaurants as signs of enjoyment and prosperity. They play an active part in Chinese folk culture and have been featured in comic books and popular movies. Each member of the group has his or her special characteristics, and He Xiangu is most commonly depicted holding a large ladle containing immortality mushrooms, peaches, and pine branches (see Fig. 8).

On her own, He Xiangu is also the key protagonist in several religious treatises of late imperial China. First, she appears in a spirit-writing text, dated to 1857, the *He Xiangu shunnei wen* (He Xiangu's Instructions on the Inner [Quarters]). A mouthpiece of Confucian morality, she teaches women how to best behave in the world, recounting her own career and expressing deep regret for her radical religious behavior, which caused her to miss the right time for marriage and led her to a lonely, desolate life in the wilderness of the mountains (Jordan and Overmyer 1986, 56-57; Grant 1995, 37-38).

何仙姑

Fig. 8: He Xiangu with her characteristic ladle containing immortality mush-rooms, peaches, and pine branches. Source: *Yuandai Liexian zhuan*.

A more religious image of the immortal is found in another popular work, the *He Xiangu xingshi funü ci* (Verses of He Xiangu to Awaken the Women of the World), a Buddhist sectarian tract of 1907. It begins with a young He Xiangu seeing the lives of her female relatives—the horrors of a girl's education, the "inexorable push towards marriage" (Grant 1995, 33), the pains of childbearing, and the inescapable subservience to the mother-in-law. She soon concludes that the spiritual path offers a much better alternative and decides: "I preserve my chastity, follow Guanyin, and refrain from marriage" (Grant 1995, 35). However, this decision is heavily contested by her family, and especially her mother tries to bribe her with worldly riches and blackmail her with thoughts of her family's reputation. She counters with Buddhist notions of transience that make it more important to strive for enlightenment than to have a family, and claims that she is already married, to the Buddha of Enlightenment and Emptiness. Her strong determination eventually wins and she embarks on a life of meditation and spiritual cultivation (Grant 1995, 38-41).

Not only a representative of women's careers from a Confucian and religious perspective, He Xiangu is also linked with inner alchemical practice through the poem *Dadao ge*. She is seen similar to Cao Wenyi in that both women have realized oneness with the Dao and inspiration for women's successful cultivation. The longer and more elaborate version of the poem is recorded in a text of the early fourteenth century and has been a classic in women's inner alchemy. It is ascribed to Cao Wenyi because of her role in the school of Clarity and Tranquility, but her authorship is by no means certain (see Chen 1939). The work consists of thirty-two stanzas of four lines. It begins:

> I am telling all you ladies straight:
> The stem of destiny grows from perfect breathing
> That irradiates the body and provides long life, whether empty or not empty,
> And brings forth the numinous mirror which contains Heaven and all beings.
> The Great Ultimate opens to the wondrous, you attain the One.
> Once you have the One, hold on to it, make sure you do not lose it.
> Your inner palaces and chambers, open and at ease, spirit naturally comes to stay.

> Your numinous center brightly burning, blood and fluids start
> to wither. (*Qunxian youyu zuanji* 2.4b; Despeux 1990, 85)

According to this, internal transformation begins with concentrating the
mind and practicing deep breathing, so that the "stem of destiny," the
central point of *qi* located near the navel, is activated. Once accomplished, the body is strengthened and radiates with long life, while the
mind becomes luminous and spirit begins to work like a "numinous mirror" (*lingjian*), containing and reflecting all, yet evaluating and classify-
ing nothing.[3] Eventually adepts attain a sense of oneness with the Great
Ultimate (Taiji), the state of the universe at creation. This causes a feeling
of inner openness and a vision of the body as consisting not so much of
flesh and bones but of palaces and chambers where universal spirit and
the various gods come to reside. The process is long and arduous, but
worthwhile. As the poem notes:

> After nine years, the work is complete, the firing time suffi-
> cient.
> Then you can go along with all in no-mind, your spirit chang-
> ing swiftly.
> The mind of no-mind: that's the perfect mind —
> Movement and rest equally forgotten, far removed from all de-
> sires . . .
> Merge all forces to join in the Dao, then forget the joining
> And you'll be able to emerge and go along with primordial
> changes.
> Penetrate metal, pierce through stone — none with difficulty,
> Sit and cast off all, stand and forget all — just be all at once!
> (2.5a)

As a result of the prolonged practice of *qi*-control and the cultivation of
inner forces, adepts develop magical powers. They are no longer limited
to their physical body but have control both over its transformations and
over things in the world outside. They gain abilities far beyond those of
ordinary people, attaining oneness with the Dao and mastery over all
things. In its description here, the poem recounts the main aspects of

---

[3] The mind as mirror is a common symbol in Chinese religion, both Buddhist and Daoist. For studies, see Kaltenmark 1974; Lai 1979; Ching 1983;
Demiéville 1987.

immortality practice already found in ancient literature, the control of *qi* through various methods, the attainment of long life, and the realization of magical faculties. However, the practice is also modified through the overall vision and terminology used, revealing an influence of Tang Daoist mysticism (see Kohn 1987) and Chan Buddhist meditation practice (see Kiyota 1978; Gregory 1986), especially in its invocation of deep meditative absorption and selfless forgetfulness.

The poem continues by emphasizing the naturalness of the method, and the difficult balancing of intentional, concentrated practice of meditation and breathing and the letting go of forgetfulness which allows the process to happen naturally. The ideal is the way of the embryo in the womb—along the lines of *Daode jing* 10, which says: "Concentrating the breath to utmost softness, can you be like an infant?" It is only in this state that one's "original destiny" can arise and shine forth (2.5b).

The second half of the poem goes on to contrast ordinary reactions with the workings of the alchemical process and urges practitioners to remain serene and at peace, "keep up the purgations and precepts, calm your mind, and moderate your speech" (2.6a). With this, a devotional element enters the picture, and it becomes clear that the poem is not just for hermits working in isolation but for women in spiritual communities that obey moral rules and perform regular rituals. Still, even these communities are separate from society and glorify the simplicity of mountain life—"eating trees and wearing grass, being alone and tranquil" (2.6b). These sentiments are echoed in the lifestyle of a twentieth-century hermit in the Zhongnan mountains who lived in isolation for over forty years, wore the same clothes for five, and never bothered to restore her hermitage to perfect shape since "good places are too comfortable and not good for practice" (Porter 1993, 130).

The poem concludes by reiterating the fleeting pleasures to be gained from worldly fame and profit and encouraging its audience to forsake them thoroughly. Practitioners can turn away from these pleasures by extinguishing the negative aspects of their lifelong habits, inner tendencies, and acquired skills. They do so gently and gradually yet relentlessly and with great persistence (2.6b). The poem ends with a recourse to female imagery:

> Diligently incite the divinities to reside in you forever,
> Establish yourself in emptiness and leisure—no need for real
> space.
> In the midst of nonbeing there is wondrous being, but holding
> on to it is hard.
> So just relax and nurture the infant within—yet also caring for
> the mother. (2.7a)

Cao Wenyi, the poet and Daoist writer of the Song dynasty, over the ages has come to be venerated as a matriarch of inner alchemical practice, associated with a detailed outline of the great work in poetic format. An inspiration to women, she appears as a great guide to alchemical transformation, describing the ideal states in glorious language and providing both warnings and admonitions. The truth of whether or not she actually wrote the poem—either in its shorter or its longer version—becomes secondary to the image she represents: the erudite, independent master and successful adept of the Dao, who acts as a guiding light to women throughout the ages.

Model of Complete Perfection

Another major inspirational figure and key model for the practice of inner alchemy and modern Daoist cultivation is Sun Buer (1119-1182; see Fig. 9), the only female in the group of the so Seven Perfected (*qizhen*), key leaders of the monastic school of Complete Perfection, a school still dominant in China today.

The school's founder Wang Chongyang (1112–1170) was born among local gentry in northwest China (Shaanxi). He received a classical education and spent most of his life as an official in the military administration of the Jurchen-Jin dynasty. The Jurchen, a people from the region of Manchuria, had conquered north China in 1125, causing Huizong's court to move south to Hangzhou and thus precipitating the beginning of the Southern Song. In 1159, at age forty-eight, Wang retired from office and withdrew to the Zhongnan mountains near Xi'an, where he built a thatched hut and led the life of an eccentric hermit.

Fig. 9: A portrait of Sun Buer. Source: *Daoyuan yiqi jing*.

During this time, he had a revelatory experience, in which he was made privy to religious Daoist secrets and became the confidant of two mysterious strangers, later identified as Zhongli Quan and Lü Dongbin, renowned alchemical heroes and leading members of the Eight Immortals. Wang intensified his dedication and asceticism to the point where he dug himself a grave called "the tomb of the living dead." In 1167, he burned his hut to the ground while dancing around it, then moved to Shandong in eastern China, where he preached his visions and began to win followers. He founded five religious communities and continued to spread his teaching until his death in 1170 (see Yao 1980; 2000; Tsui 1991).

The Seven Perfected were a group of key disciples initiated by Wang during his lifetime who, after his death, first observed the three-year mourning period for their master, then went their separate ways to spread his teaching. Each founded communities that developed into branches, the most important being the Longmen pai (Dragon Gate Branch) created by Qiu Chuji (1148–1227), better known as Qiu Changchun. Sun Buer, the only woman among them, is equally credited with the foundation of a subsect, known as the Qingjing pai (Clarity and Tranquility Branch). She was well trained and gained strong ritual powers. Both her personal cultivation and communal religious activities came to serve as a model for the role of women in Complete Perfection Daoism.

Sun Buer was born as Sun Yuanzhen in a small town in the Ninghai district of Shandong in the first month of the year 1119, under the reign of Emperor Huizong. According to the various hagiographies that detail her life,[4] this was not a natural occurrence, but was heralded by a divine

---

[4] There are five sources in the Daoist canon that describe Sun Buer's life. The oldest is the official account of the school's lineage, the *Jinlian zhenzong ji* (DZ 173), by Qin Zhi'an; it dates from 1241. This is followed, in 1271, by the *Qizhen nianpu* (Chronology of the Seven Perfected, DZ 175), compiled by Li Daoqian. After this, dated to about 1300, is her biography in the *Tongjian houji* (6.15b-19a). This, in turn, is followed by another Complete Perfection source, the *Jinlian zhenzong xianyuan xiangzhuan* (Illustrated Record of the Immortal Origins of the Perfect Lineage of the Golden Lotus, DZ 174), dated to 1326. For all these sources, see Boltz 1987, 64-68. Sun Buer also appears in a hagiography of inner alchemical

dream her mother had around the time of conception. In this dream, she saw seven cranes frolicking in her courtyard, six of which flew off, leaving the seventh to magically enter her breast. Like the mothers of sage emperors and renowned Daoists before her, she intuitively knew that she was pregnant with a child of divine powers, a baby immortal symbolized by the crane—the bird of long life and riding animal of the immortals (Despeux 1990, 111).

Little Sun's childhood was characterized by exhibitions of her saintly nature, including an exceptional intelligence, a great devotion to the rites, and happy observation of the rules of propriety. She enjoyed reciting chants and poems and practicing calligraphy, becoming an expert in the fine arts. Born into a family of literati —her father Sun Zhongjing was a scholar of some renown—she was fortunate to receive a literary education. In her teens, she was married to Ma Yu, aka Ma Danyang (1123-1183), the son of a landowning family of the same community and a descendant of Ma Yuan, a famous general under the Han dynasty.[5] The couple had three sons and lived quietly until 1167, when Wang Chongyang's arrival disrupted their lives.

When Wang came to Shandong, he set himself up in the southern gardens of Ninghai city on a piece of property owned by Ma Danyang. According to certain sources, Wang erected a hermitage and entered a 100-day retreat, which lasted from the first of the tenth month to the beginning of the new year. When he finally emerged, he began his career as a teacher and religious leader, naming his new movement Complete Perfection. Ma Danyang became his eager follower, but his wife was not pleased at all—seeing a major force disrupting her family life, social standing, and local comfort. Some accounts even suggest that rather than entering his retreat voluntarily, Wang Chongyang was incarcerated in

---

masters, compiled by Chen Zhixu, aka Shangyangzi: *Shangyangzi jindan dayao liexian zhi* (Master Shangyang's Great Principles of the Golden Elixir—Immortals' Biographies, DZ 1068), approximately dated to 1336 (see Boltz 1987, 185). Anecdotal evidence and materials pertaining to her are found in various other Complete Perfection records.

[5] On Ma and his family background, see *Ma zongshi daoxing bei* (Inscription on the Daoist Exploits of Patriarch Ma), in Li Daoqian's *Ganshui xianyuan lu* (An Account of the Origins of the Immortals of Ganshui, DZ 973), 2.18b-27a.

his hermitage by an irate Sun who wanted him out of her life so badly she tried to starve him to death. When he was still alive after a hundred days, not only had he perfected his personal sainthood but had also made a reluctant convert of Sun Buer (*Jinlian zhenzong ji* 5.9b). The story of the retreat, embellished variously, became a model for later monastic practice. It is also a classical statement on the conflict women undergo between their social role and their religious calling.

Sun's biography in the *Tongjian houji* relates another episode of a similar nature. One day Wang arrived at their house drunk and settled himself not only in Sun's room but even in her bed. Furious about this lack of propriety, Sun marched off to send for her husband who arrived promptly only to attest that he had just been chatting with Wang in the marketplace and that the latter was neither drunk nor in Sun's bed. An examination of the room found it empty, confirming Wang's magical powers over body and mind, and documenting both Sun's strong resistance against him and her reluctant acceptance of his superiority (6.16b; Cleary 1989, 21-22).

The conflict intensified when Wang demanded the separation of husband and wife, so they could both go forth and become full members of the school, which was essentially monastic and only allowed for same-sex communities. His demand came in the form of several split pears (*fenli*), a homophone for the word "to separate" (*fenli*), which he presented to the couple. Ma Danyang did not take long to follow Wang's command. At the age of forty-six, a month after the pears arrived early in 1168, he separated from his family and became a full-time renunciant, joining Wang and three other disciples in the Yunxia dong (Cloud Haze Grotto) on Mount Kunyu (*Qizhen nianpu* 8a).

Sun lingered a bit longer before leaving her home. She joined the group in the fifth month of the following year when they set themselves up in the Jinlian tang (Golden Lotus Hall) in Ninghai city, and only after Wang had urged her to convert ten times (*Xianyuan xiangzhuan* 42a). There is a poem about the situation attributed to him:

> To covert you, over these two years, I have brought you pears ten times
> On auspicious days, corresponding to favorable celestial conditions.

> But you have preferred to stay in the bosom of your family,
> Waiting patiently for the formation of the Golden Lotus.
> (*Jinlian zhengzong ji* 5.9b; *Chongyang quanzhen ji*, DZ 1153, 2.19a)

Once formally part of the group, Sun received her Daoist name Buer, "the Nondual," which indicates her oneness with the Dao and also plays upon her family position as the second child. As Wang says in another poem:

> In your family, your name was "Second."
> Leave it so your karmic fire can come to an end.
> Cultivate your being, making it subtle and fine
> And you will be ranked as an immortal.
> (*Chongyang fenli shihua ji*, DZ 1155, 2.6a)

Her reluctance to follow the call of the Dao, however predestined, was strong and not easily overcome. It was not only the severance of all family connection and security that made her so hesitant but also the change in financial and social status. This aspect is noted in yet another poem ascribed to Wang Chongyang:

> Sun the Second, you hesitate to leave the family life
> Because you might cause damage to your assets.
> But if you persist in staying home,
> The honorable Ma will not become immortal.
> (*Chongyang fenli shihua ji* 1.2b; Despeux 1990, 116)

This poem raises another important consideration in a woman's decision for the religious life: the loyalty and support for the husband who needs to be free from family obligations in order to pursue his divine path. The issue of loyalty to the husband transforms the problem from being a conflict between personal cultivation and family obligations into a tension between two different dimensions of family obedience—toward her children, native family, and social circle, on the one hand, and her husband, the mainstay of her social status, on the other. By becoming a renunciant herself, the argument states, the woman frees her husband to realize his immortal potential. Leaving the family is thus the ultimate in the fulfillment of wifely duty. The argument echoes earlier medieval propaganda in both Buddhism and Daoism, which claimed that the utmost in filial piety was to be concerned with the fate of one's parents in the afterlife and that the most filial act one could perform was to become a monk or nun—or at least give ample donations to monastic institutions (see Cole 1998).

When finally a nun of Complete Perfection, Sun Buer became a resident of the Golden Lotus Hall and received the Daoist title "Serene One of Clarity and Tranquility" (Qingjing sanren). She was made privy to several sets of transmissions, notably "secret formulas in cloud-seal script" and "celestial talismans" (*Jinlian zhenzong ji* 5.9b). These sacred writs were received in trance through spirit-writing, often with the help of the planchette, and allowed her to engage in advanced rituals, perform exorcisms, and acquire magical powers.[6]

After her ordination, Sun Buer had little contact with Wang Chongyang, who died shortly thereafter, during a visit to the capital Kaifeng. His four main disciples returned his coffin to his native village in the Zhong-nan mountains for burial and had a temple erected. According to the *Jinlian zhenzong ji*, Sun did not remain in Shandong either but moved west, fighting rain, frost, and bad terrain until she arrived three years later in Jingzhao (modern Xi'an) and was reunited with Ma Danyang. When he asserted clearly and in front of other disciples that he did not consider himself married anymore, the couple made their separation formal and permanent. As a final farewell, Ma gave her the transmission of the alchemical classic *Zhouyi cantong qi* (Tally to the Book of Changes, DZ 999), whose instructions she followed over the next seven years. Sun practiced reversed breathing (by contracting the abdomen upon inhalation), unblocked the orifices in her body, refined the *qi* in her three cinnabar fields, and eventually attained full realization. In 1179 she moved to Luoyang and began to attract disciples (*Jinlian zhenzong ji* 5.10a).[7]

---

[6] On cloud-seal script, talismans, and sacred Daoist charts, see Despeux 2000b. The Complete Perfection collection *Minghe yuyin* (Further Verses form Crane-Cry [Mountain], DZ 1100), dated to 1348, specifies trance procedures and contains a number of poems received through spirit-writing (3.11a). A contemporary Buddhist source confirms the practice in Daoist circles (T. 2116, 52.761a). For more on the planchette, see Esposito 2000, 648-50. On its modern use, see Jordan and Overmyer 1986.

[7] The *Xianyuan xiangzhuan* of slightly later provenance does not mention the final encounter with Ma Danyang and, rather than cultivating her *qi*, has her in

In Luoyang, she set herself up in the Feng xiangu dong (Grotto of the Immortal Lady Feng), named after an eccentric exorcist from Henan who had arrived there in the mid-twelfth century (*Tongjian houji* 6.17b). By choosing this residence, she symbolically inherited not only a female lineage but also a claim to exorcism and eccentricity. She died there on the 29th day of the 12th month of 1182, at high noon, having predicted the hour of her departure. Before her demise, she groomed herself, put on clean clothes, and presented herself to her disciples, sealing her life's work by reciting a poem (*Minghe yuyin* 5.7a). Sitting erect in the lotus posture, she was transformed into an immortal.

At the time of her departure, her former husband, although far away in Shandong, saw her rise up to heaven on a five-colored cloud, soaring into the empyrean. She looked down to him, smiled, and said: "I'm the first, after all, to return to Penglai." Ma reacted by tearing off his clothes and performing a shamanic dance in her honor (*Jinlian zhenzong ji* 5.10b). The final act of Sun Buer, therefore, reaffirmed both her role as part of the eternal Dao and as earthly wife to Ma Danyang. She triumphed, fully in control of her body and her life, and realized her original destiny by returning in glamour to the realm of the immortals.

This summarizes the legendary account of Sun Buer's life as it was written down in the thirteenth century. Historically her role was at first not quite as important as the stories make it seem, and she does not appear among the Seven Perfected until sixty years after her death.[8] Rising increasingly to official recognition, she received the formal title "Perfected of Clarity and Tranquility and Deep Perfection Who Follows Virtue" from Emperor Kubilai of the Mongol-Yuan dynasty in 1269. In 1310, Emperor Wuzong expanded this to include the epithet "Goddess of Mystery and Emptiness," raising her even higher in the celestial scheme (*Xianyuan xiangzhuan* 43a).

Shaanxi performing rituals for Wang Chongyang before moving to Luoyang (42a).

[8] She is first listed among them in the *Jinlian zhenzong ji* of 1241 (Boltz 1987, 65; Despeux 1990, 121-22).Other early sources, including works from 1258 and 1271, name only male leaders (*Ganshui xianyuan lu* 2.24a-25a; Chen et al. 1988, 518). However, an inscription from 1271 has her in the list (Chen et al. 1988, 604). For details on the lineage formation, see Marsonne 2001; Goossaert 2001.

Over the years Sun Buer has acted as a model and matriarch for women in the tradition of Complete Perfection, and was credited with various alchemical works. A set of fourteen poems attributed to her was arranged with commentary by Chen Yingning (1934) and translated by Thomas Cleary (1989). These verses give a general outline of the alchemical enterprise for women, beginning with the cosmic connection of the individual's *qi* and the tendency of human beings to fall into sensory entanglements. They then focus on the path to wholeness, beginning with quiet meditation, concentration on breath, reversion of *qi*, and cessation of menstruation. When the mind is completely still, *qi* is strengthened and rejuvenation is attained. In the womb, the elixir forms and gradually grows to fullness, nourished in the proper rhythm of yin and yang—"twenty-four hours a day, don't be lazy!" (Clearly 1989, 40). Once the elixir is ready, the person opens to original spirit, recovers the purity before birth, and merges with the final ultimate in cosmic emptiness. The total freedom of immortality is found, and the "jade girl rides off on a blue phoenix" (Cleary 1989, 56).

Sun Buer also plays a dominant role in dramatic and fictional accounts of the Seven Perfected, notably the late-Qing novel *Qizhen shizhuan* (The Tale of the Seven Perfected; trl. Wong 1990). Unlike in hagiographic sources, she appears here as the leading spirit in Ma Danyang's conversion. Childless, she encourages her husband to dedicate his life to the Dao, plotting variously to bring Wang Chongyang into the family compound and convince the Ma family to let the property go to the religious group (Wong 1990, 20).

The story of Wang Chongyang's simultaneous appearance in her bedroom and with her husband occurs twice, resulting in Sun's increasing trust in the powers of the Dao and showing her awakening to a proper understanding of the mutual necessity of yin and yang (Wong 1990, 47, 49). The novel also recounts her journey from Shandong to Luoyang, describing how she made herself intentionally ugly by splashing boiling oil on her face, so she could survive the trip unmolested (Wong 1990, 57; Boltz 1987, 60; Grant 1995, 42-43). In another scene, the novel focuses on Sun's death. Here she creates the image of a man and a woman from two tree branches and has them publicly embrace in the street. The local magistrate orders that these effigies be burned. During the fire three immortals appear in the flames, among them Sun Buer on her ascent to heaven. The event is followed by an auspicious rainfall that nurtures the area for several years (Wong 1990, 120).

The latter tale suggests the existence of a cult in Sun's honor in the region around Luoyang, which may also have been associated with Lady Feng, the eccentric immortal whose hermitage Sun took over. The various other stories add to her image as a successful Daoist practitioner, sectarian matriarch, and immortal, showing how Sun Buer has been highly regarded among Complete Perfection followers (see Ōyanagi 1934, 59).

The New Daoist Leaders

The prominent women of the Song and Yuan dynasties who are linked with the founding of lineages and the formulation of teachings are a completely different breed from the immortals of old and the renunciants of the middle ages. Highly visible, they play an active role in the society and interact freely and successfully with divinities (Zu Shu), emperors and aristocrats (Cao Wenyi), and leaders of new religions (Sun Buer). They are well educated and literate, coming from the upper classes and choosing the Daoist path in close relation to the society around them. Unlike medieval renunciants who tended to be social outsiders and set themselves apart to pursue their salvation, these new leaders are highly respected members of established society who remain inside the hierarchies of traditional China while pursuing their goal of enhancing the understanding of the divine, establishing perfection, and building lineages.

The dominant feature among these women is their expression in literature and especially poetry, their relation to the educated elite, and their sense of contributing to, rather than escaping from, society. Their practices are accordingly more conventional and take place in a communal and public setting. They still follow the classical practice of the immortals and focus on *qi*-control through breathing, diet, and sexual hygiene. But they also actively engage in the meditation methods made prominent in the Tang, undertaking forms of inner observation (*neiguan*), sitting in oblivion (*zuowang*), and absorption (*chan*).

These methods change the central focus of Daoist practice from the control of *qi* through longevity techniques, visualizations, and interactions with deities to a more mental practice that centers on the stilling of thoughts and the subtle perception of the inner movements of *qi*—without either abandoning or diminishing longevity practice or the interaction with the divine. On the contrary, the ritual and exorcistic aspects of practice are enhanced and developed, and many new ways of using incantations and activating talismans are developed. In addition, the movements of *qi* are increasingly expressed in alchemical terminology, creating the fullness of Daoist practice that is still dominant today.

The founders and matriarchs of the early modern period develop women's Daoist practice and the standing of female practitioners to a new level, participating more in the established society and making use of literary forms of communication and instruction. They are presented, at least in their hagiographies and in the texts attributed to them, as full participants in the Daoist enterprise and strong practitioners in their own right who are successful in every aspect of the path.

Chapter Seven

Nuns of Complete Perfection

Following the model of the great founders and matriarchs, women in Daoism strove to attain immortality and self-realization in the school of Complete Perfection, which, together with the school of the Celestial Masters, still forms the dominant organization of Daoism today. Many remained lay followers, undertaking various devotional and meditative practices at home; others became nuns and dedicated themselves to the religious enterprise. Within the wider populace nuns were classified rather derogatively as one group among the "three aunties and six grannies" (*sangu liupo*), a summary name for Daoist nuns, Buddhist nuns, and fortune-tellers plus brokers, match-makers, shaman-healers, procuresses, drug-sellers, and midwives (see Leung 1999, 102; Furth 1999, 268-69; Grant 1995, 30).

Within the Daoist organization, nuns were called "serene ones" (*sanren*) or "immortal ladies" (*xiangu*) and formed the majority of religious women. They included within their ranks widows and retired courtesans as much as devout matrons. To house these ladies of the Dao, new institutions arose, again following the leadership of Sun Buer. There were new schools and lineages that followed the example of the early founders, and formal rules were set up for both lay and monastic practitioners. The culture of nuns arose vigorously and has remained active to the present day.

Early Institutions

Under the Yuan dynasty, when China was governed by the Mongols, the country had 20,000 registered Daoists, many of them women. Institutions run by and for women arose in various parts of the country (see Fig. 10; Despeux 1990, 131-37; Goossaert 2001, 112). Shandong, where the Complete Perfection school first arose, was a major center. As recorded in the *Yunguang ji* (Collection of Cloudy Radiance, DZ 1152), its most prominent women's center was the Jinlian tang in Ninghai, where Sun Buer first joined Wang Chongyang and his disciples. This center continued to flourish and house serious adepts, as did the Weizhou guan (Monastery of Wei Prefecture) run by Tai Furen as abbot (1.2a).

According to the *Zhong'an ji* (Record of the Central Hermitage), found in the Qing-collection *Siku quanshu* (Complete Texts of the Four Repositories), the largest Daoist convent in Shandong was the Shenxiao guan (Monastery of the Divine Empyrean), located in Ren (modern Jining). It was destroyed in the wars of the early thirteenth century and reconstructed in 1259 under the leadership of Miaoqing, a local nun who requested permission for rebuilding it from the local military leader. She passed the temple on to her senior disciple Shouqing, from whom it went to Liu Huixiu. They became famous for their efficiency, exemplary discipline, and high standards of cultivation. As a result, in 1290, the local Complete Perfection administrator made Liu the formal overseer of the area and granted various honors to the temple (12a-13b).

A number of convents also became prominent in Henan. Many were populated by women of the aristocracy who tended to congregate around the capital. Among them was the Qiyun guan (Cloud Abode Monastery) in the northwest quarter of Kaifeng, constructed under the guidance of Li Miaoyuan. As recorded in the *Yunshan ji* (Compendium of Cloud Mountain, DZ 1140), she came from Nangong in Henan and after her father's death in 1263, followed her mother into the monastic life. Both women studied with Ji Zhizhen, a female disciple of Wang Qiyun, who in turn followed one of the Seven Perfected. Excelling in their studies, they were granted three acres of land to erect their own convent near the main Complete Perfection center (see also *Yangwu zhaiji* 17.20a-21b, ed. *Siku quanshu*).

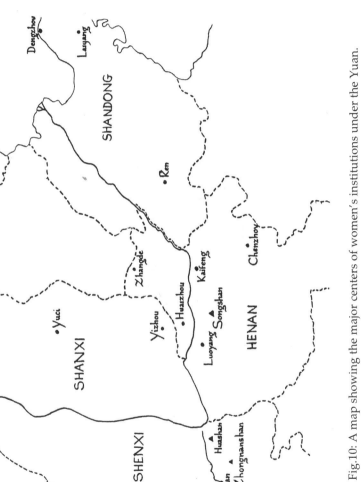

Fig.10: A map showing the major centers of women's institutions under the Yuan.

Another prominent convent in Henan was the female house of the Tian-qing gong (Temple of Heavenly Clarity) in Zhangde, under the leadership of Zuo Shouzhen, also known as Zuo Shoukuan. As described in Wang Yunwu's *Zishan daquan ji* (Complete Collection of Purple Mountain, ed. *Siku quanshu*), she was born near Anyang in 1202 as the daughter of a high official. In the 1220s, she married Wang Xin, the prefect of Anyang and Zhangde, and was widowed during a devastating army raid in 1240. After raising her children, she chose to become a Daoist nun and studied with Li Zhifang (1185-1260) [1] at the Tianqing gong, which had been the residence of Qiu Chuji until his death in 1227. Developing great spiritual competence, she was granted permission to erect her own hermitage nearby. She ran a small community here, in a hermitage whose setup included a hall to Lord Lao, a kitchen, refectory, and dormitory. She also received a formal religious title for her merits, and lived a quiet spiritual life to the ripe old age of eighty-eight (17.13a-14a).

Another convent in the same area was similarly sponsored by Li Zhifang. Run by Yang Shouhe and her daughter Shouzhen, it was known as the Jizhen guan (Monastery of the Assembled Perfected). Also widowed at an early age, Yang had opted for a religious career. She received formal ordination in 1253 and obtained the religious name Serene One of Pure Simplicity (Chunsu sanren). After her death at age seventy-two, her daughter took over the temple, and became known as Serene One of Nonaction(Wuwei sanren) (*Zishan daquan ji* 17.14b-15a).

The importance of women's religious communities in Henan is further documented in the *Lifeng laoren ji* (Compendium on the Old Man of Li Peak, DZ 1264), a collection of materials on Yu Daoxian (1168-1232), also known as Old Man of Li Peak (Lifeng laoren), a disciple of the Perfected Liu Changsheng. According to this document, Yu was originally a resident of the Changsheng guan (Monastery of Long Life) and, in the 1220s, was appointed overseer of the Taiqing gong (Temple of Great Clarity) in Haozhou. In the ensuing unrest, he fled to western Henan and died there in 1232. The text contains 319 poems of his, forty-four of which are ad-

---

[1] Li Zhifang was originally called Guo Ming. A secretary in the Ministry of Rites, he was in charge of Daoist administration. He became a monk around 1220 and was ordained by Qiu Chuji in 1224. See *Zishan daquan ji* 17.13b.

dressed or dedicated to women (2.29ab; also *Tidao tongjian xubian*, DZ 297, 2.7a).

In Shanxi, moreover, the nun Zhang Shouwei was famous for rebuilding the Xiuzhen guan (Monastery for the Cultivation of Perfection) in the city of Yizhou, which had burned down in the war of 1214. A native of Jinzheng near Yizhou, she too had been widowed early and chosen the religious path, following Yang Shouxuan, abbot of the Yuzhen'an (Hermitage of the Jade Perfected) in Taiyuan. The reconstruction of the temple began in 1241, and Zhang lived there for many quiet years.[2]

In all these cases, the tendency was for prominent Daoist women to come from an aristocratic or official background after they were widowed during the Mongol raids of the early thirteenth century. Often joined by a daughter, they entered the religious life and soon excelled, due to their extensive education and firm dedication to the path. Emerging as organizers and innovators, they become abbots and were granted titles and honors, erecting or restoring institutions and guiding younger nuns to self-realization. Like women in the Tang dynasty, those living under the Yuan made use of the religious and organizational resources at their disposal and developed both as individuals and as beneficiaries for the society around them.[3]

Schools and Lineages

After the overthrow of the Mongol-Yuan dynasty in 1368, the indigenous Ming dynasty (1368-1644) continued to follow their religious policies to a

---

[2] No details are known of any convents in Shaanxi and Beijing; some are mentioned in contemporaneous poems and Buddhist polemics. See Despeux 1990, 136.

[3] The same strength and organizational enterprise of women Daoists is also evident in the northern part of the country, under Jurchen rule. A first study of these women is currently being prepared by Shin-yi Chao (see Chao 2003). Strong women, moreover, are not found only in religion. In Yuan drama, a broader understanding of Chinese society of the time is reflected, and women are frequently portrayed as influential and competent. See Jiang 1991.

large degree, but also institutionalized a number of new administrative measures. For the most part, these remained in place through the following Qing dynasty, when China was governed by the Manchus (1644-1911). In this period, commonly known as late imperial China, all religious affairs were controlled by the Ministry of Rites, which now included a Bureau of Daoist Registration as well as various local offices that issued and monitored ordination certificates. Ordinations were allowed only in specially designated monasteries and were held only once every three, five, or ten years. The number of monks and nuns permissible in the country was restricted according to the government's needs, and the ordination of men was limited to between the ages of fourteen and twenty so that they would not join to evade draft and taxes, while women were not permitted to become nuns when still of child-bearing age.[4]

Private temples, owned and sponsored by local aristocrats, were severely curtailed and had to have an official stamp of approval from the government before they could house any religious practitioners. These measures were not always followed to the letter—nor were other administrative rules of the time, such as the prohibition of adopting a son from a family with a different surname and of marrying a concubine unless over age forty and without a male heir (Waltner 1990, 49; 147). In addition, they lost some of their effect due to the increase in female literacy and the greater acknowledgment of women's abilities and power during this period (Grant 1996, 53). Still, the overall effect of these new administrative measures was twofold: it reduced enthusiasm for the religious

---

[4] This rule was not always observed, especially when young girls joined a convent as children. A case in point is the story of a Daoist who had been given to a temple at age two and raised there. Although following the rules of a renunciant, she was never formally ordained. In 1753, she was observed by a local fruit vendor at the Lantern Festival. He raped her together with a group of drinking buddies. She raised a great commotion, and the perpetrators were severely punished. Also punished were a number of local magistrates who had not ensured that the girl was properly ordained and had failed to keep her safe. See *Xingke tiben*, sect. *Hunyin jianqing lei*, Emperor Qianlong 18/12/14. We are indebted to Janet Theiss for this information. For more on the legal status of women and their inclination toward suicide in Qing China, see Theiss 2001; 2002.

path among the population, and it caused a high level of standardization among institutions and practitioners (see DeBruyn 2000; Esposito 2000). [5]

As a result, the Complete Perfection school was organized into a number of formal lines and lineages, the most important ones going back to the Seven Perfected. As described in the *Qinggui xuanmiao* (Pure Rules of Mystery and Wonder, ZW 361; see Kohn 2002), they consisted of the following:

Lineage	Founder
Longmen pai	Qiu Chuji
Suishan pai	Liu Changsheng
Nanwu pai	Tan Changzhen
Yushan pai	Ma Danyang
Huashan pai	Hao Taigu
Yushan pai	Wang Yuyang
Qingjing pai	Sun Buer

Each lineage is centered in one specific temple or mountain and exerts influence predominantly in that area, with lesser impact in other parts of the country. They each have a specific lineage poem (*cipai*) that describes the central tenets of their doctrine and practice and is, more importantly, used as a generation marker—all lineage members of a certain generation using a specific character from the poem in their name (see Ōyanagi 1934). This method of marking lineages was also common among the great aristocratic houses of traditional China, making it easy for people familiar with the system to know who belonged to which generation.

In general, women made up about one third of the Complete Perfection clergy (Goossaert 2001, 112), and one of the seven major schools is associated with a woman founder. The Qingjing pai (Clarity and Tranquility

---

[5] For more on the education and literacy of women in the Qing, see Handlin 1975; Ropp 1976; Mann 1991; 1992; 1997; Ocko 1991; Ko 1994; Bray 1997; Widmer and Kang 1997; Cheng 2001; Widmer 1999; 2003. Widmer has also a forthcoming article in *Snakes Legs: Sequels, Continuations, Rewritings and Chinese Fiction (1600-1911)*, edited by Martin Huang (Honolulu: University of Hawaii Press), and is preparing a book on the subject.

Lineage) of Sun Buer is its most prominent women's school and has a strong lineage poem. It begins:

> Complete Perfection comes with the mystery principle;
> The virtue of the Great Dao is nonaction.
> As inner nature unifies, the body turns to ashes and is liberated,
> Completing the work of a hundred days.
> (Ōyanagi 1934, 101; Despeux 1990, 159)

Under the umbrella of these seven major lineages, many smaller groups and trends exist, and here two further female lines are found: the Yunxia pai (Morning Cloud Lineage) that traces itself back to the lady immortal He Xiangu; and another, also called Qingjing pai, affiliated with the Song poet Cao Wenyi. Their poems are as follows:

> Living on the heights beyond the Three Worlds,
> Turn around and look back at the world of dust.
> When you see a courageous woman,
> Invite her to join you in the cultivation of perfection.

And:

> Once determined to reach ascension into heaven,
> What hardship can there be in cultivation practice?
> One with Great Yang, you sublimate the body,
> Joining wondrous principle, you reach the deepest mystery.
> (Ōyanagi 1934, 111; Despeux 1990, 160)

Within these main lineages, nuns of Complete Perfection followed the model of the great founders and developed a spiritual and inspired life. They joined communities of fellow seekers and obeyed numerous rules, dressed in renunciant garb and underwent many hardships. Their main goal was the attainment of the pure Dao, reached through monastic living, karmic purification, good deeds, and internal cultivation. Their lives were simple, stark, and often hard, but they served one main purpose: overcoming the limitations of this world, finding perfection, joining the mystery, and ascending to immortality.

Basic Practice

Anyone aspiring to the religious life of Complete Perfection, even before formally joining a religious community, had to develop a devout attitude, compassion, and inner virtue, expressed in the performance of various tasks in family and society. As women were not allowed to become nuns while still of childbearing age, they had to pass through a period of family service before dedicating themselves to the Dao. For this preparatory period, a general sense of humility and dedication were encouraged, as several texts on rules for women assert.

For example, the ten rules contained in the Qing-dynasty manual *Nüdan shize* (Ten Rules for Women's Alchemy, ed. Tao 1989, 17-52; ZW 883) encouraged women practitioners, since they rarely had the opportunity to leave the family compound, to expand their practice through good deeds in the house and the development of filial piety. As the text says in its fifth rule:

> Establishing good merit and proper practice begins by looking after the parents-in-law every morning and evening. Be filial and respectful, look to their provisions and ask after their sleep. Diligently serving the parents-in-law like this is the first great merit. The first great practice, then, lies in developing the ability to exhaust the mind and put all one's strength into doing this. Thereby immortal women can establish their position and attain success.

> Always be yielding and receptive towards others, and maintain a loyal and generous heart. Never close off your heart or darken yourself. If you see someone suffering or poor, orphaned or old, develop an attitude of empathy and compassion, sympathy and commiseration.

> Always put yourself last while waiting on others at the stove, and never resent the dirty work in the kitchen. Never raise your voice. Rather, make sure to present regular offerings to the spirits and luminous [ancestors], and venerate your teachers and elders with deep respect. Be modest and humble to both old and young, be cooperative and empathetic to both villagers and neighbors. (9ab; ZW 26.459)

Women should, therefore, exhibit proper devotion, maintain a loyal and honest attitude, and develop compassion for the old, sick, and orphaned. Being content even when they had to perform dirty or menial tasks, they should strive to behave properly toward their husband and uphold good relations with the neighbors and village people.

A similar course in virtue and filial piety is also prescribed for women in the *Chuzhen jie* (Precepts of Initial Perfection, JY 292)[6], the collection of elementary rules for ordinands of the first level of the Complete Perfection system. This text was compiled in the seventeenth century, by the Baiyun guan abbot Wang Kunyang (1622-1680) as part of his formalization of the Longmen lineage (Kubo 1951, 37). Originally known as Wang Ping (aka Changyue), he was an avid Daoist traveler in his youth and, in 1628, met Zhao Fuyang, a sixth-generation Longmen patriarch, on Mount Wangwu. Having received the Longmen precepts from him, Wang continued to study with different masters for nine years, until 1655 when he went to live in the Lingyou gong (Palace-Temple of Numinous Wanderings), located in the capital. One year later he became abbot of the Baiyun guan (Esposito 2000, 629).

As abbot, Wang Kunyang reorganized Daoist religious precepts in accordance with Neo-Confucian ethics as supported by the Qing court. He outlined several sets of precepts as a key means to perfection and an important element in clerical training. He divided Daoist ordination into three ranks, each associated with a different text and level of precepts:

1. Master of Wondrous Practice—*Chuzhen jie* (Precepts of Initial Perfection, JY 292)
2. Master of Wondrous Virtue—*Zhongji jie* (Precepts of Medium Ultimate, JY 293; ZW 405)
3. Master of Wondrous Dao—*Tianxian dajie* (Great Precepts for Celestial Immortals, JY 291; ZW 403).

---

[6] The abbreviation "JY" stands for *Daozang jiyao* (Repository of the Daoist Canon), a nineteenth-century supplement to the Daoist canon that contains many works on inner alchemy. A complete catalog of the collection is found in Chen 1987. The numbering follows Komjathy 2002.

Aside from Qing-dynasty collections, these texts were also collected in manuscript form by Heinrich Hackmann, a German minister and theologian who lived in China on two separate occasions, first as pastor of the Protestant parish in Shanghai from 1894 to 1902, then as a religious traveler in 1910-11 (see Strachotta 1997; Kohn 2002). During the latter stay, he and his wife Ella spent three months in a Daoist monastery on Laoshan, near the German colony of Qingdao, where Hackmann had the opportunity to observe the daily life of monks and collect a total of twenty-eight Daoist texts. Among them were Wang Kunyang's three precepts texts, two of which Hackmann studied and translated after his return (1920; 1931; also Kohn 2004b). In his diary, Hackmann notes that he had some difficulty obtaining these texts, because they were given to monks at their ordination, then became part of their regalia, and would eventually be buried with them. He was only able to receive them because one of the monastery's flock had returned to lay life and left his ordination books with the abbot (1920, 146).

The texts provide a general outline of Complete Perfection precepts, ethics, and monastic regulations, which are essentially the same for monks and nuns. As the *Chuzhen jie* outlines, members of both sexes have to observe the basic five precepts against killing, stealing, lying, sexual misconduct, and intoxication, and follow ten further rules that encourage compassion and consideration in a larger social setting.[7]

The ten precepts are designed for people who have just made the decision to leave the family and pursue the Dao, providing both prohibitions and prescriptions. They contain admonitions to be loyal and filial, cultivate benevolence and good faith, avoid stealing and profiteering, behave with compassion and grace, and stay chaste and pure, pursuing perfection and integrity. They also insist that one should always use the Dao to help others and make sure that all clan members live in harmony, avoid slander, gossip, and defamation, stay away from wine, meat, and other

---

[7] These ten precepts go back to a medieval text, also called *Chuzhen jie* (DZ 180) and cited in Zhang Wanfu's *Sandong zhongjie wen* (Collected Precepts of the Three Caverns, DZ 178) of the early eighth century. They are reprinted in *Yunji qiqian* 40.7a-8a. See Ren and Zhong 1991, 132-33; Yoshioka 1961, 61; Kohn 2004b.

physical indulgence, as well as remain free from greed and acquisitiveness. The rules conclude:

9. Do not have any relations or exchange with the unwise or live among the mixed and defiled. Always strive to control yourself in your living assemble purity and emptiness.

10. Do not speak or laugh lightly or carelessly, increasing agitation and denigrating perfection. Always maintain seriousness and speak humble words, making the Dao and its virtue your main concern. (*Chuzhen jie*, JY 10.94)

In addition to these ten basic rules for all practitioners, the text also mentions nine precepts specifically for women. While they echo the above ten precepts, they are clearly addressed to lay women who are either devout followers or preparing for a monastic career. They emphasize loyalty, filial piety, and chastity, encourage devotees to be gentle, compassionate, and honest, and warn them against joining public ceremonies, banquets, and other festivities that might pollute the senses. They convey a sense of women pursuing a softer and more house-based path. The nine precepts for women are:

1. Be filial and respectful, soft and harmonious, careful in speech, and never jealous.

2. Be chaste and pure, controlled in body, and stay away from foul activities.

3. Develop sympathy for all beings that have life, be compassionate and friendly, and never kill.

4. During rites and recitations, be diligent and circumspect, give up all eating of meat and drinking of wine.

5. In your garments be practical and simple, never favoring floweriness or ornaments.

6. Maintain an even and harmonious disposition, never giving rise to anger and afflictions.

7. Do not frequently go out to attend purgation festivals and banquets.

8. Do not be cruel in your employment of servants and slaves.

9. Do not steal other people's things. (*Chuzhen jie*, JY 10.99; also *Nüxiu zhengtu* 3a; ZW 356, 10.534)

Once women have achieved this level of virtue and pursue self-cultivation in the family setting, they are ready to move further towards active religious practice. A set of six precepts, found in the *Nüdan shize* specifies details in this respect, encouraging women yet again to be obedient, filial, upright, and soft-spoken, but also admonishing them to develop alignment with more cosmic forces and to develop an eagerness to pursue the Dao. Here we have:

1. Be caring and nurturing towards your parents-in-law. If you do not have parents-in-law, extend this attitude towards your family and clan, and anyone older and higher ranking than yourself. Always be modest and subservient to the utmost, respectful towards the elderly and venerating the wise.

2. Be upright and steady, proper and chaste. In all your activities and rest, and especially in the clothes you wear and the ornaments you put on, always tend towards the simple and solid, the firm and steady, eschewing all luxury or fancy.

3. Be diligent and careful in your use of speech. Whether interacting with those above or below you, always be careful in what you say—especially when others debate the right and wrong of this or that. Similarly, when you receive the wondrous, true teachings from your master, be careful of your mouth and develop great humility, lest you incur a transgression of speech.

4. Be careful in how you practice. When you sit down to pursue the great work, always make sure the place is clean and away from defilements and roadsides, from dampness and noise. Observe all restrictions regarding this.

5. Be respectful towards your teacher and serious about the Dao. When you meet a lofty and enlightened [teacher], ask him to transmit his teachings with deep modesty and never voice criticism or give sharp answers. If you think yourself lofty and develop conceit, you cannot receive the benefits.

6. Be strong in determination and actively present in mind. As you enter the Dao and take up cultivation practice, make a

vow [to pursue it] for as long as you live in this body or
even for several lifetimes. Never lose that firmness of mind
and painstaking determination, lest you create an impedi-
ment to your progress. (12ab; ZW 26.461)

In this set of six precepts, women are encouraged to behave with modesty and proper civil virtue while still in the world, serving in-laws and
elders and maintaining chastity and simplicity. But they are also urged
to pursue the Dao by developing purity of speech, staying out of debates
and setting aside time and space for initial practice. They are required to
find a teacher and follow his or her instructions to see whether they are
suited to the Daoist path. Once they have made a decision to pursue the
path, they need strong determination and clear understanding, vowing
to stay with the practice for the rest of their lives. They are setting out on
the path to immortality, no longer merely cultivating social skills and
family service but taking the first step of joining the host of monastic followers in their regular practice and complete dedication to perfection.

Monastic Life

When joining monastic life, both men and women underwent initial ordination by taking the five and ten precepts and receiving the text of the
Chuzhen jie. During their novitiate, they had to prostrate themselves before the precepts master every day for one hundred days at the *si* hour
(9-11 a.m.). He heard the confession of their sins and gave them admonitions as well as suitable penances and acts of repentance, instructing
them in the details of the scriptures and rituals. Novices also had to observe special rites on all *gengshen* days (the 57th day of the 60-day cycle),
when the Three Deathbringers or Three Corpses ascended to the heavenly administration to report transgressions and misdemeanors. This
practice echoes a rite still undertaken in Japan, the so-called Kōshin vigil.
Local devotees come together to share a vegetarian feast and listen to
sermons throughout the night to prevent the Three Deathbringers from
undertaking their celestial journey. It is believed that when seven such
vigils are performed, the Deathbringers will starve and the practitioner's
longevity is extended (see Kohn 1995b).

As part of the initial training, women also received a set of twelve rules, listed and explained in the late nineteenth-century manual *Nü jindan* (Women's Golden Elixir, ed. Tao 1989, 57-122; ZW 871, 878). These rules emphasize the mental state women need to cultivate for proper attainment. They are:

1. Restrain the recurrence of inappropriate thoughts.

2. Cut off your lust and sexual indulgence.

3. Do not fly into rages or show cruelty to others.

4. Do not fall prey to annoyance and anger.

5. Avoid all melancholy, fear, and anguish.

6. Do not gawk and stare.

7. Do not listen in on others.

8. Do not chatter and prattle.

9. Do not be stingy and miserly.

10. Do not kill or harm any living being.

11. Avoid excess in eating meat.

12. Do not belittle the Dao or scorn your master. (1.4a-5a)

Thus prepared for the introduction into the monastic life, novice women joined their male counterparts in a formal, state-supported ordination ceremony, usually held on a day of the Three Primes, i.e., on the fifteenth day of the first, seventh, or tenth months of the lunar calendar. Arranged in proper order and well prepared, the ordinands appeared before a group of elders to take their vows, profess formal refuge in the Three Treasures of Dao, scriptures, and masters, and pledge their obedience to the rules and regulations of Complete Perfection.[8] They were given the text of the precepts, of which they had to make a copy for personal use. Also, in recognition of their new status, they received a set of vestments

---

[8] A list of the elders and formal statement of the ordinand's background and vows is found in the actual ordination certificate, which is attached to each of the precepts manuscripts collected by Hackmann. He offers a full translation (1920, 146-47; 1931, 6-7; also Kohn 2004b).

(a basic dark-blue robe and a yellow kerchief), a begging bowl, and various other utensils, named the "Seven Treasures." The latter include:

1. a rush mat to purify demons from outside

2. a quilted robe to support mind and inner nature

3. a single calabash to contain proper food and drink

4. a palm-leaf hat to keep off wind and rain, frost and snow

5. a palm-leaf fan to brush off worldly affairs

6. a blue satchel to store the cinnabar scriptures

7. a flat staff to point to the great Dao, pure wind, and bright moon (*Qinggui xuanmiao*, ZW 10.598)

After the ordination was over, the new Daoists were established in their proper institutions. In these centers, all monks and nuns participated regularly in the morning and evening services, and recited the *Qingjing jing* (Scripture of Clarity and Tranquility, DZ 620), *Dadong jing* (Scripture of Great Pervasion, DZ 105), and *Taigu jing* (Scripture of Great Antiquity, DZ 102), together with various refuges, prayers, and incantations. On all *xu* days, i.e., once every ten days according to the sixty-day cycle, they also chanted the *Daode jing, Wenshi jing, Tanzi, Huangting jing,* and parts of the *Zhuangzi* (*Chuzhen jie*, JY 10.97). In addition to this basic monastic curriculum, women in some lineages also had their own texts to work on, including the *Kunning jing* (Scripture of Female Peace) and the *Zhenyi jing* (Scripture of Perfect Unity).

The monastic schedule further prescribes that the periods *zi* (11 PM – 1 AM) and *wu* (11 AM – 1 PM) be used for the practice of meditation and inner alchemy (Yao 2000, 589; Yoshioka 1979). In addition, all followers had to join a 100-day retreat from the first day of the tenth month to the beginning of the new year. Also known as the mid-winter period, this was a time when everyone chanted and meditated continuously, working in proper order and following the rules with particular care (*Qinggui xuanmiao*, JY 10.599).

Once monastics rose to the intermediate level, they observed the 300 precepts of "Medium Ultimate," which consisted of three groups of rules: a set of 180 concrete and socially oriented prohibitions, thirty-six predominantly proscriptive precepts on forms of monastic behavior, and eighty-four altruistic and meditative thoughts to be cultivated (trl. Hackmann 1931; Kohn 2004b). For the hundred days of the retreat, they had to give major offerings to the Heavenly Worthy of Numinous Treasure (Lingbao tianzun) and every day, during the *si* hour (9-11 a.m.), prostrate themselves to the precepts master and repent their sins.

Those of highest ritual rank who had the power to train and ordain junior followers, followed the precepts of "Celestial Immortality." These precepts emphasized altruism and compassion, admonishing practitioners to apply themselves to the ten virtues, such as wisdom, compassion, good deeds, and universal mind, in all the different dimensions of life. Doing so, advanced monks and nuns became free from sensory entanglements and foulness, wrongness and delusion, and attained a level of comprehensive concern for all life that equals the clarity, kindness, and equanimity of the Dao itself. By going beyond all personal concerns, they realized a morally pure and karmically refined state of universal-mindedness that gave them the true immortality of the Dao. These high-level followers would recite the *Daode jing* daily at the *yin* hour (5-7 a.m.) and prostrate themselves to the worthies of the ten directions on a regular basis, emphasizing their connection with all areas of the universe. Both men and women could attain this high rank. If successful, they could conduct holy rites and lead spiritual meditations, serving as leaders of Daoist institutions and supporting the spread of the Dao.

Nuns Today

The essential equality in the status and attainment of religious men and women in Complete Perfection has continued to the present day. For example, Yin Mingdao, an elderly nun living in a Taiwanese temple, comments on the differences among the sexes in contemporary Daoist practice:

> When we worship in the temple, when we chant sacred texts aloud, it is exactly the same [for men and women], there is really no difference. The difference is in the physical and meditative practice [of inner alchemy]. Male Daoists practice "sub-

duing the white tiger" [retaining semen]. Females aim to "de-
capitate the red dragon" [ceasing menstruation]. (Paper 1997,
88)

There are still quite a number of Daoist nuns in institutions and hermit-
ages in China. As outlined in *Zhonghua xianxue* (Immortality Studies in
China, dat. 1976), they tend to follow six major Complete Perfection sub-
sects founded by and dedicated to women. They are

1. the lineage of the Old Mother of Mount Zhongtiao (Shanxi),
   a tradition that focuses on sword practice and traces itself
   back to the immortal Lü Dongbin

2. the lineage of Mother Chen, the teacher of Xu Xun of the
   Pure Brightness school, located in Jiangxi and the Nanjing
   area, with practices centering on herbs, alchemical concoc-
   tions, and the application of talismans (see *Taiping guangji*
   62.384, 67.414, and 70.437)

3. the lineage of the Lady of Southern Peak (Nanyue furen),
   Lady Wei Huacun, the ancient matriarch of Highest Clarity,
   with techniques of visualization and recitation based on the
   Huangting jing

4. the lineage of Xie Ziran, an eighth-century saint from Sichuan, with emphasis on dietary techniques and fasting,
   breathing methods and *qi*-control, as well as the worship of
   the Queen Mother of the West (*Taiping guangji* 66.408)

5. the lineage of Cao Wenyi, the Song poet, with practices focusing on meditations, purification of spirit, elimination of
   desires, and communication with the body gods

6. the lineage of Sun Buer of the Seven Perfected, whose key
   focus is the inner-alchemical transformation towards purity, beginning with the "decapitation of the red dragon."
   (Despeux 1990, 181-82)

In Taiwan, various prominent nunneries house women dedicated to the
Dao. As shown in recent research by Ho Wan-li (2003), especially the
Daode yuan (Morality Temple) in Gaoxiong and the Cihui tang (Compassion Society Temple) near Taipei are serious communities. Founded
in the 1950s and 60s, they are led by women and center on the worship of
female deities such as Xiwang mu. Renunciants follow a strict discipline

of worship and cultivation, and engage in charitable works. They support the poor, the old, and the sick, and provide medical and library services as well as disaster relief to the general populace. Their ethos joins the goal of immortality and personal cultivation with a strong urge to develop compassion and do good in the society around them.

Daoist nuns are also active in mainland China. As found during a journey Catherine Despeux undertook in 1984, nuns tended to live in mountain convents, sometimes by themselves, often with a few disciples (see Despeux 1990, 183-85). For example, the Qunxian guan (Monastery of the Host of Immortals) on Mount Hua housed three nuns, as opposed to eight in 1954. One of them, Zhang Zhiqing, was born in Lanzhou in northwest China and became a Daoist nun at age fifteen, shortly after the death of her parents. She felt she had to leave her home because her younger brother, an opium smoker, considered her a burden and treated her miserably.

Entering a Daoist temple in Lanzhou dedicated to Mazu, she joined in its martial arts practices and lived there until 1954, when a fellow sister invited her to Mount Hua. She could not remember when she had her first ordination, but the character *zhi* in her name suggests that she belongs the 21st generation of Longmen initiation. She followed the teachings of this lineage in both its liturgical and meditative, inner alchemical dimensions. She claims that at the age of twenty-eight, she succeeded in "decapitating the red dragon" and did not menstruate thereafter. But, as she noted herself, she stayed at a fairly elementary level of alchemical practice, not advancing to the higher stages.

A similar situation was also found on Mount Qingcheng, the largest Daoist mountain in Sichuan. The first temple Despeux visited there was the Tianshi dong (Celestial Master Grotto), the place where Zhang Daoling allegedly received his revelation. It housed several young men and women who, some years before, had taken their first ordination at the Baiyun guan in Beijing. They followed the standard schedule of Complete Perfection, reciting the holy texts during morning and evening services and practicing sitting meditation during regular periods.

The nearby Jieyin dian (Hall of Sojourning Yin), moreover, was dedicated entirely to women, continuing the ancient Qingdu guan (Monastery of Pure Capital), where the Tang princess Jade Perfected had made her religious home. In 1984, it was inhabited by a Daoist nun in her fifties called Zeng Shuliang. She had taken her vows in the Sanhuang miao (Temple to the Three Sovereigns) in Chengdu, then gone to study with a senior monk and Complete Perfection administrator at the Qingyang gong (Gray Sheep Temple), the leading Daoist sanctuary in the city. Like other nuns, she practiced methods of inner alchemy, including breathing exercises, self-massage, concentration, visualization, and overall refinement and sublimation of the body. Also like the other nuns, she began her training in a smaller institution before joining the greater Complete Perfection organization and coming to reside in a temple of her own.

Beyond these official members of Complete Perfection residing in better-known temples, there are also a number of hermit nuns in China. Bill Porter, who traveled around the sacred mountains in the late 1980s, met a few of them. At Louguan, for example, the major Daoist sanctuary in the Zhongnan mountains where Lord Lao supposedly transmitted the *Daode jing* to Yin Xi, he met a Daoist nun named Zhang at a solitary shrine in the back of the temple. She was sitting there all day, taking care of the shrine in exchange for flour and other necessities. Originally from the Nanyang area in Hubei, she had bound feet, which had left her crippled since childhood. Now seventy-nine years old, she had been a nun for fifty years, the last twenty of which she had spent as a hermit, first on Mount Taibai further west, then at Louguan. She said she went down the mountain once or twice a year on special occasions, but overall preferred to live alone to practice meditation. The winters were rough, she admitted, especially since the roof of the shrine leaked. Still the place gave her the solitude she needed (Porter 1993, 45).

Solitude in general was preferred over comfort by the nuns, and the Buddhist nun Chuanfu, whose roof also leaked, emphasized that it was of no importance. She said:

> You can't live in the mountains if you're still attached, if you haven't seen through the red dust. Life in the mountains is hard. But once you've seen through the illusions of this world, hardships aren't important. The only thing that matters is practice. If you don't practice, you'll never get free of the dust of delusion. (Porter 1993, 113-14)

Chuanfu had started out as a Daoist nun at age seventeen, but switched to Buddhism three years later, then spent five years near the famous Shaolin Temple in Henan. Later, she tried to live on Mount Guanyin but nearly starved to death, and returned to Shaolin. She was able to buy what she needed with money she made from collecting herbs. Nobody except the local farmers visited her and she often felt lonely.

Another nun in the same area was called Chehui. Originally from Jilin province, she had lived in the mountains since the 1950s. Unlike Chuanfu, however, she said she never felt lonely, since she had a disciple staying with her and would go to the village once a month. There—with money she made from growing walnuts or that her family sent her—she would buy cooking oil, kerosene, flour, and salt. These were the only things she needed, since she planted her own vegetables and would fast when there was nothing to eat. Like her monastic sisters, she followed a devout religious practice, meditating every night and chanting scriptures every morning and evening. She was not troubled at all by the events of the Cultural Revolution (Porter 1993, 116).

This was not the case for another Buddhist nun Porter met on his travels. Living in the mountains near Xi'an, she had been forced to return to lay life by the Red Guards. She married and had a daughter who later joined her in seclusion and had just taken her vows in a group ceremony at the Dayan ta (Big Goose Pagoda) in Xi'an (Porter 1993, 187). Her fate in some ways resembles the life of the Yuan-dynasty Daoist widows who similarly took their offspring with them to the convent, creating female lineages in the process. This shows that the tradition of nuns continues even today, albeit under slightly different auspices, in smaller settings, and certainly with much less political support.

Religious Women

The nuns of Complete Perfection show a high degree of continuity from the Yuan dynasty to the present day. Typically drawn to the Dao later in life or because of difficult family situations, they are often well educated and attain a high standing in the religious hierarchy, where they manage convents or establish institutions. In some cases they bring their daughters along, creating family-based lineages and providing a strong sense of commitment and continuity to the tradition.

Working within the organized Complete Perfection system, which in turn is tightly supervised by the state—previously by the imperial administration, today by the communist government—Daoist women had to show their moral purity and religious aptitude well before they were allowed to enter the order. When admitted, they had to undergo a period of training and probation, were formally ordained in extensive, state-sponsored ceremonies, and held to the adherence of a strict religious schedule that provided time for devotional services, meditation practice, and community work. Not all nuns lived in groups, however, even today there are a number of hermits secluded in the mountains who maintain their spiritual regimen but are essentially free from supervision.

Daoist nuns of Complete Perfection were and are strong practitioners with clear goals and a powerful motivation, a great sense of independence and self-worth. In this respect they easily match the nuns and abbots of the Chan school of Buddhism, who similarly dedicated themselves fully to a life of religious cultivation, following their chosen path with strong determination and reaching a status quite equal to that of men in spiritual attainment and monastic authority.

A classic example of a strong Chan Buddhist nun is Zhiyuan Xinggang (1597-1654), abbot and lineage holder of the Linji school. Although drawn to the religious life from an early age, she was not permitted to enter a convent because she was the only child of a Ming official and had to maintain the family line. She married and was widowed early, yet still remained a householder, serving both her parents and her in-laws until the death of her father in 1627. After fulfilling the mourning obligations, she became the disciple of Miyun Yuanwu (1565-1641), a Chan master of great renown who was famous for his discipline and eccentricity and had ordained over 300 disciples (Grant 1996, 52-56).

Struggling hard to work through a series of koans and reach enlightenment, she eventually attained awakening and, in 1638, was named a dharma-heir of one of Miyun Yuanwu's senior students. Striving for even higher spiritual powers, she went into solitary retreat for nine years, then became the abbot of a family chapel which had been converted into a convent. There she practiced meditation, built up the convent, performed rituals, instructed numerous disciples, both male and female, and gave inspiring lectures to local literati and officials. Her authority was strong and clear, and though she had more difficulty than a man in extricating herself from her family ties, she was in no way a lesser practitioner or made any suggestion that she had faced different or greater obstacles to enlightenment. After her death in 1654, she was widely venerated and left behind a flourishing lineage of female masters (Grant 1996, 63-65).[9]

Women such as Xinggang were found both in Buddhism and in Daoism in the late imperial and modern periods. Their increased presence reflects a greater degree of literacy among women as well as the fact that educated women were widely painting, writing, and publishing in late imperial China, despite the fact that women in general were still seen as inferior and subjected to footbinding, concubinage, female infanticide, and widow chastity demands (Grant 1995, 29), as well as being sold, rented, and mortgaged as if they were nothing more than inanimate pieces of property (Ocko 1991, 315). Religious women who claimed their independence created a strong counterweight to the more unfavorable images of women and dispelled the idea that all females are empty-headed and only good for secondary tasks. They actively showed that women can attain high states and be leaders of influence, at least among religious organizations.

In terms of the Daoist tradition, moreover, these strong nuns of late imperial and modern China still continue the heritage of the practitioners of old, cultivating their bodies, training their minds, and playing an active role in the organization of the religion. They follow similar practices as men and in their ritual activities are considered equal. Their inner transformation, on the other hand, relies to a large extent on the specific na-

---

[9] For more on Buddhist nuns of the late imperial period, see Grant 1994; 1999; 2001. She also has a volume forthcoming on the poetry of Buddhist nuns, *Daughters of Emptiness: Poems of Chinese Buddhist Nuns* (Wisdom Press), and an analytical study in preparation ("Remarkable Women: Female Chan Masters of Seventeenth-Century China").

ture of the female body, and is conceived and practiced in a unique and different way. Women as the representatives of cosmic yin follow different methods of internal cultivation than men. They still embody the various forces and gods of the universe, but work with them in a uniquely feminine mode. This mode is not better or worse than the masculine one, but simply other; it is a variant manifestation of the cosmic truth.

Part Three

Women's Transformation

Chapter Eight

The Inner Landscape

In this third part of the study, the focus shifts again, now towards the understanding of the female body in the Daoist religion and its role in women's transformation to immortality. Unlike the earlier sections, which focused on the lives of divine and human subjects, this part deals mainly with cosmology, the vision of inner alchemy, the processes of transcendence undergone by men and women, and the particular experiences of Daoist women in their quest toward realization.

In all these aspects, the body is central—the body not only as the inert, material base for spiritual refinement, but the body as the key expression and manifestation of individualized cosmic *qi* in this world. The vision of the body as a confluence of processes is strongly present even outside of Daoism. In Chinese representative art it is nearly impossible to find statues of the human body along the lines of ancient Greek or modern sculptors which celebrate its form with great anatomical detail. On the contrary, Chinese sculpture tends to veil the body under garments and covers, effacing its shape and displaying its overall impression, allowing the viewer an opportunity to glimpse inner movement. In the same way, Chinese paintings depict airy personages, almost transparent in looks, sketching a feeling of cosmic flow and ignoring the fleshy body of humanity. More than to its material aspects, the Chinese when regarding the body have paid attention to its inner dynamics, its energetic qualities, and patterns of *qi* circulation.

Body Cosmology

Seen dominantly in terms of *qi*, the human body in traditional China was organized and classified according to numerology and its potential medical and spiritual transformations. Ancient physicians, though well versed in human anatomy, were less interested in the solid, material structure of the body than in its energetic workings. The firm inner building blocks of bones, muscles, and organs were known and accepted, yet formed merely a framework for what really counted: the dynamic interaction of *qi* in its various forms and circulation patterns. Even the *Zhuangzi* emphasizes that "human life is the accumulation of *qi*, death is its dispersal" (ch. 27). Daoist texts on the cultivation of life echo this and heavily emphasize the refinement of *qi* for the attainment of immortality.[1]

Qi in the human body appears as the complementary forces of yin and yang, which correspond to night and day, shadow and light, resting and moving, feminine and masculine, tiger and dragon, mercury and lead, and so on. They cannot exist without one another but continuously engender and develop in mutual interaction, moving in cycles of days and seasons, of inner circulation and outer rhythm. They are further subdivided into categories of lesser and greater and associated with the five phases (*wuxing*), which are symbolic representations of their developmental patterns. In this more complex form, the phases of *qi* are set into a relationship with the key organs of the human body, its senses, structural parts, psychological agents, and emotions:

---

[1] Examples of such texts are the *Yangsheng yaoji* (Essential Collection on Nourishing Life), a fourth-century text ascribed to the *Liezi* commentator Zhang Zhan that survives in fragments and citations (see Stein 1999); the *Yangxing yanming lu* (Record of Nourishing Inner Nature and Extending Life, DZ 838), ascribed to the first Highest Clarity patriarch Tao Hongjing (456-536) or alternately to the Tang physician Sun Simiao (581-682) (see Mugitani 1987; Switkin 1977); and the *Fuqi jingyi lun* (The Essential Meaning of the Absorption of *Qi*, DZ 277) by Sima Chengzhen, dat. 730s (see Engelhardt 1987).

qi	lesser yang	greater yang	yin/yang	lesser yin	greater yin
phase	wood	fire	earth	metal	Water
organ	liver	heart	spleen	lungs	kidneys
senses	vision	touch	taste	smelling	hearing
structure	muscles	pulse	flesh	skin	bones
psych.	spirit soul	spirit	intention	material soul	will
emotions	anger	excessive joy	worry	sadness	fear

This complex map of the human body is further associated with the cosmology of the greater universe and linked, among others, with seasons, directions, colors, planets, and weather patterns:

qi	lesser yang	greater yang	yin/yang	lesser yin	greater yin
season	spring	summer	Early fall	fall	winter
direction	east	south	center	west	north
color	green	red	yellow	white	black
planet	Jupiter	Mars	Saturn	Venus	Mercury
weather	windy	hot	humid	dry	cold

Understanding the world through this correspondence chart means that things and beings are seen less as specific individual entities and more in terms of relationships and dynamic interactions. As a result, the connection between, for example, the liver and the heart is understood as analogous to that between spring and summer, green and red, vision and touch. This kind of correspondence thinking, which was also well known to the ancient Greeks before they developed formal logic, rests on synchronicity and "impulse and response" (*ganying*) rather than on linear models of causality and temporal unfolding (see Graham 1986). It places human beings into the network of the cosmos, seeing them as replicas of larger structures and patterning human existence in a wider framework. Already the Han-dynasty work *Huainanzi* (Writings of the Prince of Huainan, DZ 1184) likens the body to the cosmos, the head resembling heaven, the feet looking like the earth. It says:

> The roundness of the head is an image of heaven, the squareness of the feet is the pattern of earth. Heaven has four seasons, five phases, nine directions, and 360 days. Human beings have

four limbs, five organs, nine orifices, and 360 joints. Heaven
has wind, rain, cold, and heat. Human beings have the actions
of giving, taking, joy, and anger. The gall bladder corresponds
to the clouds, the lungs to the breath, the liver to the wind, the
kidneys to the rain, and the spleen to the thunder. (*Huainanzi*,
ch. 7)[2]

The main tradition to map the flow of *qi* through the body was Chinese
medicine, which added a set of six digestive viscera (*fu*) to the five basic
organs (*zang*) of the body. The complete set of key inner energy centers
consisted of the following:

yin organs	liver	heart	spleen	lungs	kidneys
yang viscera	gall bladder	sm. intestine	stomach	lg. intestine	bladder

Added to these five was the triple heater (*sanjiao*), a *qi*-transforming organ located above the stomach and responsible for heating the upper,
central, and lower sections of the body. The five yin organs enable the
body to center and store *qi* and are considered the more important agents
for health, long life, and immortality. The six yang viscera, due to their
more active nature, are associated with acts of moving and transforming,
such as the digestion of food and the distillation of blood and body fluids.

All organs and viscera were further associated with "meridians" (*mai*) or
conduits of *qi*, which connected the organ in the torso with the extremities (hands and feet) and charted the flow of vital energy along specific
lines (see Porkert 1974; Sivin 1988; Liu 1988). These lines were seen as
analogous to the "arteries" of the earth, described and analyzed by geo-
mancers or specialists of "wind and water" (*fengshui*). In all cases, it was
essential that *qi* flow as freely and smoothly as possible, both within the

---

[2] A similar description of the body is also found in the *Chunqiu fanlu* (Mis-
cellaneous Notes on the Spring and Autumn Annals) by Dong Zhongshu of the
Later Han (ch. 13; Chan 1963, 280-82). In Daoist texts, the same sentiments are
echoed in the *Huangting jing* (see Homann 1971, 28-31). For discussions of the
body in Daoism, see Kohn 1991; Andersen 1994; Schipper 1978; 1994; Kroll 1996;
Saso 1997; Bumbacher 2001. For studies and translations of the *Huainanzi*, see
Roth 1992; Le Blanc and Mathieu 1992; Major 1993; Larre et al. 1993.

body and within nature and the greater universe. Shamanistic dances as well as Daoist gymnastics—at times following strikingly similar patterns—both fulfill the function of opening greater and lesser energy lines on the cosmic and human levels (Despeux 1989, 238).

In more formal Daoist practice, the inner landscape of the body was further seen in terms of the palaces and passageways of the body gods, who were first visualized by medieval practitioners of Highest Clarity. According to the fourth-century *Huangting jing* (Yellow Court Scripture, DZ 331, 332), the celestial headquarters within is located in the head and matches the immortals' paradise of Mount Kunlun. It is envisioned as a large, luscious mountain surrounded by a wide lake and covered with splendid palaces and wondrous orchards. The eyes, identified as the sun and the moon, are also the Kunlun palaces of the Queen Mother of the West and the Lord King of the East (see Homann 1971; Kroll 1996; Kohn 1993, 181-88).

Between the eyes and slightly inside the skull is the Hall of Light (*mingtang*), one of nine palaces in the head (see Kalinowski 1985). It can be reached by passing through the deep, dark valley of the nose and is guarded by the two high towers of the ears. To attain entry one has to sound the gong or musical stone placed in those towers through an exercise called "beating the heavenly drum." With both palms covering the ears, the index and middle fingers are snapped to sound against the back of the skull. A sound not unlike distant drumming is produced through the reverberations, and the gates of the Hall of Light open. Passing through this important inner hall, adepts reach the Grotto Chamber (*dongfang*), and from there proceed to the central palace in the head, the residence of Lord Niwan. This is also the upper cinnabar field and a major location of elixir transformation.

Going in the opposite direction from the eyes and following the deep, dark valley of the nose downward, adepts come first to a small lake, i.e., the mouth. This lake regulates the water level of the upper lake in the head and raises or lowers it as necessary. Crossing the lower lake over a central bridge, the tongue, adepts reach the deeper regions of the body. First there is the Twelve-Storied Tower (throat), then come the Scarlet Palace (heart), the Yellow Court (spleen), the Imperial Granary (stomach), the Purple Chamber (gall), and other starry palaces transposed into the depth of the human body. Going ever deeper, another cosmic region is reached. Here is yet another representation of the sun and the moon, i.e., the left and right kidney. Beneath them, the huge ocean of energy extends with another replica of the central axis, Mount Kunlun, in its midst.[3]

Body Charts in Inner Alchemy

This vision of the body as a network of celestial palaces and passage-ways continued actively in Daoism and was a key model in inner al-chemy. It is described especially in a section of the *Chongyang zhenren jinguan yusuo jue* (Master Chongyang's Instructions on the Golden Gate and Jade Lock, DZ 1156), a record of questions and answers from the early phases of Complete Perfection (Tsui 1991, 41-48). The text outlines a mystical journey along an inner river, where the practitioner encoun-ters three torrents—representing the three teachings of Confucianism, Buddhism, and Daoism—that will carry him or her to enlightenment and immortality if use is made of the raft created by the six perfect virtues and good karma of the past. Moving steadily along through inner culti-vation, the adept will eventually come to a large mountain where he is again faced with the three teachings, this time represented by three ani-mals: a gray ox for Lord Lao, a white ram for Confucius, and a yellow deer for the Buddha. These animals lead the practitioner into the sacred city where he or she can visit grottoes, worship at temples, and attain the higher stages of the practice (18b-19a; Kohn 1993, 175-77).[4]

---

[3] The placement of two separate axes within one human body is a way of integrating the opposing meditation postures and contradictory images of the universe noted above. For a detailed discussion of the geography of the body in Daoism and its relation to various meditations, see Schipper 1994, 105-10.

[4] The three torrents and three animals are Complete Perfection variants of the Three Vehicles of Buddhism: listener, personal cultivator, and bodhisattva. For their adaptation in medieval Daoism, see Ōfuchi 1979b.

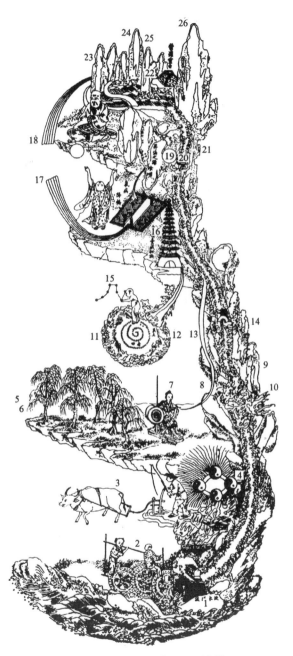

Fig. 11: The "Chart of Inner Passageways." Source: *Neijing tu*.

There are numerous charts and visual representations of the inner land-scape (see Despeux 1990, 189-98; 1994; Baryosher-Chemouny 1996). Prominent among them is the *Neijing tu* (Chart of Inner Passageways), recorded on a stone stele in the Baiyun guan in Beijing and dated to the late nineteenth century (see Fig. 11). In a body that could be either male or female, the head in this chart represents Mount Kunlun, the residence of the highest Daoist deities as well as the upper cinnabar field (*dantian*), a key processing chamber of the inner elixir. It connects to the rest of the body through a broad river, indicating the spinal column and the Gov-erning Vessel (*dumai*), the central *qi*-line along the back of the body.

At its lower end, a well-sweep with two wheels (the sun and the moon) is depicted, run by two children who stand for yin and yang. The image suggests the meditative practice of reversing the current of *qi* so that it moves upward along the spine to nourish the head.[5] In the abdomen, a symbol of four yin-yang balls shows the lower cinnabar field and essen-tial alchemical cauldron. Next to it, the ox plowing stands for the effort one makes to activate and increase one's sexual essence or *jing*, the fun-damental form of *qi* to be refined.

Above this, next to a grove of trees that represents the liver and gall bladder, the cosmic Weaver Maid is spinning her yarn, while the spiral beyond her shows the central cinnabar field with the Herd Boy wielding the Northern Dipper. Associated with two stars in Chinese folklore, the two are the archetypical lovers who, as noted earlier, meet only once a year on the seventh day of the seventh month. Here they are mythologi-cal representations of interior yin and yang. The central cinnabar field, next, is located in the solar plexus and activated by *qi* as saliva flowing down the throat, shown as a twelve-storied tower. Just as the river along the spinal column shows the ascent of *qi* towards the head, so the throat and the various centers along the front of the torso represent the down-ward movement of *qi* in preparation for the next round of refinement. In the jaw and face area, furthermore, the diagram shows two figures, a Buddhist monk with his hands raised in supplication and a Daoist mas-

---

[5] A similar design of a well-sweep is also found in the *Xiuzhen shishu* (Ten Books on the Cultivation of Perfection, DZ 363). The commentary notes that "the proper *qi* of the north strides on the wheels of the sun and the moon, activated night and day by removing the inner water and activating the inner fire" (9.3b).

ter sitting in meditation. They show the integration and cooperation of the two teachings in the attainment of inner refinement and cosmic realization.[6]

Several earlier representations of *qi*-flow in the human body depict the entire body as a mountain with a big yin-yang river on the inside. This imagery goes back to the notion of mountains as a place of retreat and a primary route to the divine. Their mediating position between heaven and earth and their vertical structure invite the ascent to otherworldly spheres (see Stein 1990; Miura 1983), so that mountains often appear as major passageways to the origin of life, cosmic chaos, and the paradises of the immortals. The agricultural imagery, moreover, shows the parallels between the interior cultivation of *qi* and the sowing, planting, and harvesting of the land, the taming and controlling of nature with the help of various devices and through regular and painstaking efforts. Only by carefully working with the flow of nature and the body can fertility and prosperity be attained, and the ideal state of cosmic harmony and transcendence be reached.

The oldest body-as-mountain image dates from 1227 and is contained in the *Duren jing neiyi* (Inner Meaning of the Scripture of Universal Salvation, DZ 90; see Fig. 12). It is entitled "Diagram of the Ascent and Descent of Yang and Yin in the Human Body" and shows the Ocean of *Qi* at the very bottom, rising up in waves on the right and left to the Yellow Court and the Gate of Life—all major acupuncture points and important locations of Daoist palaces. From there the two central meridians that run along the spine and the front of the body are depicted as a flowing river connected by a twelve-storied tower, representing the movement of *qi* as it is increasingly refined within.

In the middle of the circular stream, the image shows the divine palace of the god Wuying, serving as the immortal womb below. Above is the Jade Chamber, where further refinement takes place. The mountain on

---

[6] For more discussion, see Louis Komjathy, "Mapping the Daoist Body: The *Neijing tu* and the Daoist Internal Landscape," forthcoming in *Daoist Cultivation: Traditional Models and Contemporary Practices*, edited by Louis Komjathy.

Fig. 12: The flow of yin and yang in the human body, depicted as a mountain.
Source: *Duren jing neiyi*.

the very top is again Kunlun, rising above even the Jade Capital in the
Daoist heavens. The entire image is crowned by Mysterious Heaven, the
stage of utter oneness with the cosmic powers.

Not only showing the mystical, alchemical properties of the *qi*-flow
body, the diagram also intends to outline the spiritual process of the adepts. The *Duren jing neiyi* says:

> The body contains heaven and earth, the furnace and the stove.
> Its central place is the alchemical cauldron, while beyond it is
> the great void. Its Qian [heaven trigram] Palace is the sea of
> marrow; its Kun [earth trigram] Palace is the chamber of es-
> sence; its Divine Chamber is the alchemical cauldron. These
> are called the Three Palaces.

> Qian and Kun are the warp and woof of heaven and earth with yin and yang circulating through their midst. Heaven and earth are the great forge, yin and yang are the pivots of transformation, and the unified *qi* is the great medicine. To refine the elixir, use your inner male and female, yang and yin *qi* and circulate them all around the inner stars until they form the alchemical vessel. The Metal Mother resides right there and through wondrous transformations stimulates the *qi* of life.
>
> As yin and yang move in response with each other, we speak of refinement. As the yang essence expands daily and perfect spirit transforms, we speak of the holy womb. As yin gradually dissolves and yang comes to reside in utmost purity, we speak of the immortal embryo. This is the Great One embracing perfection, in harmony with emptiness and nonbeing, fully returning to the nonultimate state. (pref., 8b-9a)

Another, similar image is also found in the *Shangyangzi jindan dayao tu* (Shangyangzi's Illustrated Great Essentials of the Golden Elixir, DZ 1068), a major text associated with Chen Zhixu or Shangyangzi (1289-ca. 1335). Known as the "Representation of the Body of Original *Qi*," this diagram is clearly related to the one found in the *Duren jing neiyi*—either as its direct heir or as an alternate version based on the same source

The chart shows essentially the same image as the earlier one, depicting the Ocean of *Qi*, the circular flow of energy, as well as the various gates, towers, and mountainous peaks of the body. Beyond the earlier version, however, it also includes alchemical terminology for the various locations: the Ocean of *Qi* is called the Sea of Suffering and while the Yellow Court and the Gate of Life are still essential, the diagram also notes that the area behind the kidneys is the Primordial Pass, below the Chamber of Essence and the Double Pass. The solar plexus, underneath the Jade Chamber, is called the Gate of Heaven and matched by the Pass of Yang on the back of the body. Above them is the Gate of Gold, representative of the mouth, from where the stream rises up to the Jade Mountain and the Niwan Palace in the head. Mysterious Heaven is renamed Highest Mystery, still shown at the very top in the form of a craggy mountain range (3a).

In addition to seeing the body as a mountain, envisioning the mountain in the body was another way of creating a mythical, alchemical representation. A good example is found in the *Xiuzhen taiji hunyuan tu* (Illustrations of the Cultivation of Perfection to Reach the Great Ultimate and Chaos Prime, DZ 149), a collection of sacred diagrams with explanations and cultivation methods compiled by the Song master Xiao Daocun on the basis of instructions from Shi Jianwu, a ninth-century Daoist of Pure Brightness (see Baryosher-Chemouny 1996, 20-28).

According to one image found here, the body contains four sets of mountains: the peaked continent of "dust and grime" at its base and three sets of celestial realms above it. The base mountain has the Purple Prefecture towards its top, which represents the Palace of Purple Tenuity, the residence of the central ruler of the Northern Dipper and potentate of the universe. This is the starting point of celestial transformation. From here, cultivation transforms the person into a resident of three celestial mountain areas, going from the lower world of the Mysterious Pass, the Red City, and the Peach Spring through the middle realm of Mount Kunlun, with its Hanging Gardens, Hibiscus Flowers, and Turquoise Pond, to the immortals' isles of Penglai, Fangzhang, and Yingzhou. As the text says:

> Whenever a practitioner sublimates her *qi* into spirit, sheds her shell and ascends to heaven as an immortal, she first has an audience with the Great Emperor of Purple Tenuity, who evaluates her origins and bears witness to her successful endeavors. She then comes to reside on a lesser isle of the immortals and gradually ascends to the higher spheres. (8ab; Baryosher-Chemouny 1996, 150-52)

A later variant of the same theme is found in the *Daoyuan yiqi jing* (Scripture of the Unique *Qi* of Dao Origin, ZW 87), dated to 1636. Here again the entire body is a cosmic mountain, shown as it rises from the waters. The main emphasis is on the upward movement of *qi* along the spinal column, drawn by the three chariots that symbolize the three teachings or again the three energetic forces in the human body. The three chariots are also prominent in women's texts on inner alchemy, such as the Qing-dynasty manual *Nü jindan* (Women's Golden Elixir, ed. Tao 1989,57-122; ZW 871). The text says:

> In the alchemical way, we make much use of inversions, as symbolized by the hexagram Tai [Peace], where Kun [Earth] is above and Qian [Heaven] is below. Because of these inversions, heaven and earth can be rejoined and the myriad beings be pervaded. Unless you know how to pull the ram chariot in its inverted direction, all your yin *qi* will be blocked and obstructed. Then how can you ever get rid of the turbid yin and come to envision your celestial heart? . . .

> Just as the sun rises at the Fusang tree east of the great ocean, so the fiery wheel of *qi* continues to move and work without stopping. The deer chariot carries the *qi* upward to the summit of Mount Kunlun [head], and the flowing mercury returns naturally to the Spirit Hall [heart]. The deer chariot is the perfect intention that allows one to overcome all obstacles. (2.26a, 2.28a; ZW 26.423, 423-24)

The body in inner alchemy and in specific texts describing women's practice is, therefore, imagined as the seat of complex cosmic forms and patterns that interact in various ways and involve the presence and activity of deities and essential forces. It consists of flowing and moving processes that work together in a variety of ways and have to be cultivated and controlled to enable adepts to transform into immortals.

The Female Center

Within this cosmic, *qi*-flow body, both men and women have specific areas and forces that are fundamental for alchemical transformation. Inner alchemy in general aims at the transformation of the three energetic forces *jing* (essence), *qi* (energy), and *shen* (spirit), and makes strong use of the three cinnabar or elixir fields located in the head, chest, and abdomen as the major cauldrons of transmutation. In men, the fundamental force of *jing* is identified as semen and its first alchemical refinement takes place in the lower cinnabar field. In women, *jing* is replaced by *xue* (blood) and the holy enterprise begins with the middle cinnabar field in the breasts, the central area where *qi* assembles and from where it sinks down to either turn into menses or be refined along the spinal column (Despeux 1990, 203-11; see also Skar and Pregadio 2000).

The earliest emphasis on the breasts as the key spiritual center in women is found in a Tang hagiography of the Han Daoist Pei Xuanren, contained in the Song encyclopedia *Yunji qiqian*. According to this,

> after having practiced concentration and purified their thoughts, both men and women can equally practice the Dao of long life. They should maintain close secrecy of all methods and not transmit them except to the wise. Men and women equally cultivate their vital *qi*, collecting and nourishing their semen or blood respectively. (105.3a)

Both men and women begin their practice with the discipline of meditation to strengthen their intention and their *qi*, and gain spiritual detachment from the senses and all earthly affairs. To do so, they first clap their teeth to announce their practice to the gods, then chant an incantation that calls upon the divinities of the universe to fortify and support them. After this,

> men guard their kidneys and stabilize their semen, refining it into *qi* by moving it up the spine and into the Niwan Palace. This is called "return to the origin."

> Women guard their heart and nurture their spirit, refining it into fire by sitting motionless and making the *qi* descend from the nipples to the kidneys. From here they move it up along the spine to equally reach the Niwan Palace. This is called "transmutation to perfection."

> As they nourish [the *qi*], the elixir forms equally in either. After a hundred days, it opens to the numinous. Practicing over extensive periods, one naturally attains long life on this world and the state of no death. (*Yunji qiqian* 105.3b)

This shows the fundamental equality in the practice and attainment of inner alchemy for both men and women, the main difference being the location of the female center in the heart and breast area.

From the Song dynasty onward, the importance of the breasts in women's practice is well documented. For example, in the preface of the

Ziyang zhenren Wuzhen pian sanzhu (Three Commentaries on "Awakening Perfection" by the Perfected of Purple Yang, DZ 142), dated to 1169, Sun Xueshi says:

> When women cultivate immortality, they begin by focusing on their breasts [lit. "milk chambers"] as the location of vital *qi*. This method is quite simple. In men, the cultivation of immortality is called the refinement of *qi*; in women it is called the refinement of the body.
>
> When women practice cultivation and refinement, they begin by accumulating *qi* in their breasts. Then they set up the cauldron and establish the furnace. They commence the methods of refining the body through great yin. This is the easiest way of attaining the Dao. (4a)

Later texts echo this statement, frequently referring to the breasts as the center of female cultivation and emphasizing the "refinement of great yin" as the goal of the practice. They also place importance on a starting point known as the Cavern of *Qi*, which is located between the breasts. In men the equivalent point is called Yin Meeting and is located at the perineum. The *Nü jindan* has the following description:

> The Cavern of *Qi* is where the menses originate. It is found at the breasts, more precisely, in the area between them, about 1.3 inches from each. It is not identical with the nipples. In men, destiny resides in the lower cinnabar field; this is their Cavern of *Qi*. In women, it resides in the breasts; this is their Cavern of *Qi*.
>
> When yang reaches its high point it transforms into yin. From the Cavern of *Qi* the yin blood [of the menses] originates and eventually flows out of the body. This is why, in order to decapitate the red dragon, one should begin one's inner work at the place where yin [blood] originates. (2.21a; ZW 26.420)

According to other writings, another important element is the Flow of Milk (*ruxi*) located on the inside of each nipple. Two eighteenth-century manuals discuss the issue and set the trend for later works. The *Niwan Li zushi nüzong shuangxiu baofa* (Precious Raft of Women's Dual Cultivation According to Patriarch Li Niwan, ed. Tao 1989, 433-57; ZW 357), hereafter abbreviated *Shuangxiu baofa*, describes the nipple glands as the source of yin secretions to be activated in this part of the body (17b; ZW 10.541). Also called the Double Pass (*shuangguan*), these glands are further discussed in the *Xiwang mu nüxiu zhengtu shize* (Ten Rules of the Queen Mother of the West on the Proper Path of Women's Cultivation, ed. Tao 1989, 407-32; ZW 883), abbreviated *Nüxiu zhengtu*:

> When the spirit pours into the Double Pass, secretions arise on its inside and begin to emerge. Viscous like oil, they gradually transform and flow to the Southern Sea [the heart]. . .
>
> [Commentary:] The Double Pass is located behind the [spinal] column and before the [heart] palace. It has two points where secretions accumulate. (9b; ZW 10.537)

This matches the general Chinese view that breast milk is a vital fluid of high potency, cultivated even by officials under the medieval Jin dynasty, such as Zhang Cang (275-206) who is mentioned in Ge Hong's *Baopuzi neipian* (ch. 5).

Breasts in inner alchemy are the location where secretions of perfect yin originate. They normally descend into the abdomen and transform into menstrual blood.[7] According to the sixth rule in the *Nüxiu zhengtu*, "the breasts communicate above with the secretions of the heart and the lungs, below with those of the Ocean of Blood" (9b; ZW 10.537). This sets up a relationship between breast milk of a white color and menstrual blood, which is red. The great Ming-dynasty physician Li Shizhen (1518-1593) in his *Bencao gangmu* (Comprehensive Compendium of Materia Medica) says accordingly:

> Breast milk transforms into menses, just as the word for "breast" (*ru*) contains the character *fu*, which means "transformation." It is often described metaphorically as "immortals' liquor," "blood-producing agent," or "white cinnabar."
>
> Milk is a transformation of yin-blood, created in the spleen and the stomach and maintained in the Governing and Conception Vessels. After conception it comes to rest in the womb to nour-

---

[7] Some sources in regard to this issue use the term "grease" or "numinous grease" to refer to the secretions of the breasts. E.g., *Nüdan shize* 1a; ZW 26.455.

ish the embryo; after birth the red transforms into white and produces lactation. Such are the mysteries of transformation and metamorphosis. (ch. 52)

Beyond breast milk and secretions, the texts mention three key locations in the female body which appear as purple, white, and yellow lights. The yellow light corresponds to the lower cinnabar field, the place in the abdomen where the elixir is created; the white light matches the energetic position where the embryo begins to grow; and the purple light indicates the yang cavern where the blood arises. Located right above each other, in ordinary women they serve the downward move of *qi* and effect the energetic exchange of yang into yin, producing menstrual blood. In inner alchemy this is reversed. As the *Nü jindan* says: "To cultivate successfully, adepts should move the *qi* from the cinnabar field at the bottom to the yang cavern above. As they warm it regularly with inner fire, the menses will become yellow and eventually turn white, which in turn transforms into formlessness" (2.20b; 26.420).

The three lights go back to the Three Simplicities (Sansu) of the Highest Clarity school. They are the three daughters of the Goddess of Great Simplicity (Taisu yuanjun), known as the Goddesses of Purple, Yellow, and White Simplicity. They are also the mothers of the gods Wuying, Baiyuan, and Lord Lao who reside in the heart, abdomen and spleen respectively (Robinet 1984, 2:135). Another mythological link of the three lights are the Three Passes, located in women along the Conception Vessel (*renmai*) in front of the body, whereas in men they are on the Governing Vessel that runs along the spine: the coccyx, the seventh dorsal vertebra, and the occiput at the base of the skull. They, moreover, correspond to the attainment of residence on different isles of the immortals (*Xiuzhen taiji huandan tu*, 8b).

The female center in the human body is located mainly in the breast area. Here great yin resides and emerges either as secretions or as an energy flow towards the abdomen, where it transforms into menstrual blood. The alchemical process pursued by women is essentially the same as in men, but the location of their energetic base and transformative centers is different and the basic circulation of *qi* varies accordingly. Similarly, the basic forces and patterns of alchemical transformation are essentially the same yet formally different.

Basic Forces

The key force at the beginning of alchemical transmutation is *jing*, often translated as "essence" or as "semen" in men. Defined as neither yin nor yang but a force that mediates between them, *jing* is the indeterminate aspect of *qi* and can be described as *qi* in transition from one determinate form to another (Porkert 1974, 176-79; Kaptchuk 1983, 55-57; Jarrett 2000, 47-48). It can, therefore, appear as semen in the sense that it carries vital power from the parents to the growing offspring. It can also be the essence that the body takes from food during digestion, at a time when the food has not yet been fully assimilated.

Like great yin in women that arises in the breasts and descends to the abdomen, *jing* in men is a transformed form of pure *qi* that has sunk down and coalesced into sexual fluid. Ordinary people tend to emit *jing* in sexual intercourse which causes weakness over time or when done to excess. Practitioners of immortality retain and replenish it instead and attain long life and vigor. As *Shangyangzi jindan dayao* (Master Shang-yang's Great Essentials of the Golden Elixir, DZ 1067) of the thirteenth century says:

> Once *jing* is replenished, *qi* will be strong. When *qi* is strong, *shen* will be powerful. When *shen* is powerful, the whole body enjoys good health and is rarely sick. On the inside, the five organs blossom; on the outside, the skin is moist and glossy. The face is luminous and vibrant, the eyes and ears are alert and acute. Even while growing older, one still increases in vigor as one's *qi* remains firm and strong. (3.2ab)[8]

Thus *jing* is seen as the key vital force whose waste or cultivation will determine the fate and power of all other body energies as well as the overall health and aging of the individual. Only when *jing* is replenished

---

[8] The text also notes that the highest quantity of *jing* in a male is about 1.6 liters, reached at the age of sixteen. With effort it can be increased to about 3 liters, but most people instead lose it at the rate of 0.05 liters with every emission and thus decline towards death (3.1b).

and made strong can *qi* and *shen* be fully active. They in turn ensure that the body is healthy and vibrant and that long life is attained.

Jing in women, too, is predominantly sexual energy and determines physical growth and decline. It arises early in life, peaks at puberty, and weakens as menopause approaches. As the medical classic *Huangdi neijing suwen* (The Yellow Emperor's Classic of Internal Medicine, Simple Questions) says:

> When a girl is 7 years old, the kidney *qi* [*jing*] becomes abundant. She begins to change her teeth and the hair grows longer. At 14, she begins to menstruate and can get pregnant. The movement of the great pulse is strong. The menses come regularly, and the girl is able to give birth.

> At age 21, the *qi* is steady, the last tooth has come out, and she is fully grown. When she reaches the age of 28, her tendons and bones are strong, her hair has reached its full length, and her body is flourishing and fertile. At 35, her yang brightness pulse begins to slacken, her face begins to wrinkle, her hair starts falling out.

> When she reaches the age of 42, the pulse of the three yang regions deteriorates in the upper part of her body, her face is wrinkled, and her hair turns gray. At age 49, she can no longer become pregnant, and the circulation of the great pulse slows. Her menstruation is exhausted, and the gates of blood are no longer open. Her body declines, and she can bear children no more. (ch. 1; Veith 1972, 98-99; see also Ni 1995)

In inner alchemy, female *jing* or kidney *qi* is identified as menstrual blood. This emphasis matches medical thinking which attributes the growth of the embryo in the womb to the accumulation of menstrual blood and sees the sex of the baby in terms of the dominance and early arrival of either semen or menses at conception (Waltner 1990, 30). As the *Chushi yishu* (Transmitted Writings of Master Chu), a collection ascribed to the medieval physician Chu Cheng, says:

> When man and woman unite, their *jing* are both joyful. If yin-blood arrives first, yang-semen dashes against it, the blood opens to wrap around the semen. Semen enters, making bone, and a male child is formed.

If, on the other hand, yang *qi* arrives first and yin-blood later
joins it, semen opens to surround blood. Blood enters to make
the foundation, and a female child is formed. (*Shuofu* 74.14b;
Furth 1999, 210; also *Nü jindan* 2.21b, ZW 26.420)

The importance of blood as an alchemical ingredient in women first appears in the *Daoshu* of the eleventh century. It notes that the "red snow"
in women is modified by their *jing* as blood, and that they therefore can
grow children in their wombs. But this womb *jing* can also be transformed into higher forms of energy (3.5a). It is a truly wondrous substance, created in the uterus near the lower cinnabar field where during
puberty a star or pearl begins to form, called "the utmost treasure of pre-
heaven" (*Nüxiu zhengtu* 4b; ZW 10.534).

Every month at a certain time, this white pearl turns red and gives rise to
the menstrual flow, but it still remains intact as the inner reserve of primordial *qi* and can be reconstituted to permanent whiteness through alchemical practice. Menstrual blood, called the "monthly flow" or
"monthly affair" in ordinary language, is thus seen as a valuable substance in alchemical sources and named "trusted flow" (*xinshui*) or "celestial endpoint" (*tiangui*). The *Nüdan cuoyao* (Comprehensive Essentials
of Women's Alchemy), contained in the nineteenth-century collection
Nüdan hebian (Combined Works on Women's Alchemy) describes the
amounts of primordial *qi* and menstrual fluid as they change with
woman's age and spiritual activity. For example, blood dries up around
age 49, so that supplementary measures such as herbal compounds and
massages become necessary (3a).

To refine the vital force, it is circulated through the body along the microcosmic orbit (*xiao zhoutian*), made up of the Governor and Conception
Vessels running up along the spine and down in front of the torso. To do
so properly, the various outer orifices of the body have to be closed, neither allowing *jing* to escape nor outside energies to enter. Most commonly seven orifices are described in the face (ears, eyes, nostrils, and
mouth) plus two at the base of the pelvis. The seven orifices of the face
correspond to the stars of the Northern Dipper (*Huangdi neijing lingshu*,
ch. 78). In one Daoist view, as expressed in the *Huangting jing*, they are
activated by the divinities of the Dipper during gestation (DZ 332, 3.1b).

Opening the embryo to the cosmic powers, the orifices are important venues for communication and interaction, allowing different aspects of celestial nature to enter the growing human body. At the same time, once the person is in the world, the orifices become a potential source of leakage and a danger to alchemical transformation.

The same holds true for other body passageways, notably the skin and the major acupuncture points, through which negative influences might enter and empowering *qi* might escape. In alchemical literature they are called either "passes" (*guan*) or "officials" (*guan*) and considered like the sense organs, i.e., active participants in the life of the body that can be either beneficial or detrimental. This continues an understanding of the body in administrative terms that can be traced back to the ancient philosophical work *Guanzi* (Writings of Master Guan; see Roth 1999). It says:

> The heart occupies the position of the ruler. The nine orifices are his officials. The heart is the residence of the Dao, and the orifices obey its principles. As long as the heart does not actively try to direct the orifices, they are well ordered. Similarly, as long as the ruler does not try to direct the five kinds of administrators, the world is well governed. (ch. 13)

While the body functions well along its natural lines, it is essential to alchemical practice to make sure the orifices are open to the correct celestial stimuli but closed when the inner transformation is going on (Pregadio 1991, 88). There is ample literature on the dangers of leaking valuable *qi* through various openings, physical, sensory, and emotional. Already the *Daode jing* says to "block the openings, close the doors" (ch. 56), indicating the body's orifices as power points of *qi*, where essences can escape from the system. The eyes especially are regarded as a great source of potential harm. Adepts should keep them closed and direct their vision inward toward the refinement of *jing*. To be successful in the great work, the body has to become a sealed world, an integrated organism complete in itself. As the alchemical cauldron is closed during the transformation, the body has to be shuttered through the active retention of sexual fluids, breath, and emotions. Only then can the vital force be refined and the resulting *qi* circulate properly along the broad river of the inner landscape to nurture the paradise of Kunlun within.

Chapter Nine

Women's Inner Alchemy

Inner alchemy (*neidan*) grew from practices of interior cultivation under the influence of operative or "outer alchemy" (*waidan*). It replaces the physical materials of the cauldron with the internal energies of the body. It has been the dominant form of Daoist cultivation since the Song dynasty and has brought forth, especially in the last three centuries, a corpus of literature specially geared toward the transformation of women. Works of this sort rely on the same concepts as instructions written for men but add a different slant, making women's inner alchemy a highly sophisticated and unique form of religious realization.

Outer Alchemy and Inner Alchemy

Outer alchemy can be traced back to the Han dynasty, when it was practiced by the *fangshi* and supported by various emperors hopeful to find the elixir of eternal life (Despeux 1990, 71-76). Its most detailed description is found in Ge Hong's *Baopuzi neipian* of the early fourth century. A passionate seeker of alchemical and immortality methods, he spent much time researching different ways of elixir concoction, outlining various lengthy and complicated procedures that involved creating a chemical reaction on the basis of highly disparate and often poisonous substances.

They included pine needles, pine resin, mushrooms, persimmons, apricot kernels, deer antlers, mother-of-pearl, mica, aconite, realgar, sulfur, mercury, arsenic, silver, and gold. These various materials, which sometimes took years to collect, were then cooked according to revealed, cosmic instructions. They were placed in a cauldron coated with various luting compounds and surrounded by magical and protective devices to ensure the proper atmosphere for the elixir to grow (see Sivin 1968).

Over many months and even years, the right times of firing and cooling, stirring and burying had to be observed to the minutest detail. The process was thought to imitate the growth of gold in the earth on a microcosmic scale, and accordingly followed the stages of cosmic creation as it was perceived at the time (see Ware 1966). Not only was it complicated and highly secret, but the raw materials were often hard to find and very costly. As an alternative, Ge Hong suggested the creation of an elixir on the basis of "yin cinnabar" (*yindan*), a substance identified as the seminal essence that resides in the body and that later became central in inner alchemy (chs. 6, 13).

Despite these early inklings and the various meditative transformations practiced by followers of Highest Clarity, "inner alchemy" as a separate concept does not appear until the sixth century when it is mentioned in the writings of the Buddhist master Huisi (515-577; see Magnin 1979). The term also appears in the biography of the Daoist Su Xuanlang, aka Qingxiazi, who lived in the Qingxia Valley on Mount Luofu in the sixth century (Chen 1975, 2:389, 435). According to the *Luofu shan zhi* (Gazetteer of Mount Luofu), once when Su's disciples were discussing the attainment of immortality through the ingestion of a wondrous fungus, he laughed and said:

> This wondrous fungus is found inside the eight luminants of
> the human body and harvested in the Yellow Chamber. There
> is no mushroom even before heaven and earth. It is nothing
> but the product of creative imagination accompanied by su-
> preme delight. (*Gujin tushu jicheng* 240.17-9b)

To illustrate this point, Su wrote a "Guide to the Dao" and his disciples described his methods as "inner alchemy."

Despite these early references, *neidan* as an integrated and systematic practice does not appear in the literature until the late Tang dynasty and is first associated with the figure of Zhang Guo, one of the Eight Immortals. Called to court under Emperor Xuanzong, he supposedly anticipated a complex doctrine that transposed outer alchemical systems of transformation into the interior of the body (Yetts 1916, 784-89). While this information comes from later legends, the fact is that in the late Tang the cost of alchemical ingredients had risen astronomically and several emperors died from a concoction of mercury and arsenic, making the enterprise both difficult and unpopular. A shift toward internalization avoided both issues and can be clearly discerned in this period (Pregadio 2000, 170). Still, even then operative alchemy continued to be practiced, as records of the Yuan and Ming dynasties indicate.[1]

Women also engaged in the practice of outer alchemy, although details of their techniques are not commonly described. One example is the Tang Daoist Bian Dongxuan, originally from the area near Mount Mao. She refused to marry and was expelled by her family. An official's household took her in as a weaver and she worked hard day and night until she could afford the drugs and ingredients necessary for the elixir. Later she came to reside in the Dongxuan guan (Monastery of Deepest Mystery), where she erected an altar to the Heavenly Worthy and concocted the divine elixir. Upon taking it, she experienced nausea, vomiting, and diarrhea—common symptoms of mercury poisoning—but still persisted in her effort, never allowing herself to be discontented or disillusioned.

One day, an old man with a canvas bag full of "the great reverted cinnabar" arrived at the temple and told Bian Dongxuan: "The Highest Lord has sent me to call on you. Go and find a proper place, erect a shrine, and within seven days you will ascend to Heaven." She attained full realization and rose to the immortals, appearing to Emperor Xuanzong in a vision on the day of her transformation. The emperor renamed her institution Dengxian guan (Monastery of the Immortal's Ascension), gave the formal title Ziyun lou (Tower of the Purple Clouds) to the shrine she

---

[1] Outer alchemy as practiced in a Daoist monastery is mentioned in the Buddhist *Bianwei lu* of the Yuan dynasty (T. 2116, 52.767ab), and several alchemical furnaces were discovered in the tomb of a Ming Daoist from Sichuan (Despeux 1990, 73). Records of its practice are found through the ages, and even today. Among twentieth-century alchemists, especially Chen Yingning (1880-1969) and Meng Naichang (d. 1989) stand out.

erected, and had a stele inscription composed in her honor (*Taiping guangji* 63.392; Cahill 2000, 211-16).

While Bian Dongxuan is the most famous woman practitioner of outer alchemy, there are others. The *Daoxue zhuan* of the sixth century describes the practice of the Highest Clarity adept Xiao Lianzhen, who concocted a longevity drug on the basis of plant substances, such as cypress leaves, mulberry, and atractylis (Bumbacher 2000a, 504). The *Tongjian houji* notes that Lady Wang of the sixth century successfully concocted a potent cinnabar elixir; the Tang priest Li Zhenduo created an elixir on Mount Hualin; and Yang Baozong of the tenth century cured people with the help of cinnabar pills (3.2b; 2.10b; 5.19b). However, these remain isolated cases, based on anecdotal information and there is no reason to assume that there was an organized women's tradition of outer alchemy such as evolved later for the practice of women's inner alchemy.

The first traces of the latter are found in the Song dynasty, whose official records on ordained Daoists survive to the present day. According to these, women made up about three to four percent of the total Daoist population (Yoshioka 1970, 136):

Year	Men	Women
1019	7,081	89
1021	19,606	731
1033	19,548	588
1042	19,680	502
1068	18,746	738
1077	18,513	708

This represents a great reduction in numbers in comparison to the Tang dynasty, when women made up as much as one third of the ordained clergy. It was not until after the Song and with the emergence of Complete Perfection that again rose to prominence in the religion.

Works on Women's Alchemy

The most visible manifestation of this prominence is the emergence of sections or chapters in works on inner alchemy dealing specifically with women's practice. In addition, a new form of Daoist literature developed that dealt exclusively with women's inner alchemy. These texts appeared in the Ming and Qing dynasties in conjunction with a vastly expanded culture of women's literacy and publications (Ko 1994, 29-30). Some were collections of women's practice poems, associated with Sun Buer, Cao Wenyi, He Xiangu, and other famous masters (see Cleary 1989). Others were works by dedicated male adepts who, inspired by the practices of the women around them, described the methods they used.

The great bulk of texts on women's inner alchemy dates from the late eighteenth and nineteenth centuries (Despeux 1990, 163-82; 2000, 396-98). They tended to be centered on specific holy mountains and Daoist institutions, and were often revealed through the planchette (*fuji*) in spirit-writing sessions. Not unlike shamans and visionaries of Highest Clarity, practitioners would enter into trances and receive messages from gods or immortals, predicting life expectancy, good fortune, and examination topics, as well as recipes for rain-making, healing, and alchemical transformation.

Widely popular among people from all different social strata, spirit-writing was common both in Daoist monasteries and lay organizations. A given institution or group might dedicate a separate hall to the practice, offering it to its favorite celestial communicant. The hall usually contained a square table, which held the planchette, tray covered with sand or incense ashes that was connected to a three-pronged stick for writing. Before inviting the spirit to descend, devotees offered food or flowers, burned incense, drew talismans, recited incantations, and underwent ceremonies of purification. As the spirit entered the medium, his or her stick began to move automatically, tracing characters on the planchette. One person then recited the characters aloud while another wrote them down (Esposito 2000, 648).

Specialized texts on women's inner alchemy were revealed primarily by Sun Buer and to a lesser degree by He Xiangu. Commonly the teachings were traced back through the patriarchs of Complete Perfection and the sage women of Highest Clarity to their ultimate origin with the Queen Mother of the West. Surviving texts on women's alchemy include about thirty works of uneven length, both in prose and poetry and date from 1745 to 1892.

Four major centers with different compilers can be distinguished:

1. Mount Jin'gai in Jiangxi, where Shen Yibing (aka Qingyun, 1708-1786) resided as patriarch of a Longmen subsect and received Daoist teachings from the mysterious sage Li Niwan. Both he and his successor Min Yide (1758-1836) edited books that contained texts on women's alchemy.

2. Mount Zhaoyang and the Qingyang Temple in Sichuan, where Fu Jinquan (1765-1845) and He Longxiang collected numerous texts.

3. Mount Qingcheng in Sichuan, where Yi Xinying (1896-1976) served as supervisor of the Tianshi dong and assembled about ten texts on women's practice.

4. The city of Shanghai, where the Daoist master Chen Yingning (1880-1969) headed the Institute for Immortal Learning and edited numerous texts and a journal with a wide circulation.

Texts from Mount Jin'gai

The oldest known collection containing works on women's inner alchemy is Min Yide's *Daozang xubian* (Supplement to the Daoist Canon), which dates from 1834 and also contains the inner-alchemical classic *Taiyi jinhua zongzhi* (Great Unity's Instructions on [Developing] Golden Florescence, ZW 334; JHL 94), a text translated by Richard Wilhelm and C. G. Jung under the title "The Secret of the Golden Flower"(1929; see also Cleary 1992; Mori 2002).

The collection contains two major works. First is the *Xiwang mu nüxiu zhengtu shize* (Ten Rules of the Queen Mother of the West on the Proper Path of Women's Cultivation, ed. Tao 1989, 407-32; ZW 356), attributed to Lü Dongbin, revealed by Sun Buer, and transmitted to Shen Yibing in a spirit-writing séance of the year 1799 under the original title *Nü jindan jue* (Women's Formula of the Golden Elixir). Usually abbreviated *Nüxiu zhengtu*, this text presents ten rules about women's practice, beginning with the nine women's precepts of the *Chuzhen jie*. Following this, it describes the basic principles involved understanding "original destiny" and the "source of inner nature," then discusses the "cultivation of interior pathways" and the "return and recovery" of the inner elixir. Moving on to a discussion of more concrete practices, the text focuses on the "breasts," the "jade fluid," and the practice of "embryo respiration." It ends with two sections describing methods of celestial communication and various precautions to be taken in the course of the practice. Overall, the work is a comprehensive presentation of basic cultivation techniques of calming the mind and "decapitating the red dragon" with the help of breast massages, visualization of energy pathways, breathing exercises, and various meditations (Despeux 1990, 301-2; Needham 1983, 237-39).

The second women's text contained in the *Daozang xubian* is the *Niwan Li zushi nüzong shuangxiu baofa* (Precious Raft of Women's Dual Cultivation According to Patriarch Li Niwan, ed. Tao 1989, 433-57; ZW357), subtitled *Nügong zhinan* (A Compass of Women's Practice). It goes back to Li Niwan, a semi-legendary Longmen figure, whom some identify as the Tang alchemist and immortal Li Babai, others as the Imperial Lord of Lesser Yang (Shaoyang dijun). According to legend, he began to work miracles in the Song dynasty. In 1069, on his way from Sichuan to Suzhou, he passed by the house of a poor man named Wu who was deeply distraught by the death of his mother. Stopped by the moans and groans coming from the hut, Li Niwan entered, massaged the mother's body with mud and sprayed it with warm water. As a result, she revived. From this event he received his agnomen Niwan, "Mudpill" (*Jin'gai xindeng* 8.481-49b).

Li appeared variously in the following dynasties and began to communicate with Shen Yibing in 1723. After receiving formal ordination eight years later, Shen revived the local cult to Li and eventually received his work on women's practice, to which he wrote a commentary. The book was reedited by Min Yide in 1830 and included in the *Daozang xubian* (Despeux 1990, 294). Li Niwan's text consists of nine rules which systematically describe the progressive transformation of the adept's body. It begins with calming and purifying the spirit, then moves on to increas-

ing the circulation of *qi* with the help of breast massages and visualization exercises. Eventually the practice leads to the accumulation of wisdom, the increase in inner emptiness and the formation of a new body of
light within. The ninth rule emphasizes that women can undertake the
path while still actively pursuing household tasks and repeats the virtues
they are to cultivate: filial piety, obedience, meekness, softness, and so on
(Needham et al. 1983, 290-94).

Both these early texts on women's inner alchemy show a fair amount of
Buddhist tantric influence. This influence is typical for the southern
school of Daoism in the wake of Bai Yuchan (1194-ca. 1227) and also appears in other inner-alchemical texts, such as the *Xingming guizhi* (Jade
Principles of Inner Nature and Destiny, ZW 314; JHL 67), a sixteenth-
century compendium that uses numerous mantras and visualizations of
Guanyin (1.89; see Darga 1999). Similarly, the *Nüxiu zhengtu* refers to a
meditation that involves the goddess Tara, a deity—not unlike Marīcī—
popular in Buddhist and Daoist circles whose power could eliminate
desires and open the practitioner to the infinite light of the buddhas.

Another aspect of women's practice on Mount Jin'gai is documented in
Min Yide's *Jin'gai xindeng* (The Mind-Lamp Transmission of Mount
Jin'gai; see Esposito 2000, 630), which records various hagiographies of
successful female practitioners. According to this, the local Longmen
subsect had integrated a female cult of the Song, dedicated to Hu Caicai,
the daughter of a Daoist master who appeared variously in planchette
sessions, and to the Purple Lady (Zigu), known best as the mistress of
latrines.

The hagiographies also emphasize the life of Jiang Yuncheng, the wife of
the precepts master Lü Yunyin. She cultivated the Dao by reciting the
Huangting jing and received visions and texts from Wei Huacun. One of
her disciples was Wang Xiaoqi, the young daughter of a local official who,
in 1711, had a spiritual encounter with the Purple Lady and received a
sacred text from her. Another local woman, Miao Miaozhen received a
sacred revelation by Sun Buer when she visited a shrine dedicated to Lü
Dongbin on Mount Jin'gai. She followed alchemical practices and engaged in visualizations and excursions to the Dipper, ascending to
heaven in 1816 (6.27-38; 7.75-85). Overall, the record suggests that
women's practice was very much alive on Mount Jin'gai, and it is not

surprising that the first recorded texts on their alchemical techniques were collected there.

Sichuan as a Center for Women's Practice

Another major center of women's alchemical literature was Sichuan, notably the Qingyang gong (Gray Sheep Temple), the major Daoist institution in Chengdu. Here women's practice is described first in the compilations of Fu Jinquan (b. 1765): *Daoshu shiqi zhong* (Seventeen Collections of Secret Daoist Texts), a collection of inner alchemical manuals and poetry published in 1825 (Needham et al. 1983, 240; Esposito 2000, 637); and *Nü jindan fayao* (Methods and Principles of Women's Golden Elixir, JH 48), which contains poems and prose texts attributed to Sun Buer. Fu emphasizes both the importance of jointly cultivating the Dao with somebody else and the necessity of performing virtuous acts. Women must purify their karma, repent their sins, and cultivate goodness, sincerity, filial piety and proper wifely devotion.

Many of the texts found in these two collections were later integrated into the *Nüdan hebian* (Collected Edition of Works on Women's Alchemy, ed. Tao 1989, 1-188). This collection contains some of the important sources used in this study, such as the *Nüdan shize*, the *Nü jindan*, and the *Nügong lianji huandan tushuo*. The *Nüdan shize* (Ten Rules on Women's Alchemy, ed. Tao 1989, 17-52; ZW 883) consists, as the title suggests, of ten rules regarding women's alchemical practice, focusing on issues of nurturing perfection and transforming *qi*, ninefold reversion and embryo respiration, meritorious actions and strong determination, as well as recovery of spirit and ascension to heaven.

The *Nü jindan* (Women's Golden Elixir, ed. Tao 1989, 57-122; ZW 871, 878) was written in 1892 by Zhenyizi from Yongzhong in Sichuan, based on questions from his disciples. It consists of two *juan* (scrolls), the first of which deals with precepts and behavioral rules, following the model of the ten precepts of the *Chuzhen jie*. The second *juan* details interior practice in twenty-four sections. It begins with "gathering the mind," proceeds through "nourishing inner nature," "nourishing *qi*," "concentrating the spirit," and "the three centers of destiny," to a discussion of the "Cavern of *Qi*," the "firing times," the "decapitation of the red dragon," the "pursuit of the elixir," the practice of "self-cultivation," and eventually presents information on the growth of the inner embryo and ascension as an immortal.

The *Nügong lianji huandan tushuo* (Illustrated Explanation on Reverting the Cinnabar and Refining the Self in Women's Practice, ed. Tao 1989, 125-40; ZW 880), approximately dated to 1900, is a shorter treatise that begins with an illustration of a meditating woman and contains a general summary of the inner alchemical process for women (Despeux 1990, 296-98).

In addition, a number of relevant materials were included in the 1906 Qingyang gong edition of the *Daozang jiyao* (Epitome of the Daoist Canon) by He Longxiang. In his preface, He notes that he spent thirty years collecting and compiling the texts of this collection, based on the practices undertaken by the Daoist women in his family. The materials consist of twenty texts, between one and twenty pages in length and written in both prose and poetry. Practically all go back to spirit-writing séances and are attributed to gods or immortals including Lü Dongbin, Sun Buer, He Xiangu, a lady attendant of Xiwang mu, the Buddha of infinite kalpas, and the Buddha of Mount Qinglie. In some cases the transcriber's name is mentioned, such as Zhenyizi of Yongzhong, the venerable Yuexi of Guangzhou, Chen Yongqing of Shanxi, and Fu Jinquan. The texts outline the stages of the inner alchemical path and describe the energy pathways with great precision. They also make clear distinctions between men's and women's practices and, among the latter, differentiate according to their sexual status: virginal, mature, or post-menopause.

Another major location of women's practice in Sichuan is Mount Qingcheng, home of Yi Xinying (1896-1965). Originally called Liangde, he was also known as Daolilun. Born on September 26, 1896, as the son of a Sichuan farmer, he was frequently ill. In search of healing he joined the Changdao guan (Monastery of the Eternal Dao) on Mount Qingcheng in 1913. There he studied with Wei Zhiling, the twenty-first patriarch of the Dantai bidong (Turquoise Grotto of the Elixir Terrace) subsect of the Longmen branch. This subsect had been established in Sichuan in 1669 on the basis of a Daoist school from Mount Wudang and was given its formal appellation in 1700 by the Kangxi Emperor. Succeeding his master, Yi Xinying became patriarch and abbot in 1930. He was well known not only for his inner alchemical practice but also for his literary achievements and close contacts to both literati and scholars of Daoism, such as Chen Yingning, Chen Guofu, and Meng Wentong.

After the communist takeover in 1949, he dedicated himself to the rescue of Daoism. In 1956, he moved to Beijing to help organize the Chinese Daoist Association. In 1962, he became the head of the Sichuan Daoist Association and also taught a course on Daoist rituals and retreats at Beijing's Baiyun guan. A dedicated scholar, he compiled the *Nüzi daojiao congshu* (Collection of Daoist Writings for Women). This consists of eleven texts, two works from the *Daozang xubian*, one work on women's liturgy, one text on women's Daoist lineages, and several descriptions of body transmutation, interception of menses, and interior cultivation (Qing 1994, 406). In addition, he also edited the *Daojiao sanzi jing* (Daoist Three Character Classic), the *Daoxue keben* (Daoist Studies Primer), the *Qingcheng zhinan* (Guide to Mount Qingcheng), and the *Laozi tongyi* (Pervasive Explanation of the *Daode jing*) (see Li 1993).

Developed and promoted by these various masters at the great centers of the Qingyang gong and Mount Qingcheng, Sichuan was a major hub of Daoist activity and cultivation. It proved a great resource for information on women's practice and has provided the most comprehensive collections and presentations on the subject.

The Life and Work of Chen Yingning

A Daoist center of a different sort was established in Shanghai in the 1930s under the leadership of Chen Yingning (1880-1969). Originally from a small town on the Anhui-Jiangxi border, his given name was Zhixiang, aka Yuanshan. He adopted the name Yingning after becoming immersed in Daoism, using a phrase from the *Zhuangzi* that refers to the inner tranquility of the mind and its ability to overcome disturbances.

The offspring of a learned family, whose members included both medical doctors and Confucian teachers, Chen received a traditional education and took the initial state examination at age fifteen in 1895. However, at the time he was stricken by a wasting disease that left him weak and near death. Assuming it to be caused by an overindulgence in academic pursuits, he tried different healing modalities and also began to work with Daoist self-cultivation. After convalescing, he moved on to study natural sciences and even went to law school for some time. However, his disease returned in 1907, and he decided to seriously dedicate himself to Daoist learning. Financially supported by his sister's husband, he traveled to many mountains to train in immortality practices. Following his sister's household, he moved to Shanghai in 1912, where he gained access to the Daoist canon at the local Baiyun guan and immersed himself in the textual study of the tradition. Over the years, he became both erudite and accomplished in practice, also undertaking partner work with his wife Wu Yizhu, a gynecologist and professor of Western medicine.

In 1933, his disciple Zhang Zhuming founded a Daoist journal, the *Yangshan banyue kan* (Biweekly Journal to Promote the Good). Chen served as its main contributor and chief editor. Its publication was well received. It opened a broad forum for the discussion of Daoist practices nationwide, providing information and support to several thousand subscribers.

Chen also edited numerous Daoist texts and worked hard to make Daoism more accessible to the public. An alchemist and expert interior practitioner, he was well versed also in women's practice and edited and annotated a number of special texts and poems dedicated to women. He was the first to connect the *Dadao ge* with the Song poet Cao Wenyi (Chen 1939) and was a pioneer in creating a taxonomy of inner alchemy. He edited Sun Buer's poems in a collection that was partially translated by Thomas Cleary (Chen 1934; Cleary 1989), reprinted a treatise on heterodox schools and controversial practices (Chen 1939), and created the *Nüzi daoxue xiao congshu* (Elementary Collection on Women's Daoist Learning; Chen 1935-39). This important collection included the *Nügong zhengfa* (Proper Methods of Women's Practice, ed. Tao 1989, 458-70), a short text revealed by Lü Dongbin in 1880 that is based on the *Nüxiu zhengtu*, and various other works of importance, such as the *Nüdan shize* and the *Kunning jing*.

Besides his writing, Chen also served as an organizer and administrator. Although his main emphasis was on Daoism as a personal practice for health and spiritual cultivation, he also supported local temples and helped revive and expand Daoist institutions. In 1938, he founded the Institute for Immortal Learning (Xianxue yuan), where he became a frequent lecturer and seminar leader. Beyond that, he worked on a committee for the organization of the first Chinese Daoist Association, which was founded in 1936, and became a leader of the Shanghai Daoist Association, which was created in the 1930s and refounded in 1947.

Chen's life changed after the war, mainly because of the untimely death of his wife in 1945. Since he had remained childless, he took to staying with friends, disciples, and relatives, moving to a different city every few years. While continuing his theoretical and historical studies, he also got involved with the budding Qigong movement and began lecturing at rehabilitation centers and giving workshops at Qigong clinics. In 1961, he became the secretary general of the reestablished Chinese Daoist Association, working in Beijing. However, he fell severely ill after the Cultural Revolution began in 1966, and with inadequate medical care and his disciples deported to reform camps, he was left alone in his suffering. He died on May 23, 1969 (Liu 2001, ch. 1; Xu and Yuan 1976).

Chen Yingning is one of the most important Daoist figures of the twentieth century. His collections and editions of Daoist texts have inspired scholars for several generations; his personal dedication to the practice has been a leading light for masters and practitioners. His work has been reedited and reprinted since the 1980s, and his vision of women's practice shapes much of our understanding today.

Dual Cultivation

The various texts edited by these masters describe not only the procedures of women's inner alchemy but also outline the worldview at the center of the practice. They focus particularly on the two concepts *xing* and *ming*, most commonly translated as "inner nature" and "destiny." They refer to spirit and body, being and becoming, the spiritual and the sexual aspects of life. They are also correlated with the heart and kidneys, the physical organs Chinese medicine associates with spirit and sexual energy.

Historically the two concepts go back to the *Yijing* (Book of Changes; trl Wilhelm 1950), an ancient Zhou-dynasty divination manual that was revived in Song Neo-Confucianism (see Smith et al. 1990). Daoists adopted the concepts *xing* and *ming* from this background and reinterpreted them in terms of spiritual realization rather than communal and cosmic harmony. According to the Daoist understanding, it is essential to cultivate them both equally, an idea expressed in the phrase *xingming shuangxiu*, the "dual cultivation of inner nature and destiny." However, the term *shuangxiu*, especially in the Ming dynasty, also came to refer to sexual cultivation and was used as an alternative way of indicating the "arts of the bedchamber" (*fangzhong shu*). Instead of "dual" cultivation, one can therefore speak of "duo" or "twosome" cultivation (Despeux 1990, 223-27).

Some alchemical schools rejected sexual partner practice; others integrated it into their system. The Northern traditions, including Complete Perfection, generally favored celibacy and sexual abstinence; they encouraged their followers to work with their own inner sexual energies and remain independent of the outer support of a partner. For them, the union of yin and yang took place inside the adept's body, and sexual energy was not to be used outwardly. The Southern traditions, on the other hand, made use of sexual intercourse in their practice, and a few late-Ming texts document the details of their arrangements, including the set-up of the sacred chamber—a complex affair with numerous rooms and altars dedicated to a variety of deities and lineage masters—the necessity for proper worship and secrecy, the way to procure young women to be trained formally in the practice, and other concrete measures.[2]

However, as time went on, in the Ming dynasty an increasing openness regarding sexual matters developed. Both sexually explicit woodblock prints and pornographic novels rose to the fore, and in inner alchemy the two tendencies began to converge. Different strands and lineages

---

[2] See the *Xinxin xiangyin* (The Hidden Transmission Heart to Heart), *Sanfeng danjue* (Elixir Instructions of Master Sanfeng, ZW 380), *Jindan zhenzhuan* (Perfect Transmission of the Golden Elixir, ZW 398, 858), and *Daoyuan yiqi jing* (ZW 87). A study of these texts is found in Liu 2001.

evolved that could no longer be clearly identified in terms of their sexual practices. Some strongly sexual schools did not put their teachings into writing, while others publicly condemned bedroom arts yet undertook them in private. Documents emerged that rejected sexual methods up front but then discussed them in some detail in their midst. Some texts defended the practice openly and strove to delimit it clearly from marital relations and the bedroom arts. Others emphasized the spiritual dimension of twosome practice and its benefits for women, described as equal and competent partners in the great work.

In texts on women's inner alchemy, the two attitudes for and against sexual practices coexist. The earliest two texts, from Mount Jin'gai contained in the *Daozang xubian*, clearly see inner alchemy as involving the actual intercourse between partners. For example, Rule Three of Li Niwan's work addresses Sun Buer by saying: "The utmost Dao is not found in solitary practice; all things of the same type support each other in mutual interaction. Outside of your body, there is another body; once one is forgotten, the other is free from all affairs" (*Shuangxiu baofa*, 19b; ZW 10.542). Similarly the *Nüdan yaoyan* (Essential Words on Women's Alchemy), contained in the *Nüdan hebian*, emphasizes the importance of twosome cultivation. It says:

> You should know that the desire of women is stronger than that of men. Once the monthly flow stops, her heart is like a blossoming lotus bud. It benefits from rain and dew and begins to grow its fruit.

> A woman without a man is yin in isolation—it cannot bring forth a lotus blossom. Unless she receives the benefit of rain and dew, she is like a field without manure: useless. (1b; Despeux 1990)

A similar tenet is also expressed in two poems attributed to Sun Buer. The first is contained in Chen Yingning's *Sun Buer nüdan shizhu*. It says:

> Weather like in early spring, a balmy breeze is reaching out,
> The sun illuminates the Jiangnan hermit's hut,
> Encouraging the plums of winter to burst into bloom—
> Pure in mind, the man encounters the blossom of his heart.
> (2.13a; Chen 1934; Clearly 1989, 85)

The second is found in the *Sun Buer yuanjun gongfu cidi* (The Practice Stages of Lady Sun Buer, ed. Tao 1989, 282-88):

> You have to have a partner to return to Penglai.
> It is hard to climb the blue cliffs all alone.
> If you make solitary stillness your sole practice,
> You'll face the weak waters without a proper boat.
> (11a; Cleary 1989, 87; Despeux 1990)

While these texts insist on the need for a partner and favor sexual cultivation, they also give strong representation to the ritual and ascetic aspect of the practice. Thus, the physical joining of bodies is in all cases accompanied by formal offerings to the gods and masters, visualizations of protective deities, and the complete abstention from all lascivious thoughts.

Beyond the general affirmation of twosome cultivation, some texts on women's practice also condemn it. For example, the *Pangmen lu* (Record of Heterodox Schools, ed. Chen 1935) contains a prayer to the ancient Buddha of Resonating Light and Universal Transformation, accompanied by the following statement:

> Those who erroneously believe that the pursuit of perfection involves twosome activities ignore the fact that yin and yang are originally contained within the body. They accordingly acquire concubines, sleep with prostitutes, and practice the "gathering through battle," hoping to rob someone else of her primordial *qi* in order to supplement their own essence and spirit. How can they ever become the guests of the immortals on Penglai? On the contrary, such people are rascals, greedy and licentious in their deeds. (1a; Despeux 1990, 226)

The same pattern of both affirmation and negation of sexual practice is also present in the hagiography of Lü Dongbin (see Katz 2000) as described in the late-Ming novel *Dongyou ji* (Journey to the East). Written by Wu Yuantai (fl. 1566) in the mid-sixteenth century, this is a story about the Eight Immortals as they travel east toward realizing the Dao. Detailing the life of Lü Dongbin, the novel tells how he is highly attracted to the prostitute White Peony (Bai mudan) and engages in a sexual relationship with her. Discovered and reprimanded by the Chan master Yellow Dragon (Huanglong), who confiscates his sword, Lü swears off the practice and vows to remain abstinent for nine years. White Peony, in the meantime, is taught proper cultivation and attains immortality.

Within this framework the "dual cultivation" of *xing* and *ming* has several meanings. For the Northern tradition, it means beginning the alchemical work by cultivating one's inner nature through the purification of spirit. Once the vision of inner nature is sufficiently pure, certain sensations arise naturally in the body and it is time to work on physiological sublimation. For the Southern school, on the contrary, dual cultivation means taking one's first steps by refining the body through sexual methods—eventually reaching a point where one has become fully detached from desire and sensory stimuli. This is the sign that one needs partner-based techniques no longer and can move on to pursue the path of spiritual attainment and the cultivation of inner nature. A third version, moreover, asserts that "dual cultivation" is best achieved when both aspects of the human being are refined simultaneously, through the sublimation of both body and mind to higher levels of purity.

Despite these differences of opinion and the varieties of cultivation techniques, *xing* and *ming* are generally seen as closely connected. There is no essential or substantive difference between them along the lines of the Western body-mind dichotomy. The two simply indicate different aspects of the same basic phenomenon; they should be intimately linked and merged into one integrated unity. As perception becomes clearer the unfolding of the adept's spiritual side brings with it physical transformations as well as a new understanding of body and self. Similarly, all physical changes effected by the practice bring about a new evolution of the inner psychological state. Attention can then be focused on the inside of the body and create a movement of internal *qi*—integrating intention and sensation, body and spirit. In other words, even if a strong conceptual distinction between *xing* and *ming* is made in the beginning of the alchemical path, the two inevitably integrate as the work proceeds. The more the body is sublimated, the more consciousness becomes light, radiant, and open, until it dissolves into cosmic emptiness.

Meditation

However many details there may be in terms of methods and exact procedures, the foundation of all alchemical practice lies with a spiritual disposition, which is systematically strengthened through daily exercises of quiet sitting (*jingzuo*), the Complete Perfection form of meditation (Despeux 1990, 227-30). Continuing Tang-dynasty methods and adapting concrete techniques from Chan Buddhism, this involves sitting quietly in a cross-legged position, preferably the lotus posture, with the spine erect and both knees and buttocks firmly on the ground. The eyes are either closed or lowered, and the tongue is placed against the upper palate to facilitate the connection of the Governing and Conception Vessels.

Men typically rest their hands in their lap, while women who focus more on the chest area hold their hands up over their breasts to massage them (see Fig. 14).

The seated posture in Daoist meditation became standard under Buddhist influence but did not fully replace the more traditional posture, in which the adept lies on his or her side with the head supported on a folded arm, a posture still used in the twentieth century (see Eberhard and Morrison 1973, pl. 42). Other positions also included standing in a steady pose or walking slowly around—all still used in contemporary Qigong practice.

In either position, Daoist meditation begins with an exercise in concentration, usually achieved by focusing on the breath, either as it enters and leaves the nostrils or as it expands and contracts the diaphragm. This creates a focus of stillness and serenity in the body and gradually absorbs the practitioner to a point where all sensory impulses are ignored. As Wang Chongyang describes it in his *Chongyang lijiao shiwu lun* (Chongyang's Fifteen Articles on Establishing the Teaching, DZ 1233):

Fig. 14: Seated meditation, with the characteristic hand positions for men and women. Source: *Neiwai gong tushuo jiyao*.

7. Sitting Straight

"Sitting straight" does not simply mean to sit with the body erect and eyes closed. That is superficial sitting. To truly sit you must maintain a mind like Mount Tai, unmovable and unshakable at all hours of the day, whether staying, walking, sitting, or lying down, in all forms of activity and repose.

Control and shut off the four gates of the senses—eyes, ears, mouth, and nose. Never let the outside world come in! If there is even a trace of a thought about activity and repose, this is no longer quiet sitting. If you can attain such a mind, although your body may remain in the world of dust, your name has already been entered in the ranks of the immortals. (Yao 1980, 80; Reiter 1985, 42; Kohn 1993, 89-90)

Another aspect of Daoist meditation is *guan* or "observation," a practice described in Tang texts, such as Sima Chengzhen's *Zuowang lun* (Discourse on Sitting in Oblivion, DZ 1036; Kohn 1987). It means that from a strong basis in stillness and sensory absorption, practitioners learn to see the world with the new eyes of the Dao, letting their Dao-nature shine forth instead of depending on personal evaluations and egoistic desires. They begin with a critical examination of their psychological constitution, studying the state of their mind and spirit, body and physical form, to understand that they are originally pure cosmic forces that were distorted by egoistic, personal desires.

Gradually adepts overcome the ordinary mind (*xin*) and replace it with the pure mind or spirit (*shen*). Spirit is understood as the primordial, formless, and ever-changing force of life, which in connection with the physical body causes human beings to be alive. It occurs in its most concentrated form in the heart and ideally works through the human mind to govern life perfectly.

However, people get sidetracked through sensory involvement, and the pure spirit is transformed into an opinionated and limited mind, dependent on the data from the senses. Confused and defiled, human beings need to be taught how to recover the primordial state. Both spirit and mind are associated with the heart, also called *xin*, and represent different aspects of consciousness—one evaluative and critical, essential for day-to-day survival in the ordinary world, the other flowing smoothly and open to all stimuli, a manifestation of the Dao within (Kohn 1989b, 196). In inner alchemy, *xing* and *ming* are both contained in the spirit, and the mind needs to be purified—concentrated and stabilized—so that they can arise in their original form. Thus the *Neilian danjue* (Secrets of the Elixir of Inner Refinement, DZ 240), a Ming text associated with the Song master Zhang Boduan (983-1082), says:

Basically there is no other art than the ability to concentrate the mind. Thus, when demons and spirits appear in visions, this is just because there are thoughts in the mind. If the mind is free from thoughts, then the spirits' numen cannot be activated. If even the spirits do not know my mind, how much less can I myself know its workings? Thus stability and concentration of the mind are the root of practice. (1.4a)

This is a state of deep inner quietude and complete unknowing. Through prolonged practice, adepts are freed from passions and desires, thoughts and considerations, and come to realize that they are nothing but manifestations of cosmic *qi*. Gaining deep absorption into stillness they "sit in oblivion" (*zuowang*; see Kohn 1987; Liu Ming 2001) and achieve a state where they completely "drive out perception and intellect, cast off form, do away with understanding, and become identical with the Great Thoroughfare" (*Zhuangzi*, ch. 6). They recover the purity of spirit and allow it to radiate freely in all their actions, achieving a new and wider identity as part of the universe. This eventually leads to the ability to leave the ordinary self and earthly body behind and ecstatically travel to the heavens and immortals. As Wu Yun (d. 787), the Tang mystic and poet, says in his *Xinmu lun* (On Mind and Eyes, DZ 1038):

> Resting in serenity and silence,
> I listen to Pure Harmony.
> Engulfed in obscurity and darkness,
> I see the Light of Dawn.
> Going along with all beings,
> I too follow the cycle.
> Containing my inner radiance,
> I close up all the gates. (4b; Kohn 1998b, 151)

Women practitioners of inner alchemy also followed this ideal of refining the mind into spirit through meditative practice. A Complete Perfection poem contained in the *Caotang ji* (Collection of the Grass Hut, DZ 1143) is dedicated to a Maid Zhao. It says:

> On the path of cultivation, just be straight,
> Cut off cravings and desires and all wayward thoughts,
> Never submit to sensory tangles or the Three Deathbringers—
> And your body will be light.
> Sitting, lying down, standing, or walking about,
> Always rest in oblivion, tranquil and so pure,
> And one morning you will suddenly radiate with numinosity—

Clear and bright and sparkling brilliant. (27b)

This echoes the instructions in the *Chongyang lijiao shiwu lun*, which also emphasize that "whether staying, walking, sitting, or lying down, if the mind is constantly controlled, hearing and seeing, knowing and perceiving are merely sickness and affliction" and that a mind in a state of deep tranquility and rest is immovable. The text continues:

> Obscure and abstruse, it never even sees the myriad beings. Dark and vague, it never knows inside or outside. There is not the slightest trace of thought or imagination. This is the concentrated spirit, beyond the need for control. (Sect. 8)

This depth and absorption of spirit eliminates the ordinary mind from the practitioner's world. It is a state beyond all thinking and emoting, and is frequently described in texts on women's alchemy as essential for the success of the higher transformation. It also appears in poems dedicated to women, such as one by Ma Danyang to Lady Sun, found in the collection *Jianwu ji* (Anthology of Gradual Awakening, DZ 1142; Ren and Zhong 1991, 897-98). It says:

> I exhort you, Lady Sun, to cultivate the great Dao:
> Continuously hold on to your field of mind,
> To sweep away, eradicate the Three Deathbringers and six fatigues,
> Become free from all afflictions and rest in clarity and purity—
> Finally know the depth of all wonders!
> Stop asking about the different names of stove and furnace,
> Harmonize and penetrate above, below;
> Invert the flow of things—
> And through lead and mercury
> Spontaneously create the utmost treasure.
> How marvelous!
> Enveloped in hazy radiance,
> You rise up and return to Penglai isle. (1.4b)

The practice of meditation is thus essential in the attainment of inner alchemical goals. It begins with concentration and following the breath, then moves on to observation of the workings of the mind and the senses, and eventually leads to complete stillness and wondrous vision within. While there is a feeling of progress and the formal survey of meditative practices apparently provides a straightforward, linear approach to attainment, inner alchemy both employs and rejects this organized vision. It makes heavy use of meditation as a preparation for the internal transformation of *xing* and *ming*, but it also avoids seeing any particular method as the sole or even most direct path to deliverance.

In its rejection of meditation as a systematic endeavor, inner alchemy follows the Chan Buddhist model, according to which sitting in meditation in order to attain enlightenment is like polishing a brick in order to make a mirror—impossible (Despeux 1981, 34-35). The ultimate attainment is not something that results from any systematic, progressive practice but comes of itself. Practice just lays the foundation for events that occur on a completely different and more subtle plane. Most alchemical literature accordingly engages in symbolic language with multiple referents, complex images, and patterns of inversion, interpreting both Buddhist and traditional Daoist concepts in a new and often unanticipated way.

Chapter Ten

Stages of Attainment

On the solid foundation of meditative absorption, but not solely carried by it, the practitioner undergoes three major stages of attainment as described in works of the major lineages of Complete Perfection under the Ming and Qing dynasties. He or she begins by refining *jing*, sexual energy, into *qi*, cosmic energy, and from there into *shen*, spirit. Spirit eventually merges with the eternal Dao, and becomes one with the emptiness of the greater universe. This state is the attainment of transcendence and immortality, and manifests as the complete, unfettered freedom from the world.

The Male Model

For men, this means that they must avoid losing *jing* as semen through ejaculation, and instead retain it and reverse its flow, making it move up the Governing Vessel along the spinal column "to nourish the brain." The brain, according to Chinese traditional medicine, is the Ocean of Marrow, and marrow is *jing* as manifest in the bones. Every time *jing* is lost through sexual activity, therefore, the brain, the bones of the head, and the skeleton of the body are weakened and become more brittle (Despeux 1990, 237-41).

Moreover, the *jing* that travels up the spine is not the semen that would be ejaculated during sexual intercourse but its refined form, the *qi* from which the semen arose in the first place. Semen is white in color and essentially of yin quality, in that respect similar to menstrual blood in women. Once its flow is reversed and it begins to move upward, it gains a yang quality that transforms it back into *qi*. At the top of the head, the reversed *jing* unites with other yin secretions of the body and descends again through the Conception Vessel along the front of the torso to the lower cinnabar field, also known as the Ocean of *Qi* and a major energy storage center or yin repository in the body.

This process of *qi*-circulation around the torso is the microcosmic orbit. Its more extensive version, that includes also the circulation of *qi* through the extremities and all the way to the feet, is called the "macrocosmic orbit." Both are still practiced today (see Chia 1983; 1985). Accompanied by rhythmic breathing and the periodic holding of breath, this *qi*-circulation is practiced in synchronicity with the yin-yang patterns of the seasons and matched with appropriate visualizations, seeing for example the rising yang *jing* as solar, and the descending yin *qi* as lunar energies. On a macrocosmic level, moreover, the practice matches the alteration of day and night, accelerated in the internal work. As the *Ziyang zhenren Wuzhen pian sanzhu* says: "The sun and the moon meet every day of the month. In imitation of their divine efficacy, one can accomplish the work of one day in one hour" (4.2b). Parallel to this revolution, a transformative cycle occurs among the five organs, i.e., the five phases in the body, whose usual cycle of production is increasingly reversed through the union of opposites.

Through this process of refinement, the various aspects of *qi* in due course give birth to a kernel of grain or a pearl in the lower cinnabar field. Sometimes called the "mysterious pearl" (*xuanzhu*) or the "pearl of dew" (*luzhu*), this signals the first appearance of the divine elixir from which the immortal embryo will begin to grow. It indicates the successful completion of the first stage of practice.

During the second stage, the immortal embryo grows over ten months in the lower and middle cinnabar fields. It is nourished by the rhythmic ascent and descent of *qi* which creates a great abdominal openness and allows the increasing sublimation of *qi* into *shen* (*Nü jindan* 2.31ab; ZW 26.425). It requires the strongest meditative awareness yet—long periods of quiet sitting and deep inner stillness. After ten months or seventy-six cycles, the embryo is ready to be born. The yang spirit gradually moves upward along the spine until it reaches the upper cinnabar field in the head. From there it can leave the body through the top of the head, undertaking excursions to the celestial spheres. The birth of the embryo into a free-moving spirit signifies the adept's rebirth on a new level and in a new yin body: an immortal being of softness, purity, and light (2.22b-23a; ZW 26.426).

The third stage, following this spiritual rebirth, sees the yin body increasingly transformed into a body of pure yang, through deeper absorption and further meditative practice. Eventually it becomes pure, luminous spirit and is reintegrated into cosmic emptiness. In the course of this process, the adept acquires supernatural and magical powers that are, however, not considered of major importance by the tradition. The main objective is final deliverance, achieved through the overcoming of individual identity and body-mind duality.

In rough outline, these are the three stages of the inner alchemical process for men. Women undergo essentially the same, except that they begin their work with the reversal and transformation of menstrual blood.

Decapitating the Red Dragon

Women in this tradition are seen as containing pure yin, a form of *qi* most obvious and most tangible in the blood lost during menstruation. Using the "magical grease" and energy secretions of the breasts, women begin their work by transforming this blood back into *qi*, then circulate it through the interior of the body for further refinement (*Nüdan shize* 1b, ZW 26.455). By this process, the "red dragon" is slain and the outflow turned into a "white dragon," analogous to semen in men (Despeux 1990, 243-45).

Having to transform red blood into white *jing* to begin their work, women are at a slight disadvantage from men. Considered impure by nature, they are believed to be not quite as ready for alchemical transformation. On the other hand, they have a distinct advantage in the second stage, since they are by nature equipped for pregnancy. Also, once yin impurities and inherent passions are overcome, women are more adept than men at meditation, calm their spirit more effectively, and reach deeper trances for longer periods.

The women referred to as practitioners in the texts are healthy females in their reproductive years, when yin-*qi* is at its fullest. Young girls, before menstruation has set in, are considered superior for alchemical practice and may skip the entire first stage (*Nüxiu cgtu* 4a; ZW 10.534). Older women after menopause, on the other hand, are characterized as weakened in *qi* and depleted in primordial yin (Despeux 1990, 264-66). After age forty-nine, according to medical lore, the waist expands, the blood diminishes, and the overall mechanism of life gradually ceases to function. To undertake inner alchemical transformation from such a basis, older women must first practice various meditative and longevity techniques, as well as systematic breast massages that will effect rejuvenation and bring about the reappearance of menstruation (*Nü jindan* 2.24a; ZW 26.422). Only after menstruation has set in again can they proceed to stop it with alchemical means and thus enter the path of transformation.

Even women of childbearing age, though, may have to undergo some preliminary preparations, especially if they have a physical or gynecological weakness. Before undertaking the alchemical work, they must fully recuperate from their ailments and gain complete health. To do so, various breathing techniques, gymnastics, and meditations are recommended, as well as specific herbal remedies that should be taken every day to replenish the *qi* and ready the body (Despeux 1990, 266-68).

Several such remedies are described in the *Daoyuan jingwei ge* (Subtle Chant on the Origin of the Dao, ZW 826) by the nineteenth-century master Liu Mingrui, the teacher of Zhao Bichen (see Despeux 1979). They make heavy use of angelica, ginger, dates, and licorice. One recipe, for example, taken to unblock the body's orifices and enhance the blood, consists of iris flowers, safflower blossoms, ground peach kernels, red peony, ligusticum, ginger, scallions, and dates—all cut fine, meshed together, and boiled in wine, then distilled into a dense concoction. Another, used to regulate both *qi* and blood, contains angelica, white peony, ligusticum, ginseng, atractylis, digitalis, white fungus, pinella tubers, cyperus tubers, licorice root, and ginger (ZW 23.443).

Once health is restored, the first alchemical stage begins, leading to the "decapitation of the red dragon," also described as making the blood return to the void or "refining the body through great yin." To do so, women begin by massaging their breasts to stimulate *qi* secretion (Despeux 1990, 245-50). Known as "refining the fluids to transform the blood" or "transmuting the red and reverting it to the white," this involves the stoking of the internal fire and the creation of a white grease that will then circulate through the entire body (*Nüxiu zhengtu* 9b; ZW 10.537).

To prepare for breast massages, women increase the secretion of saliva, one of the fundamental substances in the body. They rotate the tongue inside the mouth or clap their teeth—just as their medieval predecessors did in preparation for meditation and ecstatic excursions. The practice not only increases fluid in the mouth but also enhances the production of inner secretions from the breasts. Next, women focus their entire attention on the chest area and begin to massage their breasts. They sit in meditative posture: legs crossed and back straight, hands held loosely over the breasts, and thoughts engaged in concentration and visualization. They practice like this every day, preferably at the turning points of yin and yang, i.e., around noon and midnight. In addition, according to the *Daoyuan jingwei ge*, women should also practice the massages when desire has arisen, making use of the naturally rising *qi* in the body (ZW 23.443).

Four specific ways of massaging are mentioned in the texts. First, the method found in the *Nüxiu zhengtu* prescribes four sets of thirty-six strokes, i.e. a total of 144 strokes,[1] undertaken with increasing speed and pressure upon each repetition. This will stimulate the internal *qi* and cause it to spread to the different parts of the body. The process should be undertaken at midnight while sitting with crossed legs and with the heels pressing against the genitals. Before beginning the practice, the adept claps her teeth thirty-six times and breathes gently through the nose thirty-six times. This serves to remove blockages from the *qi* channels in the body. Following this, she breathes softly while visualizing the

---

[1] The number 144 is associated with yin and with women, as opposed to the yang number 212, appropriate for men. The numerology goes back to the *Yijing*, and appears variously in inner alchemical literature. See Lu 1970.

qi rising up her spinal column thirty-six times, then she raises her hands up to the sky and imagines her *qi* moving upward through the crown of the head, a movement repeated altogether thirty-six times. To conclude the massages, the adept crosses her hands over the pubic bone to seal the circle of *qi* (*Nüxiu zhengtu* 9b-10a; ZW 10.537).

Another set of instructions appears in the *Nü jindan*. It involves concentrating the mind on the Cavern of Qi between the breasts, then massaging and rubbing them lightly thirty-six times with crossed hands. In the course of twenty-four breaths, while visualizing the *qi* rise up from the lower cinnabar field, the adept continues to massage her breasts and increasingly focuses her attention inward and deepens her respiration. After a certain amount of practice, perfect *qi* rises, menstruation becomes lighter and eventually disappears altogether, and the breasts shrink back to teenage size. In the long run, the massages become unnecessary, and mental concentration on the Cavern of Qi suffices to maintain perfect breath and the purity before menstruation (2.32ab; ZW26.421-22).

A third way of massaging the breasts is described in the *Nügong lianji huandan tushuo*. According to this, adepts begin by massaging first the right breast, then the left, twelve times each, followed by rubbing the navel and the abdomen thirty-six times each. Next, they swallow the saliva three times and turn their attention toward the interior of the body to observe the great calm and deep quietude that fills it. If this exercise is done daily, at noon and at midnight, within a month the perfect yin will begin to activate (6ab; ZW 26.431).

Yet another variant recorded in the *Daoyuan jingwei ge* claims that breast massages are a panacea for all ailments. It also notes that once the perfect *qi* has risen, there is a development of sexual desire that will inevitably lead to a loss of *qi*. The practitioner should therefore try to catch the *qi* as it begins to stir, availing herself of the opportunity for reversal. With the help of meditative vision, she directs the *qi* toward the right breast while massaging the left with the right hand thirty-six times, and vice versa. The exercise is complete after six full repetitions, i.e., 216 strokes. Once complete, the adept sits in silent meditation, hands held lightly over the breasts, and practices breathing and retention of breath (ZW 23.444).

All these ways of massaging the breasts are set in a larger, meditative framework that includes a preparatory period of abstention and the observance of taboos, the ritual setting of the practice in a specially designated chamber, the cleansing of the body and wearing of proper attire, as well as the correct geographical direction of the practice and its alignment in time with the rhythm of the cosmic forces. In many ways, the work of *qi*-transformation through breast massages, therefore, continues the meditation and ritual practices of medieval Daoism, developing the tradition in a new way without completely abandoning the old.

The Pearl

Whichever technique one follows, the goal in all cases is the refinement of blood into *qi* and eventual cessation of menstruation. At the same time, practitioners also begin to nurture and support the golden flower (*jinhua*), the interior pearl or "pearl of dew," the divine grain of *qi* in the abdomen that will eventually grow into the immortal embryo (Despeux 1990, 250-53). Compared to a point of light, a radiance of power in the body, the pearl is newly created from the commingling of yin and yang in men, while in women it is already present but has to be transformed and developed.[2]

To do so, women have to act at the exact moment in their cycle when the pearl is most accessible, a time described in terms of the "monthly messenger" (*yuexin*) (Despeux 1990, 253-56). About two-and-a-half days before the onset of menstruation, this "messenger" signals the impending transformation of yang *qi* into yin blood. It comes with a group of well-known symptoms, such as leg pains, headaches, loss of appetite, mood swings, depression, or hyperactivity. Women at this time can extract pure yin *qi* from the yang *qi* contained in their Cavern of *Qi*, just as men at this "time of vibrancy" pull out pure yang *qi* from their seminal *jing*.

---

[2] On the pearl in men, see *Qinyuan chundan ci* (Poems on the Cinnabar of Spring in the Garden of the Heart, DZ 156), 5b. For more on the pearl in women, see *Lifeng laoren ji* 2.4a. See also the poem by Ma Danyang in the *Dongxuan jinyu ji* (Collection of Gold and Jade of the Mystery Cavern, DZ 1149), 2.5b

The imagery used to describe this process is based on the *Yijing*: women pull the yin from the trigram *Li* (fire), while men take the yang from the trigram *Kan* (water).

Using deep, focused breaths to regulate *qi*, adepts can access the pearl and begin to gather and nourish it. The texts describe it variously. For example, the *Nü jindan* says:

> The Dao of the golden elixir begins at the time when yang first arises. At this moment concentrate the spirit and focus it on the Cavern of *Qi*. Begin to drum and lock it in firmly. Then take the cosmic wind of [the trigram] Sun and breathe rhythmically through your stove [nose], puffing and panting like a smith at his bellows. (2.23a; ZW 26.423)

The *Nügong lianji huandan tushuo* goes into a bit more detail:

> Practicing this great work, when perfect yin is not yet active and the channels of *qi* have not yet been opened, the adept will feel fatigue and need a great deal of sleep. In that case, first undertake the method of plucking the brain fluid and making it descend. What does it mean to "pluck the brain fluid and make it descend"?
>
> It means that you revert your brilliance back on yourself and reflect all light inward. Doing so, you can use your eyes to observe the brain fluid move down along the nose, cross the Bridge of Magpies [tongue], and pass through the Mysterious Sustainer [chin] and the Twelve-Storied Tower [throat]. Eventually it reaches the Central Ultimate [abdomen] and enters the Ocean of Blood [lower cinnabar field]. As its water meets the local fire, you will be completely free from all fatigue and somnolence and always remain awake and alert. Whenever an errant thought tries to arise, just focus on the central net, and it will be stilled. (2ab; 26.428-29)

This practice of inner absorption should be undertaken two to three times daily, increasingly opening up the body for the gathering of the pearl.

A first-hand report on the formation of the pearl in the body of an adept is found in Wang Shizhen's biography of Tanyangzi, the late-Ming woman saint who had an ecstatic encounter with the Queen Mother of the West and attained bodily ascension to immortality. It says:

> In her head she perceived the indistinct sound of the music of the immortals, which came from the void. The vapor of Before Heaven luminously circled through her five organs and formed an elixir pearl. First it was scarcely the size of a grain of rice. Then it grew to the size of a cross-bow pellet. Its outer appearance was like gauze; its color was perfect red and yellow. Sometimes it would rise and fall; occasionally she would take it out and hold it in the palm of her hand where it would blaze with a brilliant light, shooting forth radiance. (*Yanzhou shanren xugao* 78.7b; Waltner 1987, 113)

Once the pearl has been gathered, it is nourished through the meditative circulation of *qi* in the microcosmic orbit. Moving *qi* up along the Governing Vessel on the back of the body and down the Conception Vessel in front of the torso at regular intervals throughout day and night, adepts use visualizations, methods of concentration, and breath control to unblock the channels and create a strong stirring in the inner cauldron. Both men and women undertake this part of the practice in essentially the same way, except that in women the ultimate point of origin of the *qi* flow is the breasts and not the abdomen.

Again, different texts describe the practice differently (Despeux 1990, 256-63). The *Nüxiu zhengtu* notes that the *qi* refined through extensive breast massages will spontaneously begin to move about in the body. Once adepts become aware of this, they should guide it downward through the abdomen and divide it into two streams at the hips, turning it left and right in the course of thirty-six respirations. Getting warmer and more active, the *qi* begins to move up the spinal column, first slowly and hesitantly, then with increasing speed and vigor. To unblock hindrances along the spine, adepts clap their teeth seventy-two times and take thirty-six deep nostril breaths before the practice. To prevent *qi* from staying in the genital area and flowing out of the body, they contract the muscles of the pelvic floor and place both hands over the pubic bone, at the same time visualizing the upward flow of *qi*.

When the *qi* has begun its upward course, practitioners raise both hands overhead, spreading and releasing the fingers at regular intervals twice thirty-six times, first slowly and lightly, then a bit faster. Next, they place their hands on their hips and shrug the shoulders thirty-six times, allowing the qi to pass through the Double Pass at breast level, the upper spine, and the Jade Pillow at the occiput. Any blockages found there can be further dissolved by clapping the teeth and concentrating on the nape of the neck.

After the qi has risen through the Niwan Palace in the center of the head to its top, adepts move the lower lip above the upper to encourage the qi to descend along the front of the skull towards the nose. They roll the tongue against the upper palate to establish a connection between the Governing and Conception Vessels, allowing the sweet dew of qi to descend further. It flows down naturally towards the Purple Gate near the heart, where it is held briefly. Moving further down through the abdomen, it divides at the hips and is revolved thirty-six times as before, then concentrated in the cinnabar field and rotated thirty-six times each to the left and right.

With the arrival of the circulated qi, the abdomen is completely unblocked and feels wide and open. At this point the adept allows the qi-flow to separate once again into two streams and guides it right and left thirty-six times. Feeling as if a small grain has penetrated the womb, the adept has a sensation of warmth and vibration in this area of the body. She must now keep the gates tightly shut, lest the vibrant qi emerge and create physical numbness and emotional passions.

This phase of the process decides whether ordinary life is continued or saintliness is achieved: the vibrating qi in the abdomen creates a very pleasurable sensation not unlike an orgasm that, if emotions and desires are not fully controlled, may well entice the adept back to the pleasures of the world. If emotions are firmly restrained, on the other hand, this moment begins the growth towards immortality and signals the first reversal of qi into cosmic patterns. With the renewed ascent of qi to the head along the spinal column, a mysterious landscape opens in the body, complete with the isles of the immortals and the heights of Mount Kunlun. The entire being of the adept experiences a delightful peace, signaling the completion of the first stage (*Nüxiu zhengtu* 2ab; ZW 10.535).

Li Niwan's version of this procedure is very similar, except that adepts are encouraged to aid the ascending *qi* not only by raising their hands overhead but also by contracting the muscles of the pelvic floor. His *Shuangxiu baofa* further provides a number of detailed visualizations that help in the activation of the microcosmic orbit—such as seeing the *qi* in the heart for thirty-six respirations and moving it consciously through the abdomen and along the central vessels of the body.

The head is imagined as a vast ocean rather than the heights of Kunlun, while the abdominal resting place of the *qi* is seen as harboring the mysterious pearl. As the *qi*-cycle becomes better established, adepts visualize the interior of their body as bathed in a glowing light and enter a deep state of absorption, a place where there are no more thoughts, the breath flows with hardly any movement, and the three cinnabar fields are closely connected. Seeing the *qi* as light floating over a crystal ocean, adepts are immersed in their visions and feel as if in a deep, engaging dream. Before coming out of the practice, they rub themselves all over to bring consciousness back to the physical plane. Only then can movement be attempted in the torso, hips, legs, and toes (7b; ZW 10.545).

According to the *Nüdan shize*, the process of activating the *qi* and moving it along the microcosmic orbit tends to create dryness in the mouth. In addition to providing a general description of the overall pattern of *qi*-flow, the text encourages adepts to rinse their mouth at regular intervals and breathe through the nose. This will enhance the *qi* movement, since saliva and breath also flow down through the Twelve-Storied Tower and the chest cavity into the Ocean of Blood. From here, the *qi* is, as usual, guided through the perineum and up along the spine, to conclude yet another revolution. The method prescribes three sets of *qi* orbits, followed by a set of thirty-six breast massages with hands crossed over. The entire pattern should be repeated three times, i.e., nine revolutions of *qi* and 108 strokes of the breasts. Within a hundred days of regular practice, the text claims, women will recover perfect health and the red dragon will be slain (4ab; ZW 26.457).

Fourth and finally, the *Nügong lianji huandan tushuo* adds a different set of metaphors in describing the *qi* circulation process. It compares the secretions descending from the head with rain and sees the force and warmth of *qi* in the abdomen as similar to thunder, imaging the body as a microcosm of the earth: "Thunder rises up from the earth; rain falls from the top of the mountain." As the *qi* moves along the standard path of the microcosmic orbit, moreover, the text emphasizes the depth of concentration afforded by the adept and notes that the pearl felt in the abdomen can be true or false.

If it is a true pearl, each time the adept enters the meditation chamber for her practice, a warm fire arises in her body and a soft vapor penetrates every part. Continuing a mental fixation on the central palace in the chest area, adepts obtain the vision of a radiant pearl the size of a pea, which emerges in the Hall of Light in the head and from there rises up to hover about ten feet above them. With this vision comes a sense of emptiness, openness, and freedom from all thoughts. The head is enveloped in a brilliant pearl, the womb is warm with the fire of *qi*, and there may be sensations of trembling. The inner fire has been awakened and the first stage of the alchemical work is complete (3b; ZW 26.429).

Growing the Embryo

During the second stage, the pearl grows into an immortal embryo, continuously nourished by a regular firing cycle (*huohou*) that is calculated carefully according to the natural rhythm of yin and yang (Baryosher-Chemouny 1996, 100-03). Women at this stage have an easier time, since they are naturally endowed with wombs. Pregnancy in general is seen in terms of a cosmic event, as is documented in the *Neiguan jing* (Scripture on Inner Observation, DZ 641), a Tang manual on meditation. The text says:

> When father and mother unite in harmony, man receives life.
> In the first month, essence and blood coagulate in the womb.
> In the second month, the embryo begins to take shape.
> In the third month, yang *shen* arouses the three spirit souls to come to life.
> In the fourth month, yin *qi* settles the seven material souls as guardians of the body.
> In the fifth month, the five phases are distributed to the five organs to keep their spirit at peace.

In the sixth month, the six pitches are set up in the six viscera to nourish the *qi*.

In the seventh month, the seven essential stars open the body orifices to let in cosmic light.

In the eighth month, the eight luminant spirits descend to fill the body with perfected *qi*.

In the ninth month, the various palaces and chambers are properly arranged to keep the *jing* essence safe.

In the tenth month, the *qi* is strong enough to complete the body. (1b-2a; Kohn 1989b, 203-05)[3]

Chinese medicine takes a similar approach to human gestation, seeing the growth of the embryo as the gradual accumulation of different aspects of *qi* and the increasing influx of cosmic entities. Embryonic development is like "a potter's molding of clay or an alchemist's molding of metal"(Furth 1999, 102; Bray 1997, 219). It begins with the commingling of the parents' *jing* and blood, and thus with the water element among the five phases, shaping the kidney system, the primary residence of primordial *qi*. "Fetal life was subsequently animated by spirits (*shen*) and souls (*ling*) from an eclectic popular pantheon. There were the three *hun* souls in the third month, and the seven *po* souls in the fourth month, followed by the spirits of the five *zang* organ systems in the fifth month, the navel anima in the sixth, and the primal spirit in the eighth" (Furth 1999, 102).

The embryo's development was also determined to a great degree by the activities of the mother, the things she ate, saw, and with which she had contact (Despeux 2003). Instead of seeing the mother only as a vessel for the nurturing of the child, this process made her "the mediator between the natural world and the child" (Waltner 1990, 39). In a similar way, women in the second stage of inner alchemy are mediators between the embodied world of humanity and the transcendent realm of the immortals. They should be very careful in what they eat, feel, and think, to en-

---

[3] The same passage describing the is also found in *Hunyuan shubing pian* (Chaos Prime Describes Human Endowment), *Yunji qiqian* 29.1ab. An earlier version is contained in the *Yinyuan jing* (Scripture on Karma and Retribution, DZ 336), 8.1b-2a. Before that, see *Huainanzi* 1 (Major 1993).

234 / Women in Daoism

sure the proper development of the immortal embryo (*Nüxiu zhengtu* 10.534).

The second stage of the alchemical process can generally be described as a balancing of yin and yang in practitioners of both sexes. According to the eighth rule of the *Nüxiu zhengtu*, when women attain the first stage by making their menstrual blood white like semen they effectively realize a male or yang-quality body. But to complete the alchemical process, both sexes must fully realize the female or yin-quality body. This is the purpose of the second stage, when men achieve the state of pregnancy and women return to womanhood, but on a higher, more cosmic and *qi*-based level. They nurture the immortal embryo in proper accordance with the seasons and the phases of the planets, creating a new self in their own bodies.

The key practice undertaken in this stage is embryo respiration (*taixi*) or perfect respiration (*zhenxi*), a technique well known already in the middle ages (Despeux 1990, 269-73; Baryosher-Chemouny 1996, 96-98). The embryo in the womb is independent of outer breath and nourishment, fully sustained by the closed circuit of energy that links it with the mother's body. By analogy, ideal Daoist adepts, as they increasingly merge with the Dao, no longer need to breathe or eat. Instead, they can regulate and nurture the *qi* within, creating a closed world of energetic transformation. Daoists were well aware that embryo breathing in the inner alchemical context was a metaphor, chosen because adepts would focus their attention predominantly on the abdomen and concentrate on the *qi* moving in the lower part of the torso. It meant the continuous circulation of *qi* and light within, the full focus on the internal transformation and increased loosening of ties to the outer world (*Nüxiu zhengtu* 13ab; ZW10.539).

As the *qi* was purified and made perfect, so the blood was transformed into breast secretions that increasingly moved through the meridians and began to irrigate the fluid system of the body. These secretions, known poetically as "jade milk" (*yuru*), are none other than *qi* that is brought forth within the body through internal respiration. Women thus sublimated their inner *qi* through continuous circulation into a new and purer flow (*Nüdan shize* 7b; ZW 26.458).

One method included the use of a mantra, whose rhythmic recitation allowed the *qi* to move in the desired pattern. The *Nügong zhengfa* mentions the tantric mantra *om mani padme hum* as a suitable vehicle for this effort. Each of its syllables, the text explains, is oriented toward one direction, radiating outward from the center of the body, centered on *om*. As the adept chants the mantra, so the five syllables and the five phases, matching the bodily organs, circulate and merge, increasing the *qi*-flow to the womb (sect. 8; Tao 1989, 466-67). They successfully mix and exchange the wood *qi* of the liver and the metal *qi* of the lungs, creating a reversal of the ordinary production cycle of the phases and gradually returning to cosmic origins. In alchemical language this phase of the process is described in terms of a battle between the dragon (wood) and the tiger (metal) in the Lotus Chamber at the center of the body. The process is likely to give rise to fears and worries and to a mind like a monkey with its wildly galloping thoughts. However, once it is over, "the seven emotions do not stir, the five robbers [senses] do not cause disturbance, the six roots [of the senses] are greatly stabilized, and sensuality and outside thinking are both forgotten" (*Nü jindan* 2.25a; ZW 26.422).

Another way of describing the firing cycle is with the help of the trigrams and hexagrams of the *Yijing*. The four elementary trigrams (heaven, earth, water, fire) come to stand for the basic materials, for the framework of the alchemical work, as well as for its tools. Various hexagrams, moreover, symbolize the movements and increasing changes in embryonic growth and mark the progress of the work in terms of time and cosmic constellations (Robinet 1989b, 316; Baryosher-Chemouny 1996, 56-59).

Alchemists typically arrange the hexagrams in two major groups, one of which stands for the "yang-ization," the other for the "yin-ization" undertaken in the work. They establish an order of hexagrams entirely of their own, an order different from the standard system of the *Yijing*. To begin, they symbolize the first unfolding of yang with the hexagram *Fu*, "The Return" (Wilhelm 1950, 97), which consists of only one unbroken yang line at the bottom, above which there are five broken yin lines. Gradually the yang lines of the hexagram increase until the state of complete yang is reached, which is the hexagram *Qian*, "Heaven."

The line of six hexagrams from *Fu* to *Qian* shows in a graphic manner the process of rising yang, which is parallel to the waxing of the moon, the rising of the sun, and the warming of the year. When *Qian* is reached, the work pauses for a moment, after which the process is reversed. Then it begins with the hexagram *Gou*, "Coming to Meet" (Wilhelm 1950, 179), which has one yin line at the bottom and five yang lines on top. Gradually increasing yin and decreasing yang, the hexagram changes into *Kun*, "Earth," the complete yin. The relationship between the rising and waning yin and yang is also expressed in terms of the dosage of lead and mercury or in terms of the activation of fire and the use of water (Robinet 1989b, 316).

The goal of this practice is to vitalize and increase original spirit, leading eventually to a prolonged state of deep absorption. As Liu Mingrui describes it in a poem:

> Yin and yang evolve through the intervention of clear speech,
> But feelings and preferences ultimately meet with silence.
> As the starved tiger sucks the marrow of the young phoenix,
> The red serpent glides into the nest of the black tortoise.
> The colors mix, obstacles evaporate.
> As you plunge towards the source, the waves begin to calm.
> At the heart of the clouds, the dragon whistles and the snow twirls,
> To the sound of the flute, the Weaver Maid climbs toward the western slope. (*Daoyuan jingwei ge*, ZW 23.446-47)

In the second stage of the great alchemical work, therefore, the embryo undergoes ten months of gestation, growing in the same way as a human child develops in the womb and incorporating all the different cosmic forces and aspects. Adepts nurture the embryo through breathing and the circulation of *qi*, following the proper rhythm of yin and yang, matching the seasons and placing themselves in the correct directions. As they do so, cosmic fire commingles with water, lead merges with mercury, and the dragon joins the tiger. The procedure is symbolized with the help of these various metaphors, indicating yin and yang at higher alchemical levels, but in essence it consists of a continued refinement of the inner body and enhanced growth of the adept's spirit nature.

The Birth of the Spirit

The third stage commences with the birth of the immortal embryo through the head of the practitioner. The *Dadao ge* of Cao Wenyi describes the alchemical work as leading to a state of complete mystical oneness with the universe and the attainment of both magical powers and an easy flowing-along with primordial, cosmic transformations. It says:

> Spirit is inner nature; *qi* is destiny.
> So spirit does not gallop far away, let the *qi* be firm.
> Originally the two are mutual and close,
> How could they ever be dispersed—the primordial handle of all life.
> Merge all forces to join in the Dao, then forget the joining,
> And you'll be able to emerge and go along with primordial changes.
> Penetrate metal, pierce through stone—none with difficulty,
> Sit and cast off all, stand and forget all—just be all at once!
> (2.5a)

According to this, as adepts merge with the One, they overcome all duality—body-mind, subject-object, heaven-humanity. At this stage, the *qi*-embryo is complete and takes birth. To do so, it is transposed from the middle to the upper cinnabar field, gently moved up from the chest area to the head—either through rhythmic breathing or with the help of a mantra (*Nügong zhengfa* 8; Tao 1989, 466-47). Still a body of yin, it has not quite achieved its final state of pure yang. But it will gradually attain this level as *qi* is further sublimated into *shen*, and the entire person is reintegrated with cosmic emptiness (Despeux 1990, 275-78).

During the second stage, as the golden flower blossoms forth and the embryo grows toward completion, a primordial light begins to shine through the entire body. The adept enters into a state of deep absorption, lying immobile as if dead, pale in complexion, and apparently not breathing at all. She needs a helper at this time who watches over her day and night for however long the state persists, which may be up to six days. All noise and shouting that might startle her must be avoided, lest the tenuously growing spirit-embryo be injured and the adept be afflicted by madness or demonic forces. When she comes out of this absorption, nostril breathing begins very subtly and the divine light opens. One can call out to her in a low voice. She begins to move and will gradually rise, get dressed, and take some nourishment, still remaining vigilant since the process is not yet over. Rather, the most important part is still to come: the exiting of the spirit into the celestial realm (*Nüdan shize* 13b-14a; ZW 26.461-62).

The first exiting of the spirit embryo is known as "deliverance from the womb" (*tuotai*). It is the adept's celestial rebirth and is accompanied by the perception of a deep inner rumbling, like a clap of thunder. Then the celestial gate at the top of her head bursts free and opens wide, and a white smoky essence can be seen hovering above her (see Fig. 15). The spirit passes through the top of the head and begins to communicate with the celestials, transcending the limitations of the body.

In men, the color white rises first into the head, followed by the colors black, green, red, and yellow. In women, the order differs, and the first color to arise is black, followed by red, white, green, and yellow. The five colors, representative of the five phases, unite and the gate of heaven opens with a clap of thunder (*Nügong zhenfa* 10; Tao 1989, 468). A poem by Ma Danyang describes it:

> Maintain yourself quite firmly in repose and patience,
> See refined *qi* spread over the Three Terraces,
> The dragon hisses, the tiger roars, coming at each other—
> Under the bright moon, a clear breeze arises.
> The hazy radiance of the five realms [of rebirth] covers and envelopes you;
> The spirit pearl, well nurtured, leaves the womb.
> With a clap of thunder, the Grotto Gate is opened:
> Only now you notice mountain and companions—all quite strange. (*Jianwu ji* 1.27b)

Here the inner experience of the spiritual rebirth is described, beginning with a vision of the spiraling *qi* within and the dragon and tiger forces battling. As their fight ends, the scene calms and a clear breeze and heavenly haze arise, and the embryo begins its ascent. The Grotto Gate at the top of the head bursts ajar and the new spirit being passes through—

端拱冥心圖

Fig. 15: The immortal embryo emerges from the head of the practitioner. Source: *Xingming guizhi*.

while the awareness of the practitioner, as if from great distance, comes back to the surroundings of the world.

Until the adept enters a state of deep absorption, the embryonic spirit cannot fully detach from the *qi* circulating in the body. Once absorption is attained and the spirit has begun to move on its own, the adept easily maintains concentration and may experience various strong internal states. For example, she may have a vision of a shower of heavenly flowers, perceive divine perfumes, or see an image of a seven-storied pagoda. In addition, as the *Nüdan shize* notes, men have to wait for the attainment of highest yang before the spirit can exit. Women, on the contrary, can achieve this stage more easily and much sooner. Again the main point is the effort at purification in women. Her body has to become "like a vessel of ice" and her spirit "as limpid as autumn rain" (14b; ZW 26.463).

After its first exit, the spirit learns to come and go freely and communicate widely with the otherworld. At first it moves rather slowly and does not go far away from the body, then, supported by further meditative exercises known as "nursing for three years" (*rufu sannian*), it gradually gets used to its new powers, moves faster and travels further afield until it can go far and wide without limit (Despeux 1990, 278-81). As the spirit enters into these cosmic ventures, the adept exhibits supernatural powers: she can be in two places at once, move quickly from one place to another, know the past and the future, divine people's thoughts, procure wondrous substances, overcome hazards of fire and water, and has control over life and death. Known as "spirit pervasion" (*shentong*), this indicates the freedom achieved by the spirit and also manifest in the practitioner (*Nüdan shize* 14b; ZW 26.463; *Nü jindan* 2.33b; ZW 26.426).

There is a great contrast in the states before and after the spirit's exit. Before, the adept is immovable and in deep trance. After, she moves about freely, lightly, and with great energy, undertaking ecstatic excursions and manifesting wondrous abilities. She gains a new level of rapport with the Dao and with the universe, a new freedom, and the great transcendence of the immortals. A first-hand report on such an experience is found in the biography of Tanyangzi. According to this, she instructs her father to guard her body while she goes off on a spirit excursion.

> "Don't go out; stay for a while and look after me. As the daylight fades and my face becomes red, and the breathing from

my mouth and nose becomes faint, this will mean that my spirit is departing. Take care that no one from the household spies on me."

At noon, her spirit really did depart. Her father held his breath and guarded her, protecting her while he waited. In late afternoon, an icy sound like chimes came from the void.

Tanyangzi woke up. She smiled and said to her father: "Luckily nothing went wrong. In an instant I travelled hundreds of thousands of miles. I beheld all sorts of things: mountains, rivers, grasses, trees, dragons, snakes, birds, and bees. And all of them are spirits within my body!" (*Yanzhou shanren xugao* 78.8ab; Waltner 1987, 114)

However, even this high level of attainment, with its complete freedom of the spirit and universal vision of the body, is not the ultimate goal of inner alchemy, which is only realized after further meditative practice, known as "wall gazing" (*mianbi*). This technique is adopted from Chan Buddhism, whose first patriarch Bodhidharma is said to have realized full enlightenment by sitting in a cave and gazing at a wall for nine years. In this final phase of the process, the adept whose body is already transformed into pure light has yet to fully overcome its limits and melt into cosmic emptiness. The process takes nine years or 3,000 days, a number that is symbolic of highest yang and great completion.

A poem attributed to Sun Buer, entitled "Wall Gazing" and found in the collection *Sun Buer yuanjun fayu* (Dharma Saying of Primal Lady Sun Buer, ZW 370; JY 212) describes it as follows:[4]

> All the myriad tasks already well fulfilled,
> Sit down unmoving in a corner.
> Light in body, rise on purple *qi*,
> Calm within, float off on clear waters.
> *Qi* merges, yin and yang unite,
> Your spirit joins with heaven and with earth.
> The great work done, you visit the Jade Towers,
> Giving a long whistle, emerge from smoke and vapors.[4]

---

[4] ZW 10.805; *Sun Buer yuanjun gongfu cidi* 1.13a *Nü jindan* 2.34a, ZW.26.427; Chen 1934; Cleary 1989, 51-52.

Fig. 16: Ascension to immortality on a phoenix. Source: *Xingming guizhi*.

The deep meditative absorption in this stage, perfected over long years of practice, involves the attainment of complete clarity, tranquility, and nonaction. Mind and spirit are no longer of this world but illuminate the infinite. However, since women are part of cosmic yin, unlike men who at this stage attain the diamond body of pure yang, they are still partly yin and need to perform further virtuous actions—even if these actions only occur on a celestial and superhuman plane.

Eventually the day comes when the adept is real for the heavenly spheres and ascends upward, mounting a cloudy chariot or riding on an immortals' bird (see Fig. 16).

She has received formal empowerment from the palaces above and is now an acknowledged member of the heavenly host. Received by the immortal ladies at the court of the Queen Mother, she is led to the immortals' paradise on Penglai or Kunlun. All beings at this auspicious moment receive great blessings, and the world itself for a short instant is nothing but a celestial paradise. Another poem attributed to Sun Buer describes it:

> On this auspicious day, you leave the vale [of earth],
> Striding on a batch of wondrous clouds
> With jade maidens reining a team of blue phoenixes
> And gold lads offering rosy peaches.
> Accompanied by tunes of lutes, the spread of flower petals,
> The sound of jade flutes, and clear rays of moonlight,
> Leave your sheath of flesh on a fine, bright morning
> And peacefully traverse the cosmic flows.[5]

The spirit, thus united completely with Heaven and cosmic emptiness; it moves along freely and openly with the flow of the Dao. The gods are present everywhere and nowhere, not attained through outward efforts, but found deep within, through the cultivation and complete transformation of the inner powers of body and mind.

---

[5] *Sun Buer yuanjun fayu*, ZW 10.806; *Sun Buer yuanjun gongfu cidi* 1.13b; Tao 1989, 288; Chen 1934; Cleary 1989, 56-57.

Conclusion

Women in Daoism as presented in this volume are a multifaceted, complex, and intricate group. They include goddesses, immortals, renunciants, and lay practitioners, and in all cases represent a vision and an ideal of the female as portrayed in the religion, that is to say, by the men of the religion who wrote the texts and documented the events. Few of the women, therefore, are merely historical figures, and only occasionally do the sources come close to being chronicles of actual events. This means that the data on women in the Daoist tradition, are colored by the interests and visions of the writers of the texts, who were for the most part male. These interests can be personal, as in the description of an exceptional female of one's own lineage and clan; they may reflect community interests if the writer wished to enhance the prestige of a certain village, temple, or area by recording the extraordinary feats of a local woman; or they may be theoretical, when the author is trying to prove the factual reality of certain magical or physical abilities.

Despite the possibility that the motivations of those who have authored the historical record have obscured it, and even acknowledging the possibility that some authors have propagandized women's exploits to enhance the standing and image of women—the basic fact remains that whatever gets recorded in the literature of traditional China serves to show something significant, unusual, and noteworthy. This, of course, holds true for all historical writing and is also the case for biographies of men. Ordinary events, normal people, and undistinguished workers do not make exciting subjects worthy of recording for posterity or extolling in the present. Still, it is those ordinary individuals that make up the majority of people, and the majority of women. As Daniel Overmyer says:

> In traditional China, the overwhelming majority of women were poor, illiterate, and had to work hard every day to survive. . . . The religious activities of most women were confined to worshiping their husband's ancestors and occasionally visiting a local temple to pray for healing or sons. . . . Even if a

> woman were a pious Buddhist the values in sermons she
> might hear would emphasize frugality, obedience, chastity, ac-
> ceptance of her lot, hope for paradise after death. For all but a
> few, religion was socially conservative. (1981, 92)

When talking about women in Daoism, therefore, we should not forget that the cases presented in the literature and highlighted in this volume only make up a small portion of the Daoist population which mainly consisted of ordinary, lay followers. They were deeply ensconced in traditional Chinese society and ethics and found some solace and support in their prayers and devotions. This form of devotion can be described as "domestic religion" and was, as Dorothy Ko points out, "a dominant motif in gentrywomen's domestic life" (1994, 198). Women would pray at the family altar, visit the local temple, and join other women for scripture study or recitation. "Daily devotion fostered communities of women, as sisters gathered to study the sutras, or a mother interpreted a daughter's dreams and recited chants" (1994, 198). Women might also find religious value in simple ethical commands, such as nonkilling and compassion, and many would gear their households toward vegetarianism and practice good deeds in their neighborhoods from a religious motivation (Ko 1994, 199).

The domestic religion practiced by the overwhelming majority of lay women in China was and is supportive of the established society and centers on ancestor worship and the care for family and community deities, such as the Stove God, the Village God, and the City God. Beyond that, deities that proved efficacious in healing, protection, and support would be addressed, as well as gods that showed particular aptitude for serving the concerns of women, such as Guanyin, Doumu, Mazu, and other goddesses. While there may be some awareness of sectarian differences among popular practitioners, there is only minimal concern for them. It is thus not surprising that the visionary Tanyangzi practices devotion to Guanyin, recites the name of Amitābha, attains immorality through the forming of an inner elixir, and ends up on an ecstatic journey to the Queen Mother of the West.

Such conflation of sectarian boundaries has been described as "syncretism," but is better understood as the practical appropriation of suitable vehicles for specific situations and purposes (see Berling 1980; Orzech

2002). There is also nothing much new about it. In fact, the earliest Daoist statues surviving from the Northern Wei dynasty in the fourth and fifth century C.E. show the integration of Daoist and Buddhist motifs, deities, and prayers. Erected by ordinary people, they served to secure peace for the ancestors and good fortune for the living. Next to an image of Lord Lao, they easily could place a prayer invoking the powers of the Buddha Maitreya (see Kamitsuka 1998; Liu 2001).

Women in Daoism must be understood within this context of specific interests guiding the writers of historical and hagiographic records as well as of the practice among the majority of women of a multifaceted and highly integrative popular religion. The figures and practices described in this volume, therefore, represent an ideal vision of Daoist women, showing what both historical writers and popular practitioners most admired in women following the Daoist path or representing the Daoist religion.

The most fundamental characteristic of Daoist women is their cosmic nature of yin. This nature is a major aspect of cosmic unfolding and without this quiet, latent, preserving, supporting part of universal *qi*, all the activities and high flights of yang would not be possible. Yin is dark, shady, sinking, soft, and weak, but it is also empowering and necessary, a force in its own right that all, not only women, have to attain so that self-realization can be complete. Inherently part of this power of yin, women have sexual power and potency which can be exploited by men, but which can also be used to control others and to create energetic cycles in accordance with the Dao.

Since they represent half of the cosmic powers, women have the ability to run households, manage affairs, supervise palaces, and take on major responsibilities. They can be well educated and write lofty poems, be in charge of the sacred scriptures, and educate sons and give sage advice to elders and rulers. Women can attain magical powers just as well as men, and in some cases even surpass them; they can reach immortality, appear as teachers, and reveal scriptures; they can undergo full ordination, occupy high priestly ranks, and serve as abbots of communities. The women described in the literature are competent and confident, strong characters who will do whatever is necessary to fulfill their destiny in the Dao and thereby enhance the harmony of the cosmos.

The actions necessary to accomplish these feats tend to involve a disentanglement from the family and mainstream society, which in some cases was a smooth process desired by the family, but most of the time presented a difficult barrier. Women as much as men were required to continue the family line, serve their parents and their communities, and were not free to leave at will. Men in classical hagiographies, unless they were younger sons and let go more easily, tended to marry and produce offspring, then leave their wives and children. Similarly, women in most cases were widowed when they entered the religion. If they wished to leave the family at a younger age, they had more difficulty, needing to resist the pressures of marriage and gain as much control over their lives as possible. Often this happened with the help of radical fasting, food being one area where they could exert control (Waltner 1987, 123). The gods, favoring the girl's actions, helped by giving her the ability to survive without nourishment, causing the parents to face unbending resistance and the potential danger of losing their daughter to emaciation. Many parents did give in eventually, some gracefully, some with great reluctance.

The drama of disentanglement is a classic motif in hagiographies and popular stories. It shows the strong determination and supernatural connection of the future Daoist and follows a classic outline:

> The main plot is that of a girl, often of wealthy if not aristo-cratic birth, born to childless parents. Hearing of the miseries of motherhood in this life and the horrors of hell in the next, she decides to pursue the religious life. Her parents, in particular her father, oppose this decision and pressure her into marriage, often resorting to physical violence to make their point. . . . With a combination of unshakable determination and supernatural help, she eventually becomes a bodhisattva or an immortal and, in a final act of reintegration, returns to save the family that had initially ostracized her. (Grant 1995, 45-46)

Despite all contrariness during the breaking-away from family and society, religious women come back to serve the community, often having gained powers of healing, divine contact, and prognostication.

The concern of many hagiographies with the relation of Daoist women to family and society reflects the mainstream tendency to see women in relational terms. Women are yin, men are yang; women are inside, men are outside. They belong to different spheres, but they interact and both are necessary (Mann 1997, 15; Ko 1994, 13). Women relate to men as daughters, wives, mothers, widows, and concubines, and have their identity determined by these connections and their relative positions. In mainstream society the vision of women, therefore, includes erotic images of dominance and submission of sexual partners, the understanding of the mother as indulgent and caring, the ideal of the determined widow who will sacrifice everything for chastity and family loyalty, the contrast between the jealous wife and the smitten husband, as well as the general image of the emotion-ridden female versus the man who follows a rigorous code of ethics and social rules (Ebrey 1993, 261-62).

Although these images and ideals could provide women with a sense of purpose and self-worth, and while there was room to attain a degree of happiness and comforts within the social constraints, the satisfaction of women was understood as occurring exclusively in connection with family and society, through the flourishing of her clan, the success of her husband, and the growth of her children. Women, in short, were seen to define themselves entirely in relation to others, preferably males.

In contrast to this understanding, the ideal women of Daoism define themselves through others only in a secondary way. Their primary identity comes from creating a relationship both narrower and wider than family and society: by concerning themselves with their own bodies and with the greater universe of the Dao. The two, of course, coincide in the Daoist vision, where the gods of the stars reside also in the body, and where the cultivation of bodily qi leads to complete control over self and nature. Daoist women are more inward-looking than their mainstream counterparts, either because they are born with "immortals' bones" and inherently gifted for the religious life or because they are so disillusioned with mainstream life that they turn to the Dao. The turning to the Dao, then, is primarily a turning away from the outside world of relationships and towards the inner world of monthly cycles, energy flow, meditations, and ecstatic visions. Through this turning-away, Daoist women achieve a competence and independence far beyond their mainstream counterparts. They engage in celestial visions and journey to the heavens, reach ordination ranks, and gain magical and ritual powers.

For women in Daoism, the distinction between yin and yang, inner and outer, is not between male and female, or society and family: It shifts to family and body, submission to others and dominance over oneself, outer obedience and inner determination, ethical demands and religious urges. What was yin before, the inner circle of the family, is yang now—the family as the outer sphere in contrast to the cosmic body within. Obedience and submission, yin virtues and positive traits in mainstream culture, similarly have shifted to being yang attitudes of betrayal to the true values of yin—dominance over the self and determination in the Dao. The Daoist path, therefore, moves the yin-yang, inner-outer dichotomy of Chinese mainstream society into a new set of yin-yang, inner-outer values, making women more yin, more inner, more focused on themselves. In this respect, then, women are the ideal practitioners of the Dao, realizing their cosmic nature of yin by moving closer towards the inner circle of the Dao.

The shift away from the relation to society and towards a greater concern with inner states and cosmic attainments holds true not only for Daoist, but also for Buddhist women in traditional China. Still, women in Buddhism are seen much differently from their Daoist counterparts. They are described as essentially imperfect, helpless victims of sensuality and desire, seats of lasciviousness and lewdness (Faure 1998, 79). Women are dirty and foul, seductive and enticing, uncontrollable and wild. As a result, Buddhist nuns were considered dangerous and placed in a position of dependence and control. They had to observe many more rules than monks and had to be extremely careful to avoid all contact with them.

Daoists similarly were admonished to avoid all casual contact with the opposite sex, and several rules of the *Laojun yibai bashi jie* (The One Hundred and Eighty Precepts of Lord Lao, in DZ 786, YJQQ 39), the main code of the early Celestial Masters that influenced all later sets of Daoist precepts (Penny 1996; Kohn 2004b), prohibit being secluded, traveling, or speaking with a woman alone (nos. 139, 161, 162). It also says: "When in mixed company, do not sit together for a shared meal nor touch the hands of a person of the opposite sex" (no. 164; see Hendrischke and Penny 1996, 22). In the monastic institutions of the high middle ages, moreover, men and women were strictly segregated and prohibited from all casual contact or discussions because, as stated in the *Qianzhen ke*

(Rules for a Thousand Perfected, DZ 1410, 7a) of the early seventh century, "if they do not even see an attractive person of the opposite sex, their minds will not get agitated."

However, the rule had exceptions. Male Daoists were allowed to lecture lay women on the scriptures as long as they were not alone with one of them. At the time of ordination it was permitted for men and women to enter each other's quarters after receiving permission from the masters. They were admonished, however, to behave with dignity and were neither allowed to go off individually by themselves or in groups of two, nor to enter any private quarters (*Qianzhen ke* 16a). If a monk came across a woman in danger of drowning or burning, he must not "hesitate to reach out a hand to help," because this contact was "not in violation of the rules" (*Qianzhen ke* 11b). Similarly, when his own mother, sister, or aunt was "sick or in some kind of distress at home, he could go and serve to support her" (11b). He could also in special cases bring her to the monastery and set up a hut for her nearby (Bumbacher 2000a, 246; Kohn 2003, 122).

The contact of male Daoists with women was therefore circumscribed but not prohibited, Daoist rules for women were not excessive beyond those of men, and nowhere do Daoist texts denounce women as lascivious and evil. Why is this? Why such misogyny in Buddhism—and Christianity or Islam? Why not in Daoism? The answer lies in the understanding of the body, and particularly of men's sexuality, in these traditions. In India and the West the body is seen as an obstacle to salvation and as an enemy to the purity of the soul, and sexuality is the most pronounced and most difficult force to tame within the body. In Daoism, on the contrary, the body is the basis for transformation, and sexual energy is highly valued as the one form of *qi* that can be actively aroused and consciously felt at the beginning of the path. Thus celibacy in Daoism was predicated on the retention, inner circulation, and refinement of *jing* or "essence," and the avoidance of sexual intercourse was not to subdue the body but to enhance its inner strength and cosmic connection (Eskildsen 1998, 67).

Men in Daoism had to actively confront and use their sexuality rather than deny, suppress, and eradicate it. Women, representative of sexual enticement in all cultures, were accordingly seen in a positive light—as sources of sexual fluids, partners in the arousal and enhancement of sexual energies, and teachers of sexual methods and bodily control. More than that, women were admired for their inherent power of yin, a power men wished to refine and cultivate, and for their natural ability of pregnancy, a state men needed to attain in a spiritual way while pursuing immortality. The very substances and states in a woman's body most polluting and most offensive in mainstream society and Buddhism—her menstrual blood and the birth of a child—in Daoism come to be key factors in the cultivation of immortality: blood as the female form of *jing* and thus the equivalent of semen; the birth of the embryo as the ultimate liberation of the spirit from the constraints of this world.

Sexual union, moreover, was part of the practice in all forms of Daoism, whether with real women in rituals of the "harmonization of *qi*," with celestial deities in pure, otherworldly encounters among the stars, with partners in the preparation of inner alchemy, or within the self in the rhythmic circulation and mingling of yin and yang. While it is regretful that the vision of women in religion often has more to do with men's relation to their own sexuality than with the appreciation of a fellow human being, in Daoism this trait has played out positively: women are for the most part described in the literature as being valued as individuals and seats of cosmic yin, respected for their natural gifts, and acknowledged for the capabilities and strengths they can attain.

Bibliography

Akizuki Kan'ei 秋月觀英. 1978. *Chūgoku kinsei dōkyō no keisei* 中國近世道家の形. Tokyo: Sōbunsha.

Ames, Roger. 1981. "Taoism and the Androgynous Ideal." In *Women in China: Current Directions in Historical Scholarship*, edited by Richard W.Guisso and Stanley Johannesen, 21-45. Lewiston, NY: Edwin Mellen Press.

Andersen, Poul. 1994. "The Transformation of the Body in Taoist Ritual." In *Religious Reflections on the Human Body*, edited by Jane Marie Law, 181-202. Bloomington: Indiana University Press.

Baldrian-Hussein, Farzeen. 1984. *Procédés secrets du joyau magique: Traité d'alchimie taoïste du XIe siècle*. Paris: Les Deux Océans.

_____. 1986. "Lü Tung-pin in Northern Sung Literature." *Cahiers d'Extrême-Asie* 2: 133-70.

Barrett, T. H. 1996. *Taoism Under the T'ang: Religion and Empire During the Golden Age of Chinese History*. London: Wellsweep Press.

Baryosher-Chemouny, Muriel. 1996. *La quête de l'immortalité en Chine: Alchimie et payasage intérieur sous les Song*. Paris: Dervy Livres.

Benhamouda, A. 1972. *Etoiles et constellations*. Madrid: Altamira-Rotopress.

Benn, Charles D. 1987. "Religious Aspects of Emperor Hsüan-tsung's Taoist Ideology." In *Buddhist and Taoist Practice in Medieval Chinese Society*, edited by David W. Chappell, 127-45. Honolulu: University of Hawai'i Press.

_____. 1991. *The Cavern Mystery Transmission: A Taoist Ordination Rite of A.D. 711*. Honolulu: University of Hawai'i Press.

_____. 2000. "Daoist Ordination and *Zhai* Rituals." In *Daoism Handbook*, edited by Livia Kohn, 309-38. Leiden: E.Brill.

Berling, Judith A. 1980. *The Syncretic Religion of Lin Chao-en*. New York: Columbia University Press.

Berthier, Brigitte. 1988. *La Dame du bord de l'eau*. Nanterre: Société d'ethnologie.

Biallas, Leonard J. 1986. *Myths: Gods, Heroes, and Saviors.* Mystic, Conn.: Twenty-third Publications.

Birrell, Anne. 1993. *Chinese Mythology: An Introduction.* Baltimore: Johns Hopkins University Press.

Black, Alison H. 1986. "Gender and Cosmology in Chinese Correlative Thinking." In *Gender and Religion: On the Complexity of Symbols,* edited by Carolyn Walker Bynum, Stephen Harrell and Paula Richman. Boston: Beacon Press.

Bland, John O. P. 1910. *China Under the Empress Dowager.* Philadelphia: J. B. Lippincott Company.

Blofeld, John. 1978. *Bodhisattva of Compassion: The Mystical Tradition of Kuan Yin.* Boulder: Shambhala.

Bodde, Derk. 1975. *Festivals in Classical China.* Princeton: Princeton University Press.

Bokenkamp, Stephen R. 1997. *Early Taoist Scriptures.* Berkeley: University of California Press.

Boltz, Judith M. 1986. "In Homage to T'ien-fei." *Journal of the American Oriental Society* 106: 211-32.

_____. 1987. *A Survey of Taoist Literature: Tenth to Seventeenth Centuries.* Berkeley: University of California, China Research Monograph 32.

Bray, Francesca. 1997. *Technology and Gender: Fabrics of Power in Late Imperial China.* Berkeley: University of California Press.

Bremmer, Jan N. 1993. *The Early Greek Concept of the Soul.* Princeton: Princeton University Press.

Bumbacher, Stephan Peter. 1998. "Abschied von Heim und Herd: Die Frau im mittelalterlichen Daoismus und Buddhismus." *Asiatische Studien / Etudes Asiatiques* 52: 673-94.

_____. 2000a. *The Fragments of the Daoxue zhuan.* Frankfurt: Peter Lang.

_____. 2000b. "On the *Shenxian zhuan.*" *Asiatische Studien/Etudes Asiatiques* 54.4:729-814.

_____. 2001. "Zu den Körpergottheiten im chinesischen Taoismus." In *Noch eine Chance für die Religionsphänomenologie?,* edited by D. Peoli-Olgiati, A. Michaels, and F. Stolz, 151-72. Frankfurt: Peter Lang.

Burton, Janet. 1994. *Monastic and Religious Orders in Britain, 1000-1300.* Cambridge: Cambridge University Press.

Bynum, Caroline Walker. 1987. *Holy Feast and Holy Fast: The Religious Significance of Food to Medieval Women*. Berkeley: University of California Press.

Cahill, Suzanne. 1985. "Sex and the Supernatural in Medieval China: Cantos on the Transcendent Who Presides Over the River." *Journal of the American Oriental Society* 105: 197-220.

_____. 1986a. "Reflections on a Metal Mother: Tu Kuang-t'ing's Biography of Hsi-wang-mu." *Journal of Chinese Religions* 13/14: 127-42.

_____. 1986b. "Performers and Female Taoist Adepts: Hsi Wang Mu as the Patron Deity of Women in Medieval China." *Journal of the American Oriental Society* 106: 155-68.

_____. 1990. "Practice Makes Perfect: Paths to Transcendence for Women in Medieval China." *Taoist Resources* 2.2: 23-42.

_____. 1992. "Sublimation in Medieval China: The Case of the Mysterious Woman of the Nine Heavens." *Journal of Chinese Religions* 20: 91-102.

_____. 1993. *Transcendence and Divine Passion: The Queen Mother of the West in Medieval China*. Stanford: Stanford University Press.

_____. 2000. "Pien Tung-hsuan: A Taoist Holy Woman of the T'ang Dynasty (618-907 A.D.)." In *Women Saints in World Religions*, edited by Arvind Sharma, 205-20. Albany: State University of New York Press.

_____. 2001. "Biography of the Daoist Saint Wang Fengxian by Du Guangting (850-933)." In *Under Confucian Eyes: Writings on Gender in Chinese History*, edited by Susan Mann and Yu-yin Cheng, 17-30. Berkeley: University of California Press.

_____. 2002. "Material Culture and the Dao: Textiles, Boats, and Zithers in the Poetry of Yu Xuanji (844-868)." In *Daoist Identity: History, Lineage, and Ritual*, edited by Livia Kohn and Harold D. Roth, 102-26. Honolulu: University of Hawai'i Press.

Campany, Robert F. 2002. *To Live As Long As Heaven and Earth: A Translation and Study of Ge Hong's Traditions of Divine Transcendents*. Berkeley: University of California Press.

Carmody, Denise Lardner. 1979. *Women and World Religions*. Oxford: Abingdon Press.

Cedzich, Angelika. 1987. "Das Ritual der Himmelsmeister im Spiegel früherer Quellen." Ph. D. Diss., University of Würzburg, Germany.

_____. 1995. "The Cult of the Wu-t'ung/Wu-hsien in History and Fiction: The Religious Roots of the Journey to the South." In *Ritual and Scripture in Chinese Popular Religion*, edited by David Johnson, 137-218. Berkeley: Chinese Popular Culture Project.

Chamberlayne, J.H. 1962. "The Development of Kuan Yin: Chinese Goddess of Mercy." *Numen* 9: 45-52.

Chan, Alan. 1990. "Goddesses in Chinese Religion." In *Goddesses in Religions and Modern Debate*, edited by Larry W. Hurtado, 9-81. Atlanta: Scholars Press.

_____. 1991. *Two Visions of the Way: A Study of the Wang Pi and the Ho-shang-kung Commentaries on the Laozi*. Albany: State University of New York Press.

Chan, Wing-tsit. 1963. *A Source Book in Chinese Philosophy*. Princeton: Princeton University Press.

Chang, Jolan. 1977. *The Tao of Love and Sex: The Ancient Chinese Way to Ecstasy*. New York: Dutton.

Chang, Kang-yi Sun, and Haun Saussey, eds. 1999. *Women Writers of Traditional China*. Stanford: Stanford University Press.

Chao, Shinyi. 2003 "The Perfection of Daoist Priestesses in the Song-Yuan Era." Paper Presented at the international conference on "Daoism and the Contemporary World," Boston University, Boston.

Chavannes, Edouard. 1919. "Le jet des dragons." *Mémoires concernant l'Asie Orientale* 1919, 55-214.

Chen Guofu 陳國符. 1975. *Daozang yuanliu kao* 道藏源流考. Taipei: Guting chubanshe.

Chen Yingning 陳櫻寧. 1934. *Sun Buer nüdan shizhu* 孫不二女丹釋註. Shanghai: Yihuo tangshan shuju.

_____. 1935. *Pangmen xiaoshu lu* 旁門小術錄. Shanghai: Yihuatang.

_____. 1935-39. *Nüzi daoxue xiao congshu* 女子道學小叢書. Shanghai: Yihuatang.

_____. 1939. *Lingyuan dadao ge baihua zhujie* 靈元大道歌白話註解. Shanghai: Yihuatang.

Chen Yuan 陳垣, Chen Zhichao 陳智超, and Zeng Qingying 曾慶瑛, eds. 1988. *Daojia jinshi lue* 道家金石略. Beijing: Wenwu.

Chen, Ellen M. 1969. "Nothingness and the Mother Principle in Early Chinese Taoism." *International Philosophical Quarterly* 9.3: 391-405.

_____. 1973. "Is There a Doctrine of Physical Immortality in the *Tao-te-ching*?" *History of Religions* 12: 231-49.

_____. 1974. "Tao as the Great Mother and the Influence of Motherly Love in the Shaping of Chinese Philosophy." *History of Religions* 14.1: 51-64.

Chen, William Y. 1987. *A Guide to Tao Tsang chi yao*. Stony Brook, NY: Institute for the Advanced Study of World Relgions.

Cheng, Yu-yin. 2001. "Letters by Women of the Ming-Qing Period." In *Under Confucian Eyes: Writings on Gender in Chinese History*, edited by Susan Mann and Yu-yin Cheng, 169-78. Berkeley: University of California Press.

Chia, Mantak. 1983. *Awaken Healing Energy Through the Tao*. Huntington, NY: Healing Tao Books.

_____. 1985. *Taoist Ways to Transform Stress into Vitality*. Huntingto, NY: Healing Tao Books.

Chia, Mantak, and Michael Winn. 1984. *Taoist Secrets of Love: Cultivating Male Sexual Energy*. Santa Fe: Aurora Press.

Ching, Julia. 1983. "The Mirror Symbol Revisited: Confucian and Taoist Mysticism." In *Mysticism and Religious Traditions*, edited by Michael Katz. Oxford and New York: Oxford University Press.

Chow, Rey. 1991. *Women and Chinese Modernity*. Minneapolis: University of Minnesota Press.

Chu, Valentin. 1994. *The Yin-Yang Butterfly: Ancient Chinese Sexual Secrets for Western Lovers*. Los Angeles: J. P. Tarcher.

Cleary, Thomas. 1987. *Understanding Reality: A Taoist Alchemical Classic by Chang Po-tuan*. Honolulu: University of Hawai'i Press.

_____. 1989. *Immortal Sisters: Secrets of Taoist Women*. Boston: Shambhala.

_____. 1992. *The Secret of the Golden Flower: The Classic Chinese Book of Life*. San Francisco: Harper.

Cole, Alan. 1998. *Mothers and Sons in Chinese Buddhism*. Stanford: Stanford University Press.

Corless, Roger J. 1993. "Pure Land Piety." In *Buddhist Spirituality: Indian, Southeast Asian, Tibetan, and Early Chinese*, edited by Takeuchi Yoshinori, 241-74. New York: Crossroad.

Daly, Mary. 1973. *Beyond God the Father: Toward a Philosophy of Women's Liberation*. Boston: Beacon Press.

Darga, Martina. 1999. *Das alchemistische Buch von innerem Wesen und Lebensenergie: Xingming guizhi*. Munich: Diederichs.

Davis, Edward L. 2001. *Society and the Supernatural in Song China*. Honolulu: University of Hawai'i Press.

DeBruyn, Pierre-Henry. 2000. "Daoism in the Ming (1368-1644)." In *Daoism Handbook*, edited by Livia Kohn, 594-622. Leiden: E. Brill.

DeGroot, J. J. M. 1892. *The Religious System of China*. 6 vols. Leiden: E. Brill

_____. 1910. *The Religions of the Chinese*. New York.

Demiéville, Paul. 1987. "The Mirror of the Mind." In *Sudden and Gradual: Approaches to Enlightenment in Chinese Thought*, edited by Peter N. Gregory, 13-40. Honolulu: University of Hawai'i Press.

DePee, Christian. 1999. "The Ritual and Sexual Bodies of the Groom and the Bride in Ritual Manuals of the Sung Dynasty." In *Chinese Women in the Imperial Past*, edited by Harriet T. Zurndorfer, 53-100. Leiden: E. Brill.

DeRotours, Robert. 1968. "Les grands fonctionnaires des pronvinces en Chine sous la dynastie des T'ang." *T'oung Pao* 25: 219-332.

Despeux, Catherine. 1979. *Zhao Bizhen: Traité d'alchimie et de physiologie taoïste*. Paris: Guy Trédaniel.

_____. 1981. *Les entretiens de Mazu, maître de Chan du VIIIe siècle*. Paris: Les Deux Océans.

_____. 1986. "L'ordination des femmes taoïstes sous les Tang." *Etudes chinoises* 5: 53-100.

_____. 1988. *La moélle du phénix rouge. Santé et longue vie dans la Chine du seizieme siècle*. Paris: Editions Trédaniel.

_____. 1989. "Gymnastics: The Ancient Tradition." In *Taoist Meditation and Longevity Techniques*, edited by Livia Kohn, 223-61. Ann Arbor: University of Michigan, Center for Chinese Studies Publications.

_____. 1990. *Immortelles de la Chine ancienne: Taoïsme et alchimie féminine*. Puiseaux: Pardès.

_____. 1994. *Taoïsme et corps humain: Le Xiuzhen tu*. Paris: Guy Trédaniel.

_____. 2000a. "Women in Daoism." In *Daoism Handbook*, edited by Livia Kohn, 384-412. Leiden: E. Brill.

_____. 2000b. "Talismans and Sacred Diagrams." In *Daoism Handbook*, edited by Livia Kohn, 498-540. Leiden: E. Brill.

_____. 2003. "Bien débuter dans la vie: l'éducation prénatal en Chine." In *Education et instruction en Chine*, edited by Christine Nguyen Tri and Catherine Despeux, 61-98. Paris: Editions Peeters.

DeWoskin, Kenneth J. 1983. *Doctors, Diviners, and Magicians of Ancient China*. New York: Columbia University Press.

Doi Takeo. 1973. *The Anatomy of Dependence*. Tokyo: Kōdansha International.

Doub, William C. 1971. "A Taoist Adept's Quest for Immortality: A Preliminary Study of the *Chou-shih Ming-t'ung chi* by T'ao Hung-ching." Ph.D. Diss., University of Washington, Seattle.

Dudbridge, Glen. 1978. *The Legend of Miao-shan*. London: Ithaca Press.

Duyvendak, J. J. L. 1954. *Tao Te Ching*. London: John Murray.

Eberhard, Wolfram, and Hedda Morrison. 1973. *Hua Shan: The Taoist Sacred Mountain in West China, Its Scenery, Monasteries and Monks*. Hong Kong: Vetch and Lee Ltd.

Ebrey, Patricia B. 1991. "Shifts in Marriage Finance from the Sixth to the Thirteenth Century." In *Marriage in Inequality in Chinese Society*, edited by Rubie S. Watson and Patricia B. Ebrey, 25-57. Berkeley: University of California Press.

_____. 1993. *The Inner Quarters: Marriage and the Lives of Chinese Women in the Sung Period*. Berkeley: University of California Press.

_____. 2000. "Taoism and Art at the Court of Song Huizong." In *Daoism and the Arts of China*, edited by Stephen Little and Shawn Eichman, 95-111. Berkeley: University of California Press.

Ebrey, Patricia B., and Peter N. Gregory, eds. 1993. *Religion and Society in T'ang and Sung China*. Honolulu: University of Hawai'i Press.

Engelhardt, Ute. 1987. *Die klassische Tradition der Qi-Übungen. Eine Darstellung anhand des Tang-zeitlichen Textes Fuqi jingyi lun von Sima Chengzhen*. Wiesbaden: Franz Steiner.

_____. 2000. "Longevity Techniques and Chinese Medicine." In *Daoism Handbook*, edited by Livia Kohn, 74-108. Leiden: E. Brill.

Eskildsen, Stephen. 1998. *Asceticism in Early Taoist Religion*. Albany: State University of New York Press.

Esposito, Monica. 2000. "Daoism in the Qing (1644-1911)." In *Daoism Handbook*, edited by Livia Kohn, 623-58. Leiden: E. Brill.

Falk, Nancy Auer, and Rita M. Gross, eds.1980. *Unspoken Worlds: Women's Religious Lives in Non-Western Cultures*. San Francisco: Harper & Row.

Faure, Bernard. 1987. "Space and Place in Chinese Religious Traditions." *History of Religions* 26: 337-56.

_____. 1998. *The Red Thread: Buddhist Approaches to Sexuality*. Princeton: Princeton University Press.

Field, Stephen L. 1999. "The Numerology of Nine Star Fengshui." *Journal of Chinese Religions* 27: 13-34.

Fitzgerald, C.P. 1955. *The Empress Wu*. Melbourne: Australian National University.

Forte, Antonino. 1992. "Chinese State Monasteries in the Seventh and Eighth Centuries." In *E Chō Ō Gotenchikukyō den kenkyū* 慧超往五天竺國傳研究, edited by Kuwayama Seishin 桑山正進, 213-58. Kyoto: Kyoto University, Jimbun kagaku kenkyūjo.

Fracasso, Ricardo. 1988. "Holy Mothers of Ancient China: a New Approach of the Hsi-wang-mu Problem." *T'oung-pao* 74: 1-46.

Franke, Herbert. 1972. "Einige Drucke und Handschriften der frühen Ming-Zeit." *Oriens Extremus* 19: 55-64.

_____. 1990. "The Taoist Elements in the Buddhist *Great Bear Sutra (Pei-tou ching)*." *Asia Major* 3.1: 75-112.

Frühauf, Manfred. 1999. *Die Königliche Mutter des Westens: Xiwangmu in den alten Dokumenten Chinas*. Bochum: Project Verlag.

Fukui Kōjun 福井康順. 1964. "Genmyō naihen ni tsuite" 玄妙內篇について. In *Iwai hakase koseki kinen tenseki ronshū* 岩井博士古稀記念典籍論集, 560-67. Tokyo: Dai'an.

Fung, Yu-lan, and Derk Bodde. 1952. *A History of Chinese Philosophy*. 2 vols. Princeton, Princeton University Press.

Furth, Charlotte. 1994. "Rethinking Van Gulik: Sexuality and Reproduction in Traditional Chinese Medicine." In *Engendering China*, edited by Christina Gilmartin et al., 125-46. Cambridge, Mass.: Harvard University Press.

_____. 1999. *A Flourishing Yin: Gender in Chinese Medical History, 960-1665*. Berkeley: University of California Press.

Getty, Alice. 1962 [1914]. *The Gods of Northern Buddhism*. Tokyo: Charles Tuttle.

Giles, Herbert A. 1916. *Strange Stories from a Chinese Studio*. Shanghai: Kelly & Walsh.

Giles, Lionel. 1948. *A Gallery of Chinese Immortals*. London: John Murray.

Goossaert, Vincent. 2001. "The Invention of an Order: Collective Identity in Thirteenth-Century Quanzhen Taoism." *Journal of Chinese Religions* 29: 111-38.

Graham, A. C. 1960. *The Book of Lieh-tzu*. London: A. Murray.

_____. 1986. *Yin-Yang and the Nature of Correlative Thinking*. Singapore: The Institute for East Asian Philosophies.

_____. 1990. "The Origins of the Legend of Lao Tan." In *Studies in Chinese Philosophy and Philosophical Literature*, edited by A. C. Graham, 111-24. Albany: State University of New York Press.

Granet, Marcel. 1932. *Festivals and Songs in Ancient China*. New York: E.P. Dutton.

Grant, Beata. 1994. "Who is this I? Who is that Other? The Poetry of an Eighteenth Century Buddhist Laywoman." *Late Imperial China* 15.1:1-40.

_____. 1995. "Patterns of Female Religious Experience in Qing Dynasty Popular Literature." *Journal of Chinese Religions* 23: 29-58.

_____. 1996. "Female Holder of the Lineage: Linji Chan Master Zhiyuan Xinggang (1597-1654)." *Late Imperial China* 17.2: 51-77.

_____. 1999. "Severing the Red Cord: Buddhist Nuns in Eighteenth-Century China." In *Buddhist Women Across Cultures: Realizations*, edited by Karma Lekshe Tsomo, 91-103. Albany: State University of New York Press.

_____. 2001. "Behind the Empty Gate: Buddhist Nun-Poets in Late-Ming and Qing China." In *Cultural Intersections in Later Chinese Buddhism*, edited by Marsha Weidner, 81-113. Honolulu: University of Hawai'i Press.

Gregory, Peter N., ed. 1986. *Traditions of Meditation in Chinese Buddhism*. Honolulu: University of Hawai'i Press, Kuroda Institute Studies in East Asian Buddhism 4.

Grünwedel, Albert. 1900. *Mythologie des Buddhismus in Tibet und der Mongolei*. Leipzig: F. A. Brockhaus.

Guisso, Richard W. 1981. "Thunder Over the Lake: The Five Classics and the Perception of Women in Early China." In *Women in China: Current Directions in Historical Scholarship*, edited by R. W. L. Guisso and Stanley Johannesen, 47-62. Lewiston, NY: Edwin Mellen Press.

Guisso, Richard W., Stanley Johannesen, eds. 1981. *Women in China: Current Directions in Historical Scholarship*. Lewiston, NY: Edwin Mellen Press.

Gulik, Robert van. 1961. *Sexual Life in Ancient China*. Leiden: E. Brill.

Güntsch, Gertrud. 1988. *Das Shen-hsien-chuan und das Erscheinungsbild eines Hsien*. Frankfurt: Peter Lang.

Hackmann, Heinrich. 1920. "Die Mönchsregeln des Klostertaoismus." *Ostasiatische Zeitschrift* 8: 141-70.

_____. 1931. *Die dreihundert Mönchsgebote des chinesischen Taoismus*. Amsterdam: Koninklijke Akademie van Wetenshapen.

Handlin, Johanna. 1975. "Lü Kun's New Audience: The Influence of Women's Literacy on Sixteenth-Century Thought." In *Women in Chinese Society*, edited by Margery Wolf and Roxanne Witke, 13-38. Stanford: Stanford University Press.

Harper, Donald. 1987. "The Sexual Arts of Ancient China As Described in a Manuscript of the Second Century B.C." *Harvard Journal of Asiatic Studies* 47: 459-98.

_____. 1999. *Early Chinese Medical Manuscripts: The Mawangdui Medical Manuscripts*. London: Wellcome Asian Medical Monographs.

Hawkes, David. 1959. *Ch'u Tz'u: The Songs of the South*. Oxford: Clarendon Press.

_____. 1967. "The Quest of the Goddess." *Asia Major* 13: 71-94.

Hendrischke, Barbara. 2000. "Early Daoist Movements." In *Daoism Handbook*, edited by Livia Kohn, 134-64. Leiden: E. Brill.

Hendrischke, Barbara, and Benjamin Penny. 1996. "*The 180 Precepts Spoken by Lord Lao*: A Translation and Textual Study." *Taoist Resources* 6.2: 17-29.

Henricks, Robert G. 2000. *Lau Tzu's Tao Te Ching: A Translation of the Startling New Documents Found at Guodian*. New York: Columbia University Press.

Hervouet, Yves, ed. 1978. *A Sung Bibliography; Bibliographie des Sung*. Hong Kong: The Chinese University Press.

Hiltebeitel, Alf, and Barbara D. Miller. 1998. *Hair: Its Power and Meaning in Asian Cultures*. Albany: State University of New York Press.

Hirohata Sukeo 廣田輔雄. 1965. "Nihon ni okeru hokushin shūhai ni tsuite" 日本における北辰崇拜訪について. *Tōhōshūkyō* 東方宗教 25: 36-50.

Ho, Wanli. 2003. "Daoist Nuns in Contemporary Taiwan." Paper Presented at the international conference on "Daoism and the Contemporary World," Boston University, Boston.

Holmgren, Jennifer. 1981. "Widow Chastity in the Northern Dynasties: The Lieh-nü Biographies in the *Wei-shu*." *Papers on Far Eastern History* 23: 165-86.

_____. 1995. *Marriage, Kinship and Power in Northern China*. Aldershot, UK: Variorum.

Homann, Rolf. 1971. *Die wichtigsten Körpergottheiten im Huang-t'ing-ching*. Göppingen: Alfred Kümmerle.

Hsieh, Evelyn Ding-hwa. 1999. "Images of Women in Chan Buddhist Literature of the Sung Period." In *Buddhism in the Sung*, edited by Peter Gregory and Daniel Getz, 148-87. Honolulu: University of Hawaii Press.

_____. 2000. "Buddhist Nuns in Sung China." *Journal of Sung-Yuan Studies* 30: 63-96.

Huntington, Rania. 1993. "Tigers, Foxes, and Other Animals in Tang-Dynasty Chuanqi." *Papers on Chinese Literature* 1: 42-59.

Hymes, Robert. 2002. *Way and Byway: Taoism, Local Religion, and Models of Divinity in Sung and Modern China*. Berkeley: University of California Press.

Ishihara, Akira, and Howard S. Levy. 1970. *The Tao of Sex*. New York: Harper & Row.

Jarrett, Lonny S. 2000. *Nourishing Destiny: The Inner Tradition of Chinese Medicine*. Stockbridge: Spirit Path Press.

Jiang, Tsui-fen. 1991. "Gender Reversal: Women in Chinese Drama Under Mongol Rule (1234-1368)." Ph. D. Diss., University of Washington, Seattle.

Johnson, T. W. 1974. "Far Eastern Foxlore." *Asian Folklore Studies* 33: 35-68.

Jordan, David K. and Daniel Overmyer. 1986. *The Flying Phoenix: Aspects of Chinese Sectarianism in Taiwan*. Princeton: Princeton University Press.

Kalinowski, Marc. 1985. "La transmission du dispositif des Neuf Palais sous les Six-dynasties." In *Tantric and Taoist Studies*, edited by Michel Strickmann, 3:773-811. Brussels: Institut Belge des Hautes Etudes Chinoises.

Kaltenmark, Maxime. 1953. *Le Lie-sien tchouan*. Peking: Universite de Paris Publications.

_____. 1974. "Miroirs magiques." In *Melanges de Sinologie offers a M. P. Demiéville*, 2: 91-98. Brussels: Institut Belge des Hautes Etudes Chinoises.

_____. 1980. "Chine." In *Dictionnaire des mythologies*, 1-75. Paris: Flammarion.

Kamitsuka Yoshiko 神塚淑子. 1992. "Dōkyō girei to ryū" 道教儀禮と龍. *Nihon bunka kenkyū* 日本文化研究 3: 126-34.

_____. 1998. "Lao-tzu in Six Dynasties Sculpture." In *Lao-tzu and the Tao-te-ching*, edited by Livia Kohn and Michael LaFargue, 63-85. Albany: State University of New York Press.

Kaptchuk, Ted J. 1983. *The Web that Has No Weaver: Understanding Chinese Medicine*. New York: Congdon & Weed.

Karetzky, Patricia E. 1992. *The Life of the Buddha: Ancient Scriptural and Pictorial Traditions*. Lanham, MD: University Press of America.

Katz, Paul R. 2000. *Images of the Immortal: The Cult of Lü Dongbin at the Palace of Eternal Joy*. Honolulu: University of Hawaii Press.

Kelleher, Theresa. 1987. "Confucianism." In *Women in World Religions*, edited by Arvind Sharma, 135-60. Albany: State University of New York Press.

King, Karen. 1997. *Women and Goddess Traditions*. Minneapolis: Fortress Press.

Kirkland, J. Russell. 1986. "Taoists of the High T'ang: An Inquiry into the Perceived Significance of Eminent Taoists in Medieval Chinese Society." Ph.D. Diss., Indiana University, Bloomington.

_____. 1991. "Huang Ling-wei: A Taoist Priestess in T'ang China." *Journal of Chinese Religions* 19: 47-73.

Kiyota, Minoru. 1978. *Mahāyāna Buddhist Meditation: Theory and Practice*. Honolulu: Hawai'i University Press.

Kleeman, Terry F. 1994. *A God's Own Tale: The Book of Transformations of Wenchang, the Divine Lord of Zitong*. Albany: State University of New York Press.

_____. 1998. *Great Perfection: Religion and Ethnicity in a Chinese Millenarian Kingdom*. Honolulu: University of Hawai'i Press.

Kloppenborg, Ria, and Wouter J. Hanegraff, eds. 1995. *Female Stereotypes in Religious Traditions*. Leiden: E. Brill.

Ko, Dorothy. 1994. *Teachers of the Inner Chambers: Women and Culture in Seventeenth-Century China*. Stanford: Stanford University Press.

_____. 2001. "The Sex of Footbinding." In *Good Sex: Feminist Perspectives from the World's Religions*, edited by Patricia Beattie Jung, Mary E. Hunt, and Radhika Balakrishnan, 140-57. New Brunswick, NJ: Rutgers University Press.

_____. 2002. "Footbinding as Female Inscription." In *Rethinking Confucianism: Past and Present in China, Japan, Korea, and Vietnam*, edited by Benjamin A. Elman, John B. Duncan, and Herman Ooms, 147-77. Berkeley: University of California Press.

Kobayashi Masayoshi 小林正美. 1990. *Rikuchō dōkyōshi kenkyū* 六朝道教史研究. Tokyo: Sōbunsha.

_____. 1992. "The Celestial Masters Under the Eastern Jin and Liu-Song Dynasties." *Taoist Resources* 3.2: 17-45.

Kohn, Livia. 1987. *Seven Steps to the Tao: Sima Chengzhen's Zuowanglun*. St. Augustin / Nettetal: Monumenta Serica Monograph XX.

_____. 1989a. "The Mother of the Tao." *Taoist Resources* 1.2: 37-113.

_____. 1989b. "Taoist Insight Meditation: The Tang Practice of *Neiguan*." In *Taoist Meditation and Longevity Techniques*, edited by Livia Kohn, 193-224. Ann Arbor: University of Michigan, Center for Chinese Studies.

_____. 1989c. "Guarding the One: Concentrative Meditation in Taoism." In *Taoist Meditation and Longevity Techniques*, edited by Livia Kohn, 123-56. Ann Arbor: University of Michigan, Center for Chinese Studies Publications.

_____. 1991. "Taoist Visions of the Body." *Journal of Chinese Philosophy* 18: 227-52.

_____. 1993. *The Taoist Experience: An Anthology*. Albany: State University of New York Press.

_____. 1995a. *Laughing at the Tao: Debates among Buddhists and Taoists in Medieval China*. Princeton: Princeton University Press.

_____. 1995b. "Kōshin: A Taoist Cult in Japan. Part II: Historical Development." *Japanese Religions* 20.1: 34-55.

_____. 1996a. "Laozi: Ancient Philosopher, Master of Longevity, and Taoist God." In *Religions of China in Practice*, edited by Donald S. Lopez Jr., 52-63. Princeton: Princeton University Press.

_____. 1996b. "The Looks of Laozi." *Asian Folklore Studies* 55.2: 193-236.

_____. 1997a. "Yin and Yang: The Natural Dimension of Evil." In *Philosophies of Nature: The Human Dimension*, edited by Robert S. Cohen and Alfred I. Tauber, 91-105. New York: Kluwer Academic Publishers, Boston Studies in the Philosophy of Science.

_____. 1997b. "The Taoist Adoption of the City God." *Ming Qing Yanjiu* 5 (1997), 68-106.

_____. 1998a. *God of the Dao: Lord Lao in History and Myth*. University of Michigan, Center for Chinese Studies.

_____. 1998b. "Mind and Eyes: Sensory and Spiritual Experience in Taoist Mysticism." *Monumenta Serica* 46 (1998), 129-56.

_____. 1998c. "The Lao-tzu Myth." In *Lao-tzu and the Tao-te-ching*, edited by Livia Kohn and Michael LaFargue, 41-62. Albany: State University of New York Press.

_____. 2000. "The Northern Celestial Masters." In *Daoism Handbook*, edited by Livia Kohn, 283-308. Leiden: E.Brill.

_____. 2001a. *Daoism and Chinese Culture*. Cambridge, Mass.: Three Pines Press.

_____. 2001b. "Doumu: The Mother of the Dipper." *Ming Qing Yanjiu* 8:149-95.

_____. 2002. "Monastic Rules in Quanzhen Daoism As Collected by Heinrich Hackmann." *Monumenta Serica* 51.

_____. 2003. *Monastic Life in Medieval Daoism: A Cross-Cultural Perspective*. Honolulu: University of Hawai'i Press.

_____. 2004a. *The Daoist Monastic Manual: A Translation of the Fengdao kejie*. New York: Oxford University Press.

_____. 2004b. *Daoist Precepts*. Cambridge, Mass.: Three Pines Press.

Kohn, Livia, and Russell Kirkland. 2000. "Daoism in the Tang (618-907)." In *Daoism Handbook*, edited by Livia Kohn, 339-83. Leiden: E. Brill.

Kominami Ichirō 小南一朗. 1991. *Seiōbo to tanabata denshō* 西王母と七夕傳承. Tokyo: Hirakawa.

Komjathy, Louis. 2002. *Title Index to Daoist Collections*. Cambridge, Mass.: Three Pines Press.

Krappe, Alexander. 1944. "Far Eastern Foxlore." *California Folklore Quarterly* 3: 124-47.

Kristeva, Julia. 1986. *About Chinese Women*. New York: Marion Boyars.

Kroll, Paul W. 1996. "Body Gods and Inner Vision: *The Scripture of the Yellow Court*." In *Religions of China in Practice*, edited by Donald S. Lopez Jr., 149-55. Princeton: Princeton University Press.

Kubo Noritada 窪德忠. 1951. "Dōkyō no shingi ni tsuite" 道教の清規について. *Tōhōshūkyō* 東方宗教 1: 28-44.

Kusuyama Haruki 楠山春樹. 1979. *Rōshi densetsu no kenkyū* 老子傳説の研究. To-kyo: Sōbunsha.

LaFargue, Michael. 1992. *The Tao of the Tao-te-ching*. Albany: State University of New York Press.

Lagerwey, John. 1981. *Wu-shang pi-yao: Somme taoïste du VIe siecle*. Paris: Publica-tions de l'Ecole Française d'Extrême-Orient.

———. 1992. "The Pilgrimage to Wu-tang Shan." In *Pilgrims and Sacred Sites in China*, edited by Susan Naquin and Chün-fang Yü, 293-332. Berkeley: Uni-versity of California Press.

Lai, Whalen. 1979. "Ch'an Metaphors: Waves, Water, Mirror, Lamp." *Philosophy East and West* 29: 243-255.

Larre, Claude, Isabelle Robinet, and Elisabeth Rochat de la Vallee. 1993. *Les grands traites du Huainan zi*. Paris: Editions du Cerf.

Lau, D. C. 1982. *Chinese Classics: Tao Te Ching*. Hong Kong: Hong Kong Univer-sity Press.

Le Blanc, Charles, and Remi Mathieu, eds. 1992. *Mythe et philosophie a l'aube de la Chine imperial: Etudes sur le Huainan zi*. Montreal: Les Presses de l'Universite de Montreal.

Leung, Angela Ki Che. 1999. "Women Practicing Medicine in Premodern China." In *Chinese Women in the Imperial Past*, edited by Harriet T. Zurndorfer, 101-34. Leiden: E. Brill.

Levering, Miriam. 1989. "Studies of Enlightened Women in Ch'an and the Chi-nese Buddhist Female Bodhisattva/Goddess Tradition." In *Women and God-dess Traditions in Antiquity and Today*, edited by Karen L. King, 137-76. Min-neapolis: Fortress Press.

———. 1992. "Lin-chi (Rinzai) Ch'an and Gender: The Rhetoric of Equality and the Rhetoric of Heroism in the Ch'an Buddhist Tradition." In *Buddhism, Sexuality, and Gender*, edited by José Ignacio Cabézon, 137-56. Albany: State University of New York Press.

———. 2000. "Women Ch'an Masters: The Teacher Miao-tsung as Saint." In *Women Saints in World Religions*, edited by Arvind Sharma, 180-204. Albany: State University of New York Press.

Levy, Howard S. 1956. "Yellow Turban Rebellion at the End of the Han." *Journal of the American Oriental Society* 76:214-27.

———. 1966. *Chinese Footbinding*. New York: Rawls.

Lewis, Mark E. 1990. *Sanctioned Violence in Early China*. Albany: State University of New York Press.

Li Yangzheng 李養正 993. *Dangdai Zhongguo daojiao* 當代中國道教. Beijing: Zhongguo shehui kexue chubanshe.

Li Yuzhen 李玉珍. 1989. *Tangdai de biqiuni* 唐代的比丘尼. Taipei: Xuesheng.

Little, Stephen, and Shawn Eichman. 2000. *Taoism and the Arts of China*. Berkeley: University of California Press.

Liu, Ming. 2001. "Zuowang." *Frost Bell — Newsletter of Orthodox Daoism in America*. Winter 2001: 1-11.

Liu, Xun. 2001. "In Search of Immortality: Daoist Inner Alchemy in Early Twentieth-Century China." Ph. D. Diss., University of Southern California, Los Angeles.

Liu, Yang. 2001. "Origins of Daoist Iconography." *Ars Orientalis* 31: 31-64.

Liu, Yanzhi. 1988. *The Essential Book of Traditional Chinese Medicine*. 2 Vols. New York: Columbia University Press.

Loewe, Michael. 1979. *Ways to Paradise. The Chinese Quest for Immortality*. London: George Allen and Unwin.

Loon, Piet van der. 1984. *Taoist Books in the Libraries of the Sung Period*. London: Ithaca Press.

Lu, Kuan-yü. 1970. *Taoist Yoga — Alchemy and Immortality*. London: Rider.

Magnin, Paul. 1979. *La vie et l'oeuvre de Huisi (515-577)*. Paris: Ecole Française d'Extrême-Orient.

Main, John. 1975 [1913]. *Religious Chastity*. New York: AMS Press.

Major, John S. 1993. *Heaven and Earth in Early Han Thought: Chapters Three, Four, and Five of the Huainanzi*. Albany: State University of New York Press.

Mann, Susan. 1987. "Women in the Kinship, Class, and Community Structures of Qing-Dynasty China." *Journal of Asian Studies* 46: 37-56.

_____. 1991. "Grooming a Daughter for Marriage: Brides and Wives in the Mid-Ch'ing Period." In *Marriage in Inequality in Chinese Society*, edited by Rubie S. Watson and Patricia B. Ebrey, 204-30. Berkeley: University of California Press.

_____. 1992. "*Fuxue* (Women's Learning) by Zhang Xuecheng (1738-1801): China's First History of Women's Culture." *Late Imperial China* 13.1: 40-62.

_____. 1997. *Precious Records: Women in China's Long Eighteenth Century.* Stanford: Stanford University Press.

Mann, Susan, and Yu-yin Cheng, eds. 2001. *Under Confucian Eyes: Writings on Gender in Chinese History.* Berkeley: University of California Press.

Marinatos, Nanno. 1998. "Goddess and Monster: An Investigation of Artemis." In *Ansichten griechischer Rituale,* edited by Fritz Graf, 114-25. Stuttgart: B. G. Teubner.

Marsone, Pierre. 2001. "Accounts of the Foundation of the Quanzhen Movement: A Hagiographic Treatment of History." *Journal of Chinese Religions* 29: 95-110.

Martin-Liao, Tianchi. 1985. "Traditional Handbooks of Women's Education." In *Women and Literature in China* edited by Anna Gerstlacher et al. Bochum: Brockmeyer.

Maspero, Henri. 1981. *Taoism and Chinese Religion.* Translated by Frank Kierman. Amherst: University of Massachusetts Press.

Mather, Richard B. 1979. "K'ou Ch'ien-chih and the Taoist Theocracy at the Northern Wei Court, 425-451." In *Facets of Taoism,* edited by Holmes Welch and Anna Seidel, 103-22. New Haven, Conn.: Yale University Press.

Mathieu, Rémi. 1978. *Le Mu Tianzi zhuan.* Paris: Mémoires de l'Institut des Hautes Etudes Chinoises 9.

_____. 1983. *Etude sur la mythologie et l'éthnologie de la Chine ancienne.* 2 vols. Paris: Collège de France.

_____. 1987. "Chamanes et chamanisme en Chine ancienne." *L'Homme* 101 : 10-34.

Matsumoto Kōichi 松本浩一. 1983. "Dōkyō to shūkyō girei" 道教と宗教儀禮. In *Dōkyō* 道教, edited by Fukui Kōjun 福井康順 et al., 1:189-238. Tokyo: Hirakawa.

_____. 1997. "Taihokushi no shimyō to reido hōkai" 臺北市の祠廟と靈斗法會. *Tōhōshūkyō* 東方宗教 90: 22-44.

Matsumoto Shoji. 1985. "Early Pure Land Buddhism in China." *Pure Land* (NS) 2: 135-44 and 3: 121-34.

Miura Kunio 三浦國雄. 1983. "Dōten fukuchi kōron" 洞天福地小論. *Tōhōshūkyō* 東方宗教 61: 1-23.

Miyakawa Hisayuki. 1979. "Local Cults around Mount Lu at the Time of Sun En's Rebellion." In *Facets of Taoism*, edited by Holmes Welch and Anna Seidel, 83-102. New Haven, Conn.: Yale University Press.

Mori, Yuria. 2002. "Identity and Lineage: The *Taiyi jinhua zongzhi* and the Spirit-Writing Cult to Patriarch Lü in Qing China." In *Daoist Identity: History, Lineage, and Ritual*, edited by Livia Kohn and Harold D. Roth, 165-84. Honolulu: University of Hawai'i Press.

Mugitani Kunio 麥谷國雄. 1987. "Yōsei enmei roku kunchu" 養性延命錄訓註. *Report of the Study Group on Traditional Chinese Longevity Techniques*, no. 3. Tokyo: Mombushō.

Murcott, Susan. 1991. *The First Buddhist Women: Translations and Commentary of the Therigatha*. Berkeley: Parallax Press.

Naquin, Susan. 1992. "The Peking Pilgrimage to Miao-feng Shan: Religious Organizations and Sacred Site." In *Pilgrims and Sacred Sites in China*, edited by Susan Naquin and Chün-fang Yü, 333-77. Berkeley: University of California Press.

Needham, Joseph, et al. 1956. *Science and Civilisation in China, vol. II: History of Scientific Thought*. Cambridge: Cambridge University Press.

_____. 1983. *Science and Civilisation in China, vol. V.5: Spagyrical Discovery and Invention—Physiological Alchemy*. Cambridge: Cambridge University Press.

Neumann, Erich. 1963. *The Great Mother: An Analysis of the Archetype*. Translated by Ralph Manheim. Princeton: Princeton University Press.

Ngo, Van Xuyet. 1976. *Divination, magie et politique dans la Chine ancienne*. Paris: Presses Universitaires de France.

Ni, Maoshing. 1995. *The Yellow Emperor's Classic of Medicine*. Boston: Shambhala.

Nienhauser, William H., ed. 1986. *The Indiana Companion to Traditional Chinese Literature*. Bloomington: Indiana University Press.

Noguchi Tetsurō 野口鐵朗 et al., eds. 1994. *Dōkyō jiten* 道教事典. Tokyo: Hirakawa.

O'Hara, Albert Richard. 1980. *The Position of Women in Early China According to the Lieh nü chuan*. Westport, Conn.: Hyperion Press.

Ocko, Jonathan K. 1991. "Women, Property, and Law in the People's Republic of China." In *Marriage in Inequality in Chinese Society*, edited by Rubie S. Watson and Patricia B. Ebrey, 313-46. Berkeley: University of California Press.

Ōfuchi Ninji 大淵忍爾. 1979a. *Tonkō dōkei: Zuroku hen* 敦煌道經圖錄篇. Tokyo: Kokubu shoten.

_____. 1979b. "The Formation of the Taoist Canon." In *Facets of Taoism*, edited by Holmes Welch and Anna Seidel, 253-68. New Haven, Conn.: Yale University Press.

Ōgata Tōru 大形徹. 1995. "Hihatsu kō" 被髪考. *Tōhōshūkyō* 東方宗教 86: 1-23.

Orzech, Charles D. 2002. "Fang Yankou and Pudu: Translation, Metaphor, and Religious Identity." In *Daoist Identity: History, Lineage, and Ritual*, edited by Livia Kohn and Harold D. Roth, 213-34. Honolulu: University of Hawaii Press.

Overmyer, Daniel L. 1976. *Folk Buddhist Religion: Dissenting Sects in Late Traditional China*. Cambridge, Mass: Harvard University Press.

_____. 1991. "Women in Chinese Religions. Submission, Struggle, Transcendence." In *From Benares to Beijing: Essays on Buddhism and Chinese Religion*, edited by Kōichi Shinohara and Gregory Schopen, 91-120. Oakville: Mosaic Press.

Ōyanagi Shigeta 小柳司氣太. 1934. *Hakuunkan shi* 白雲觀史. Tokyo: Tôhôbunka gakuin.

Paper, Jordan, ed. 1997. *Through the Earth Darkly: Female Spirituality in Comparative Perspective*. New York: Continuum.

Pas, Julian F. 1995. *Visions of Sukhavati: Shan-tao's Commentary on the Kuan wu-liang-shou fo-ching*. Albany: State University of New York Press.

Paul, Diana Y. 1985. *Women in Buddhism: Images of the Feminine in Mahayana Tradition*. Stanford: Stanford University Press.

Penny, Benjamin. 1996. "Buddhism and Daoism in *The 180 Precepts Spoken by Lord Lao*." *Taoist Resources* 6.2: 1-16.

Plaskow, Judith. and Joan Arnold Romero, eds. 1974. *Women and Religion*. Missoula: Scholars' Press.

Porkert, Manfred. 1961. "Untersuchungen einiger philosophisch-wissenschaftlicher Grundbegriffe und -beziehungen im Chinesischen." *Zeitschrift der deutschen morgenländischen Gesellschaft* 110: 422-52.

_____. 1974. *The Theoretical Foundations of Chinese Medicine: Systems of Correspondence*. Cambridge, Mass.: MIT Press.

Porter, Bill. 1993. *The Road to Heaven: Encounters with Chinese Hermits*. San Francisco: Mercury House.

Porter, Deborah Lynn. 1996. *From Deluge to Discourse: Myth, History, and the Creation of Chinese Fiction*. Albany: State University of New York Press.

Pregadio, Fabrizio. 2000. "Elixirs and Alchemy." In *Daoism Handbook*, edited by Livia Kohn, 165-95. Leiden: E. Brill.

_____. 1991. "Review of *Les Immortelles de la Chine ancienne*." *Taoist Resources* 3.1: 85-93.

Preston, James J., ed. 1982. *Mother Worship: Theme and Variations*. Chapel Hill: University of North Carolina Press.

Puett, Michael J. 2002. *To Become a God: Cosmology, Sacrifice, and Self-Divinization in Early China*. Cambridge, Mass.: Harvard University Asia Center.

Qing Xitai 卿希泰. 1994. *Zhongguo daojiao shi* 中國道教史. Chengdu: Sichuan renmin.

Raphals, Lisa. 1998. *Sharing the Light: Representations of Women and Virtue in Early China*. Albany: State University of New York Press.

Reed, Barbara E. 1987. "Taoism." In *Women in World Religions*, edited by Arvind Sharma, 161-80. Albany: State University of New York Press.

_____. 1992. "The Gender Symbolism of Kuan-yin Bodhisattva." In *Buddhism, Sexuality, and Gender*, edited by Jose Ignacio Cabezon, 159-80. Albany: State University of New York Press.

Reid, Daniel P. 1989. *The Tao of Health, Sex, and Longevity*. New York: Simon & Schuster.

Reiter, Florian C. 1985. "Ch'ung-yang Sets Forth His Teachings in Fifteen Discourses." *Monumenta Serica* 36: 33-54.

_____. 1998. *The Aspirations and Standards of Taoist Priests in the Early T'ang Period*. Wiesbaden: Harrassowitz.

Ren Jiyu 任繼愈. 1990. *Zhongguo daojiao shi* 中國道教史. Shanghai: Shanghai Renmin.

Ren Jiyu 任繼愈, and Zhong Zhaopeng 鐘肇鵬, eds. 1991. *Daozang tiyao* 道藏提要. Beijing: Zhongguo shehui kexue chubanshe.

Robinet, Isabelle. 1984. *La révélation du Shangqing dans l'histoire du taoïsme*. 2 vols. Paris: Publications de l'Ecole Francaise d'Extrême-Orient.

_____. 1988. "Sexualité et taoïsme." In *Sexualité et religion*, edited by Marcel Bernos, 51-71. Paris: Cerf.

_____. 1989a. "Visualization and Ecstatic Flight in Shangqing Taoism." In *Taoist Meditation and Longevity Techniques*, edited by Livia Kohn, 157-90. Ann Arbor: University of Michigan, Center for Chinese Studies Publications.

_____. 1989b. "Original Contributions of *Neidan* to Taoism and Chinese Thought." In *Taoist Meditation and Longevity Techniques*, edited by Livia Kohn, 295-38. Ann Arbor: University of Michigan, Center for Chinese Studies Publications.

_____. 1993. *Taoist Meditation*. Translated by Norman Girardot and Julian Pas. Albany: State University of New York Press.

_____. 1995. *Introduction a l'alchimie interieure taoïste: De l'unité et de la multiplicité*. Paris: Editions Cerf.

Robson, James. 1995. "The Polymorphous Space of the Southern Marchmount." *Cahiers d'Extrême-Asie* 8: 221-64.

Ropp, Paul S. 1976. "The Seeds of Change: Reflections on the Condition of Women in the Early and Middle Ch'ing." *Signs* 2.1: 5-23.

Roth, Harold D. 1992. *The Textual History of the Huai-Nan Tzu*. Ann Arbor: Association of Asian Studies Monograph.

_____. 1999. *Original Tao: Inward Training and the Foundations of Taoist Mysticism*. New York: Columbia University Press.

Russell, Terence C. 1985. "Songs of the Immortals: The Poetry of the *Chen-kao*." Ph.D. Diss., Australian National University, Canberra.

Sakade Yoshinobu 扳出祥伸 and Masuo Shin'ichirō 增尾伸一朗. 1991. "Chūsei Nihon no shintō to dōkyō" 中世日本の神道と道教. In *Nihon, Chūgoku no shūkyō bunka no kenkyū* 日本中國の宗教文化の研究, edited by Sakai Tadao 酒井忠夫 et al., 53-80. Tokyo: Hirakawa.

Saso, Michael. 1978. *The Teachings of Taoist Master Chuang*. New Haven, Conn.: Yale University Press.

_____. 1997. "The Taoist Body and Cosmic Prayer." In *Religion and the Body*, edited by Sarah Coakley, 231-47. Cambridge: Cambridge University Press.

Schafer, Edward H. 1973. *The Divine Women. Dragon Ladies and Rain Maidens in Tang Literature*. Berkeley: University of California Press.

_____. 1977a. "The Restoration of the Shrine of Wei Hua-ts'un at Lin-ch'uan in the Eight Century." *Journal of Oriental Studies* 15: 124-37.

_____. 1977b. *Pacing the Void: T'ang Approaches to the Stars.* Berkeley: University of California Press.

_____. 1978a. "The Capeline Cantos: Verses on the Divine Love of Taoist Priestesses." *Asiatische Studien/Etudes Asiatiques* 32: 5-65.

_____. 1978b . "The Jade Women of Greatest Mystery." *History of Religions* 17: 387-97.

_____. 1980. *Mao-shan in T'ang Times.* Boulder: Society for the Study of Chinese Religions.

_____. 1985. "The Princess Realised in Jade." *T'ang Studies* 3: 1-23.

Schipper, Kristofer M. 1965. *L'empereur Wou des Han dans la légende taoïste.* Paris: Ecole Française d'Extrême-Orient.

_____. 1975. *Concordance du Tao Tsang: Titres des ouvrages.* Paris: Publications de l'Ecole Francaise d'Extrême-Orient.

_____. 1978. "The Taoist Body." *History of Religions* 17: 355-87.

_____. 1979. "Le Calendrier de Jade: Note sur le *Laozi zhongjing.*" *Nachrichten der deutschen Gesellschaft für Natur- und Völkerkunde Ostasiens* 125: 75-80.

_____. 1984. "Le monachisme taoïste." In *Incontro di religioni in Asia tra il terzo e il decimo secolo d. C.,* edited by Lionello Lanciotti, 199-215. Firenze: Leo S. Olschki.

_____. 1985. "Taoist Ritual and Local Cults of the T'ang dynasty." In *Tantric and Taoist Studies,* edited by Michel Strickmann, 3: 812-34. Brussels: Institut Belge des Hautes Etudes Chinoises.

_____. 1994. *The Taoist Body.* Translated by Karen C. Duval. Berkeley: University of California Press.

Seaman, Gary. 1987. *Journey to the North: An Ethnohistorical Analysis and Annotated Translation of the Chinese Folk Novel 'Pei-you chi'.* Berkeley: University of California Press.

Seidel, Anna. 1969. *La divinisation de Lao-tseu dans le taoïsme des Han.* Paris: Ecole Française d'Extrême-Orient.

_____. 1982. "Tokens of Immortality in Han Graves." *Numen* 29: 79-122.

Sharma, Arvind, ed. 1987. *Women in World Religions*. Albany: State University of New York Press.

———, ed. 1994. *Religion and Women*. Albany: State University of New York Press.

———, ed. 2000. *Women Saints in World Religions*. Albany: State University of New York Press.

Sivin, Nathan. 1968. *Chinese Alchemy: Preliminary Studies*. Cambridge, Mass.: Harvard University Press.

———. 1988. *Traditional Medicine in Contemporary China*. Ann Arbor: University of Michigan, Center for Chinese Studies Publications.

Skar, Lowell. 2000. "Ritual Movements, Deity Cults, and the Transformation of Daoism in Song and Yuan Times." In *Daoism Handbook*, edited by Livia Kohn, 413-63. Leiden: E. Brill.

Skar, Lowell, and Fabrizio Pregadio. 2000. "Inner Alchemy (*Neidan*)." In *Daoism Handbook*, edited by Livia Kohn, 464-97. Leiden: E. Brill.

Smith, Kidder et al., eds. 1990. *Song Dynasty Uses of the I-ching*. Princeton: Princeton University Press.

Smith, Thomas E. 1990. "The Record of the Ten Continents." *Taoist Resources* 2.2: 87-119.

———. 1992. "Ritual and the Shaping of Narrative: The Legend of the Han Emperor Wu." Ph.D. Diss., University of Michigan, Ann Arbor.

———. 1994. "The Ritual of Scriptural Transmission as Seen in the *Han Wudi neizhuan*." Paper presented at the 46th Annual Meeting of the Association for Asian Studies, Boston.

———. 1998. "Rikuchō ni okeru butsudō ronsō to Ressenden no denshō" 六朝における佛道論爭と列仙傳の傳承. In *Dōkyō no rekishi to bunka* 道教の歴史と文化, edited by Yamada Toshiaki 山田利明 and Tanaka Fumio 田中文雄, 145-66. Tokyo: Hirakawa.

Sōfukawa Hiroshi 曾布川寬. 1981. *Konronsan e no shōsen* 崑崙山えの昇仙. Tokyo: Chūōkōron sha.

Stein, Rolf A. 1963. "Remarques sur les mouvements du taoïsme politico-religieux au IIe siècle ap. J.-C." *T'oung Pao* 50:1-78.

———. 1986. "Avalokitesvara/Kuan-yin: Un example de transformation d'un dieu a en deesse." *Cahiers d'Extrême-Asie* 2: 17-77.

_____. 1990. *The World in Miniature: Container Gardens and Dwellings in Far Eastern Religious Thought*. Translated by Phyllis Brooks. Stanford: Stanford University Press.

Stein, Stephan. 1999. *Zwischen Heil und Heilung: Zur frühen Tradition des Yangsheng in China*. Uelzen: Medizinisch-Literarische Verlagsgesellschaft.

Strachotta, Fritz Günter. 1997. *Religiöses Ahnen, Sehnen und Suchen: Von der Theologie zur Religionsgeschichte*. Frankfurt: Peter Lang.

Stranghair, Anna. 1973. *Chang Hua: A Statesman-Poet of the Western Chin Dynasty*. Canberra: Australian National University.

Strickmann, Michel. 1978a. "A Taoist Confirmation of Liang Wu-ti's Suppression of Taoism." *Journal of the American Oriental Society* 98: 467-74.

_____. 1978b. "The Longest Taoist Scripture." *History of Religions* 17: 331-54.

_____. 1978c. "The Mao-shan Revelations: Taoism and the Aristocracy." *T'oung Pao* 63: 1-63.

_____. 1979. "On the Alchemy of T'ao Hung-ching." In *Facets of Taoism*, edited by Holmes Welch and Anna Seidel, 123-92. New Haven, Conn.: Yale University Press.

_____. 1981. *Le taoïsme du Mao chan: chronique d'une révélation*. Paris: Collège de France, Institut des Hautes Etudes Chinoises.

Sun, Seung-hye. 2003. "Transformation of Taoism: The Queen Mother of the West in Korean and Japanese Art." Paper Presented at the international conference on "Daoism and the Contemporary World," Boston University, Boston.

Sunayama Minoru 沙山捻. 1987. "Ku Dō tōsenkō" 瞿童登仙考. *Tōhōshūkyō* 東方宗教 69: 1-23.

Sung, Marina H. 1981. "The Chinese *Lieh-nü* Tradition." In *Women in China: Current Directions in Historical Scholarship*, edited by R. W. L. Guisso and Stanley Johannesen, 63-74. Lewiston, NY: Edwin Mellen Press.

Switkin, Walter. 1977. *Immortality: A Taoist Text of Macrobiotics*. San Francisco: H. S. Dakin Company.

Tao Bingfu 陶秉福, ed. 1989. *Nüdan jicui* 女丹集萃. Beijing: Beijing shifan daxue.

Tay, C. N. 1976. "Kuan-Yin: The Cult of Half Asia." *History of Religions* 16: 147-77.

Thatcher, Melvin P. 1991. "Marriages of the Ruling Elite in the Spring and Autumn Period." In *Marriage in Inequality in Chinese Society*, edited by Rubie S. Watson and Patricia B. Ebrey, 1-24. Berkeley: University of California Press.

Theiss, Janet. 2001. "Managing Martyrdom: Female Suicide and Statecraft in Mid-Qing China." In *Passionate Women: Female Suicide in Late Imperial China*, edited by Paul S. Ropp, Paola Zamperini, and Harriet T. Zurndorfer, 47-76. Leiden: E. Brill.

_____. 2002. "Femininity in Flux: Gendered Virtue and Social Conflict in the Mid-Qing Courtroom." In *Chinese Femininities/Chinese Masculinities: An Introductory Reader*, edited by Susan Brownell and Jeffrey Wasserstrom, 47-66. Berkeley: University of California Press.

Tsai, Kathryn A. 1981. "The Chinese Buddhist Monastic Order for Women: The First Two Centuries." In *Women in China: Current Directions in Historical Scholarship*, edited by R. W. L. Guisso and Stanley Johannesen, 1-20. Lewiston, NY: Edwin Mellen Press.

_____. 1994. *Lives of the Nuns: Biographies of Chinese Nuns*. Honolulu: University of Hawai'i Press.

Tsui, Bartholomew P. M. 1991. *Taoist Tradition and Change. The Story of the Complete Perfection Sect in Hong Kong*. Hong Kong: Christian Study Centre on Chinese Religion and Culture.

Veith, Ilza. 1972. *The Yellow Emperor's Classic of Internal Medicine*. Berkeley: University of California Press.

Verellen, Franciscus. 1989. *Du Guangting (850-933)—taoïste de cour à la fin de la Chine médiévale*. Paris: Collège de France, Mémoires de L'Institut des Hautes Etudes Chinoises 30.

_____. 1992. "Evidential Miracles in Support of Taoism: The Inversion of a Buddhist Apologetic Tradition in Tang China." *T'oung Pao* 78: 217-63.

Waddell, L. Austine. 1972. *Tibetan Buddhism*. New York: Dover.

Wädow, Gerd. 1992. *Tien-fei hsien-sheng lu: Die Aufzeichnungen von der manifestierten Heiligkeit der Himmelsprinzessin. Einleitung, Übersetzung, Kommentar*. St. Augustin/Nettetal: Steyler Verlag, Monumenta Serica Monograph 29.

Waltner, Ann. 1981. "Widows and Remarriage in Ming and Early Qing China." In *Women in China: Current Directions in Historical Scholarship*, edited by Richard W. Guisso and Stanley Johannesen, 129-46. Lewiston, NY: Edwin Mellen Press.

_____. 1987. "T'an-yang-tzu and Wang Shih-chen: Visionary and Bureaucrat in the Late Ming." *Late Imperial China* 8: 105-33.

_____. 1990. *Getting an Heir: Adoption and the Construction of Kinship in Late Imperial China.* Honolulu: University of Hawai'i Press.

Wang, Robin. 2003. *Women in Chinese Thought and Culture.* Cambridge: Mass.: Hackett Publishing.

Ware, James R. 1966. *Alchemy, Medicine and Religion in the China of AD 320.* Cambridge, Mass.: MIT Press.

Watson, Burton. 1968. *The Complete Works of Chuang-tzu.* New York: Columbia University Press.

Watson, Rubie S. 1991. "Wives, Concubines, and Maids: Servitude and Kinship in the Hong Kong Region, 1900-1940." In *Marriage in Inequality in Chinese Society,* edited by Rubie S. Watson and Patricia B. Ebrey, 231-55. Berkeley: University of California Press.

Watson, Rubie S, and Patricia B. Ebrey, eds. 1991. *Marriage in Inequality in Chinese Society.* Berkeley: University of California Press.

Watters, T. 1874. "Chinese Fox Myths." *Journal of the Royal Asiatic Society, North China Branch* 8: 45-58.

Widmer, Ellen. 1999. "The Trouble with Talent: Hou Zhi and her *Tanci zao zaotian* of 1828." CLEAR 21: 131-50.

_____. 2003. "Considering a Coincidence: The "Female Reading Public" circa 1828." In *Writing and Materiality in China: Essays in Honor of Patrick Hanan,* edited by Judith T. Zeitlin and Lydia H. Liu, 273-316. Cambridge, Mass.: Harvard University Asia Center.

Widmer, Ellen, and Kang-I Sun, eds. 1997. *Writing Women in Late Imperial China.* Stanford: Stanford University Press.

Wijayaratna, Mohan. 1990. *Buddhist Monastic Life.* Cambridge: Cambridge University Press.

Wile, Douglas. 1992. *Art of the Bedchamber: The Chinese Sexology Classics Including Women's Solo Meditation Texts.* Albany: State University of New York Press.

Wilhelm, Richard. 1950. *The I Ching or Book of Changes.* Princeton: Princeton University Press, Bollingen Series XIX.

_____. 1984 [1929]. *The Secret of the Golden Flower: A Chinese Book of Life.* Harmondsworth: Penguin Books.

Witke, Roxanne. 1977. *Comrade Chiang Ching*. Boston: Little & Brown.

Wolf, Margery. 1972. *Women and the Family in Rural Taiwan*. Stanford: Stanford University Press.

Wolf, Margery, and Roxane Witke, eds. 1975. *Women in Chinese Society*. Stanford: Stanford University Press.

Wong, Eva. 1990. *Seven Taoist Masters*. Boston: Shambhala.

Wu, Hung. 2000. "Mapping Early Taoist Art: The Visual Culture of Wudoumi Dao." In *Taoism and the Arts of China*, edited by Stephen Little and Shawn Eichman, 77-94. Berkeley: University of California Press.

Xu Boying 徐伯英, and Yuan Jiegui 袁介圭. 1976. *Zhongguo xianxue* 中國仙學. Taipei: Zhenshanmei.

Yan Shanzhao 嚴善炤. 2001. "Shoki dōkyō to kōshi konki hōchūjutsu 初期道教と黄赤混氣房中術." *Tōhōshūkyō* 東方宗教 97: 1-19.

Yanagisawa Taka 柳澤孝. 1967. "Tōhon hokuto mandara no ni irei" 唐本北斗曼荼羅の二遺例. *Dōkyō kenkyū* 道教研究 2: 205-35.

Yao, Tao-chung. 1980. "Ch'üan-chen: A New Taoist Sect in North China During the Twelfth and Thirteenth Centuries." Ph.D. Diss., University of Arizona, Phoenix.

Yao, Ted. 2000. "Quanzhen—Complete Perfection." In *Daoism Handbook,* edited by Livia Kohn, 567-93. Leiden: E. Brill.

Yetts, Percifal. 1916. "The Eight Immortals." *Journal of the Royal Asiatic Society* 1916, 773–807.

Yoshioka Yoshitoyo 吉岡義豐. 1961. "Bukkyō jūkai shisō no Chūgoku teki shūyō" 佛教十戒思想の中國的受容. *Shūkyō kenkyū* 宗教研究 35.1:51-72.

_____. 1970. *Chōsei no negai: Dôkyô* 長生の願い：道教. Tokyo: Tankosha.

_____. 1979. "Taoist Monastic Life." In *Facets of Taoism,* edited by Holmes Welch and Anna Seidel, 220-52. New Haven: Yale University Press.

Young, Serinity, ed. 1999. *Encyclopedia of Women and World Religions*. New York: Macmillan.

Yü, Chün-fang. 1990a. "Feminine Images of Kuan-Yin in Post-T'ang China." *Journal of Chinese Religions* 18: 61-89.

_____. 1990b. "Images of Kuan-yin in Chinese Folk Literature." *Hanxue yanjiu* 8: 221-85.

_____. 1992. "P'u-t'o Shan: Pilgrimage and the Creation of the Chinese Potalaka." In *Pilgrims and Sacred Sites in China*, edited by Susan Naquin and Chün-fang Yü, 190-245. Berkeley: University of California Press.

_____. 2001a. *Kuan-yin: The Chinese Transformation of Avalokiteśvara*. New York: Columbia University Press.

_____. 2001b. "Biography of the Great Compassionate One of Xiangshang by Jiang Zhiqi (1031-1104)." In *Under Confucian Eyes: Writings on Gender in Chinese History*, edited by Susan Mann and Yu-yin Cheng, 31-46. Berkeley: University of California Press.

Yü, Ying-shih. 1964. "Life and Immortality in the Mind of Han-China." *Harvard Journal of Asiatic Studies* 25: 80-122.

Yūsa Noboru 遊左昇. 1983. "Dōkyō to chūgoku bungaku" 道教と中國文化. In *Dōkyō* 道教, edited by Fukui Kōjun 福井康順 et al., 2: 311-69. Tokyo: Hirakawa.

Zürcher, Erik. 1959. *The Buddhist Conquest of China: The Spread and Adaptation of Buddhism in Early Medieval China*. 2 vols. Leiden: E. Brill.

Zurndorfer, Harriet T. 1999. "Introduction." In *Chinese Women in the Imperial Past*, edited by Harriet T. Zurndorfer, 1-18. Leiden: E. Brill.

Index/Glossary

administration, celestial, 36-37, 58, 110; of Daoists, 156
agriculture, 184
alchemy, 116, 188, 198-201
altar, 126
amae, 3
Amitābha, 43, 65, 245
Anhui, 96, 208
animals, 16-17, 26, 61, 101, 182, 184
Anyang 安陽, 154
art, 28, 68, 72, 177, 246
ascension, 60-62, 124-25, 147, 149, 241-43
Avalokitesvara, 72
Bai mudan 白牡丹, 213-15
Bai Yuchan 白玉蟾, 205
baifeng sui 白鳳髓, 21
Bailian pai 白蓮派, 43
Baiyuan 白元, 193
Baiyun guan 白雲觀, 18, 160, 169, 208
Ban Gu 班固, 26
Ban Zhao 班照, 15
baojuan 寶卷, 43
Baopuzi neipian 抱朴子內篇, 58, 70, 86-88, 192, 198-199
baxian 八仙, *see* Eight Immortals
Beidou 北斗, see Dipper
Beidou bensheng zhenjing 北斗本生真經, 69
Beijing 北京, 58, 169, 208, 210
Bencao gangmu 本草綱目, 192
Bi 弼, 69, 72
Bian Dongxuan 邊洞玄, 200
Bian Shao 邊邵, 62

Bianwei lu 辯偽錄, 200
Bianzheng lun 辯正論, 107
bigu 避穀, 91
Biqiuni zhuan 比丘尼傳, 109, 115
birth, natural, 96; of spirit, 223; 236-40; supernatural, 50, 56, 62, 69, 78, 142
Bixia yuanjun 碧霞元君, 66
blood, 189-92, 196, 222, 234
Bo Shanfu 伯善甫, 88
Bodhidharma, 241
body, 6, 8-9, 12, 135, 138, 177-98; goddess in, 37-38; new, 223; transformation of, 86-90, 138, 236-40; vision of, 58, 228, 250-52
Bowu zhi 博物志, 29
Boyang 伯陽, 54
Bozhou 亳州, 62
breasts, 189-93, 204-06; massages of, 116, 225-27, 231
breathing, 87, 107, 216, 222, 229, 231, 234, 236
Buddha, 182, 207; birth of, 51, 55-56
Buddhism, 22, 67, 113, 115-16, 120, 130, 137, 151, 170-73, 182, 184, 199, 205, 215, 245-46, 249-51
Cai Jing 蔡經, 94
Cainü 蔡女, 15
calendar, 165
Cao Cao 曹操, 13
Cao Daochong 曹道沖, 133